BRITANNIA'S CALENDAR OF HEROES

GEORGE ALLEN & SONS
PUBLISHERS
LONDON
RUSKIN HOUSE

The Victoria Cross.

The New Zealand Cross.

BRITANNIA'S
CALENDAR OF HEROES

COMPILED BY

KATE STANWAY

WITH AN INTRODUCTION BY

REV. THE HON. E. LYTTLETON, M.A., D.D.

HEADMASTER OF ETON

The Naval & Military Press Ltd

published in association with

FIREPOWER
The Royal Artillery Museum
Woolwich

Published by
The Naval & Military Press Ltd
Unit 10 Ridgewood Industrial Park,
Uckfield, East Sussex,
TN22 5QE England
Tel: +44 (0) 1825 749494
Fax: +44 (0) 1825 765701
www.naval-military-press.com

in association with

FIREPOWER
The Royal Artillery Museum, Woolwich
www.firepower.org.uk

INSCRIBED

TO

THE HEROES OF ALL AGES

AND TO

THE FRIENDS OF HEROES

*

INTRODUCTION

WE are probably accustomed to associate the word Calendar with something not particularly interesting or enlivening. Dates are generally thought to be dry, and Almanacks are used more frequently to fix business engagements than to enrich our ideas of human life; but here is a Calendar which is of quite another kind—it is interesting and enlivening. It is based upon a happy idea conceived by a very noble-minded man, and prefaced by a great saying of one of England's most gifted women. I cannot help commending it most cordially and sincerely to the notice of the public, especially of those among us who are inclined to believe that the decadence of the country has begun.

E. LYTTELTON.

November 1909.

PREFACE

In this age of toil and bustle the acts — no matter how noble or heroic they may be—of men, women, and children are too apt to receive only passing recognition.

For some days—and occasionally, in specially sensational instances, perhaps for some weeks—these deeds of self-sacrifice are eulogised as "splendid," "grand," "magnificent," then buried in files of Gazettes and newspapers, and forgotten.

The compiler hopes, by placing permanently on record some of the noblest acts of men and women, to gain for them at least a small measure of the loving remembrance they so richly merit.

Over one hundred and sixty signatures of Heroes of the Victoria Cross are included, also those of the first two recipients of the Edward Medal (see September 12 and November 23), and the second recipient of the Albert Medal (see June 20), all of which have been given to the compiler, either by the wearers of the Decorations themselves, or (in cases where these have passed away) by near relatives who have kindly allowed them to be reproduced. The work of collecting these signatures has been considerably increased—in the case of living heroes —by that modesty which ever goes with high courage.

Several officers of varying rank have refused permission for their autographs to be used. One Crimean hero, whose name stands high on the roll-call of honour, doubtless voiced the feelings of others when he wrote: "I cannot refuse the request you make for my autographic scribble, though hitherto—obsessed by the terror of being jeered at as a self-advertiser—I have refrained from complying with a request of the kind; but now, as an octogenarian who may any day join the majority, I can risk a taunt which may fall harmless on the 'cold, dull ear of death.'"

Following the mention of the Victoria Cross comes the not less nobly-merited award, aptly described as "the Miners' V.C.," which has been recently instituted by H.M. King Edward VII. In connection with the perils encountered underground, not one of the least is the possibility of starvation (see March 4 and August 26), and the following letter appeared in the *Daily Telegraph* in March 1908:—

"Your leading article in to-day's issue contains a vivid portrayal of the awful position of entombed miners who are suddenly cut off from all communication with the world. One of the horrors of such a position is summed up by the writer in the words, 'They have no food.' Would it not be possible to remedy this defect in every mine? Could not food in some concentrated form be stored in various parts of the mine? Suppose sufficient food to last fifty men, say, a fortnight, were stored in twelve different parts of the mine, would this not, perhaps, be the means of relieving the horrors, and possibly of saving lives? The cost would be comparatively small, and would seem infinitesimal when compared with the possible good that might arise. A regulation of the

Home Office making such a provision compulsory might be passed with advantage.—I am, Sir, your obedient servant, RICHARD A. WITTY.

"6 DOWGATE HILL, CANNON STREET,
LONDON, *March* 11."

Besides the gallant 522, who for their deeds of courage and compassion have been gazetted to the famous Bronze Cross "For Valour," holders of all the Royal Medals and many other Decorations are given.

Then there are the workaday heroes and heroines whose martyrdom to their highest impulses is inscribed under the simple cloister in Postman's Park (St. Botolph's Churchyard, Aldersgate Street, London, E.C.), on tablets erected by G. F. Watts, R.A., and by Mrs. Watts, who helped the compiler with accounts of a large number of similar cases well-authenticated, and covering a long period.

By a singular coincidence the first cases—those of Grace Darling and her father—occurred on September 7, 1838, and the last recorded is on the same day of this year (1909).

Both sexes, all ranks, many occupations, and ages ranging from four (see August 15) to eighty-two years (see October 18), find a place in these pages, which glow with the Divine fire of self-sacrifice. Rescues from drowning, foul air, flaming mines, burning houses, broken ice, and shipwreck are all chronicled; also one case of transfusion of blood (see May 17), and one of a man who deliberately starved himself to feed his little children (see April 17).

Every day has at least one fine deed—most have two, and many are crowded.

The ruling note of the book is the saving of life; and the compiler has in this matter earned the approval of

Mr. Andrew Carnegie, who recently wrote to her: "You do well thus to commemorate the Heroes of civilisation who serve or save their fellows." Mr. Carnegie has given considerably over six hundred thousand pounds, divided equally between America, England, and France. The first Hero Fund was instituted at Pittsburg in March 1904; the second (our own) on September 21, 1908; and the third (the French) in the early part of the present year (1909). There is also a separate fund confined to the inhabitants of Dunfermline.

The following extract is from the Deed of Trust instituting the English Carnegie Hero Fund Commission:—

"The success of the Hero Fund upon the North American Continent has been so great that I have decided to extend its benefits to my native land. Not seldom are we thrilled by deeds of heroism where men or women are injured or lose their lives in attempting to preserve or rescue their fellows; such are the heroes of civilisation."

Chivalric souls are all of one brotherhood; and although the book is of necessity confined to deeds of the British Empire, it will be seen that there is an International *Entente Cordiale;* and that men of one and all nationalities stretch out helping hands to their fellow-men in distress. (See January 17 and 31, and June 20.)

It is also noteworthy that on April 15, 1806, the Emperor Alexander of Russia received from our own Royal Humane Society the first Gold Medal ever awarded. The Decoration was given for an act of resuscitation at Wilna, probably toward the end of 1805.

The compiler desires to express most cordial thanks to those ladies and gentlemen who have helped her in collecting material for her work.

To Mr. W. Graham Greene, at the Admiralty, for

supplying names of naval recipients of the Albert Medal; to Mr. J. G. Ashley and the authorities at the War Office for assistance in tracing wearers of the Victoria Cross; to Mr. A. H. Eggett of the Home Office for information concerning recent awards of the Edward and Albert Medals, and details of the warrant of the new Decoration, "The King's Police Medal."

To General Sir James Hills-Johnes, V.C., for particulars of awards of the New Zealand Cross; and to members of the Services and their relatives for information, autographs, addresses, &c.

She is grateful to the Authorities of the Mint for permission to photograph and reproduce the Royal Decorations, the Foreign Office Medal, and the Board of Trade Medal; and to the following gentlemen who have given information about the various Societies and Institutions they represent, and for the generous loan of blocks of medals, &c.:—

Lloyds (Mr. E. F. Inglefield); the Royal National Lifeboat Institution (Mr. Charles Dibdin); the Royal Humane Society (Mr. R. McAdam); the Liverpool Shipwreck and Humane Society (Staff-Commander E. C. Dubois Phillips, R.N.); the Glasgow Humane Society (Dr. T. S. Meighan); the London Fire Brigade (Mr. G. Gamble); the Order of St. John of Jerusalem in England (Colonel Sir Herbert Perrott, Bart.); the Carnegie Hero Fund (Mr. W. George and Mr. F. Murland).

In conclusion, she wishes to express her appreciation of the kindness of the following authors and publishers for permission to quote copyright poems:—Miss Muloch (Mrs. Craik), Sir A. Conan Doyle and Sir Francis Hastings Doyle, and Messrs. Macmillan & Co.; Mr. Rudyard Kipling and Messrs. Methuen & Co. for three verses from "Recessional," taken from "The Five Nations"; Messrs. Kegan Paul, Trench, Trübner & Co., for permission to use extract from the late Sir Edwin Arnold's poem on the Victoria Cross, verses from Dr. Goodchild's poem on "The Birkenhead," and lines from Mr. Richard Trench's poem on "Alma"; Messrs. Wells Gardner, Darton & Co., for leave to use extract from "The Boy Hero," by the late Bishop Walsham How; the proprietors of *The People*, for permission to quote the lines by Miss Madge St. Maury; and to the proprietors of *Punch*, for permission to reproduce verbatim poems "The Critic on the Hearth" and "Binns of the Republic." Also to Mrs. Clement Scott for her cordial permission to quote from Clement Scott's lines on "The Lifeboat"; to Miss Christabel Massey for leave to quote lines by the late Gerald Massey; to Canon H. D. Rawnsley, for numerous quotations from his "Ballads of Brave Deeds," which emphasise and adorn the plain recital of some of the choicest instances of self-sacrifice in the Calendar; to Mr. James Rhoades for a verse of his; and to Mr. Charles Dibdin, for permission to quote poems from the *Lifeboat Journal*.

KATE STANWAY.

134 ABBEY FOREGATE, SHREWSBURY,
October 1909.

DESCRIPTIONS OF THE MEDALS ILLUSTRATED

WITH SOME ACCOUNT OF THE RULES UNDER WHICH THEY ARE AWARDED, AND OF THEIR INSTITUTION

THE VICTORIA CROSS

Instituted January 29, 1856, by Her late Majesty Queen Victoria at the end of the Crimean War. Awards of this were made retrospective.

The coveted Decoration is a small bronze Maltese Cross with the brief inscription "For Valour," surmounted by a lion standing on the Royal Crest. The Crosses are cast from a Russian gun captured at Sevastopol, the ribbon being blue for Naval and red for Military recipients. In the Royal Warrant mention was made of an additional Bar to be placed above the Cross for each successive Act of Valour, but no such Bar has ever been granted.

Originally awards were confined to the two Services, all ranks being eligible for the Decoration, which was bestowed *solely* on those who "in the presence of the enemy had performed some signal act of valour or devotion to their country."

There have been exceptions to the rule confining awards to the Services. Four civilians (see January 22, July 30, and November 8), many doctors serving with our troops, and one clergyman (see December 11) have received the Cross "For Valour."

The award has also been made for a deed not "performed in the presence of the 'enemy'" (see June 9).

Apart from the "Regulars," Colonial troops, the Imperial Yeomanry, and three men of colour have been admitted to the noble brotherhood, which numbers 522; additions having been made from time to time to the Royal Warrant in order to allow of these concessions.

The list, which covers a period of fifty years and includes forty-two campaigns, may seem a meagre one, but it must be remembered that a large proportion of the awards have been made under Rule XIII. of the Royal Warrant, which runs as follows :—

> "*Thirteenthly.*—It is ordained that, in the event of a gallant and daring act having been performed by a squadron, ship's company, a detached body of seamen or marines, not under fifty in number, or by a brigade, regiment, troop, or company, in which the Admiral, General, or other Officer commanding such forces, may deem that all are equally brave and distinguished, and that no special selection can be made by them : then in such case, the Admiral, General, or other Officer commanding, may direct, that for any such body of seamen or marines, or for every troop or company of soldiers, one Officer shall be selected by the Officers engaged for the Decoration ; and in like manner one Petty Officer or Non-Commissioned Officer shall be selected by the Petty Officers and Non-Commissioned Officers engaged ; and two Seamen or Private Soldiers or Marines shall be selected by the seamen, or private soldiers, or marines, engaged, respectively, for the Decoration ; and the names of those selected shall be transmitted by the Senior Officer in command of the Naval force, brigade, regiment, troop, or company, to the Admiral or General Officer commanding, who shall in due manner confer the Decoration as if the acts were done under his own eye."

The Senior Service claims forty-two recipients of the Cross "For Valour," and of our own Regulars in the junior branch the 9th Lancers head the Cavalry Regiments with thirteen awards, while in the Infantry the South Wales Borderers (the "noble 24th" of Rorke's Drift fame) take the lead with sixteen ; the Rifle Brigade running them close with fifteen.

Members of the Medical Profession claim twenty-eight Crosses.

Among the autographs appearing in the following pages all ranks from Admiral and Field-Marshal to Able-Seaman and Drummer are represented.

The first deed which gained the honour was that of throwing a "live" shell overboard H.M.S. *Hecla*, on June 21, 1854, and the last deed was recorded on July 6, 1904.

The Victoria Cross confers a pension of £10 per annum on those below commissioned rank, which sum was increased in 1908 to £50 in respect of those "who from old age, or infirmity, not due to their own fault, may be in poor circumstances and unable to earn a living."

On June 26, 1857, sixty-two men of varying rank and both Services were publicly decorated in Hyde Park by the august and beloved Royal Lady whose name graces the most famous Decoration in the world.

The roll-call of honour has sadly diminished, but the list of survivors is sometimes represented as being less than is the case, as the following letter from Colonel W. Hope, **V.C.**, which appeared in the *Daily Telegraph* on July 3, 1908, and is here reproduced by permission of the writer, will show :—

"*To the Editor of the 'Daily Telegraph.*'

"SIR,—It is doubtless to that wonderful man, the doyen of war correspondents, my friend—if he will allow me to call him so—Mr. Bennet Burleigh, that I owe my exhumation from the tomb in your list of Crimean V.C.'s still living. It is with a sharp pain that I find the list is so terribly shrunk, and think of my comrades who have passed away. But, at all events, I am truly thankful to be able to add one more to the list, namely, 'Alma Jones,' shot through the jaw carrying the Queen's Colour at the Alma, shot in the shoulder during the six assaults during the night of June 7–8, 1855, on the 'Quarries,' which we had to deliver, or attacks which we had to repel, before we could hold the work. We had attacked at dusk—a forlorn hope of 600—and Lord Raglan's excellent orders provided for our being supported, if we effected a lodgment, by 1800, to be followed again by a working party of 1000 to 'turn' the work. But the headquarter staff did not carry out Lord Raglan's orders, and our 'supports' only came to relieve us, at least the remains of us, at about nine on the morning of the 8th. But to come back to 'Alma Jones,' he was again wounded in the chest on Sept. 8 (final assault on the Redan), being struck by a large shell splinter on the glacis of the work. He is, I am happy to say, still alive and wonderfully well. I expect to see him very shortly on a flying visit to London. Thus the list of survivors is increased to six, and it is not a little remarkable that half of those were Royal Fusiliers.

"We began the war with twenty-nine officers, and had fifty-six casualties, the entire staff of the regiment being swept away on June 7 and 18, 1855. 'Alma Jones' and I were both killed by the War Office many years ago, when it was discovered that neither of us had any pension, and therefore no right to live, so the young gentleman told off to keep the list in the War Office promptly killed us both.—I am, Sir, yours faithfully,

"W. HOPE,
"Colonel, formerly commanding
No. 1 Company, Royal Fusiliers."

The following announcement appeared in the *London Gazette* of August 8, 1902 :—

"The King has been graciously pleased to approve of the Decoration of the Victoria Cross being delivered to the *representatives* of the under-mentioned officers, non-commissioned officers, and men who fell during the recent operations in South Africa in the performance of acts of valour, which would, in the opinion of the Commander-in-Chief of the Forces in the Field, have entitled them to be recommended for that distinction had they survived :—

"D. R. Younger, Captain, Gordon Highlanders.
"R. J. T. Digby-Jones, Lieutenant, R.E.
"H. Albrecht, Trooper, 459, Imp. Light Horse.
"G. H. B. Coulson, Lieut.-Adjt., K.O.S.B., 7th M.I.
"A. Atkinson, Sergt., 3264, Yorkshire Regiment.
"J. Barry, Pte., 3733, 1st Batt. Royal Irish Regiment."

EDWARD MEDAL

(The Miners' and Quarrymen's V.C.)

Instituted by His Majesty King Edward VII., on July 13, 1907.

First Class.—A circular Medal of Silver with the King's effigy on the obverse, and on the reverse a design representing the rescue of a miner, with the inscription "For Courage."

Second Class.—A replica of above in Bronze. Ribbon for each Class : dark blue, with narrow yellow stripe on each side.

THE EDWARD MEDAL ("The Miners' V.C.").

THE ALBERT MEDALS FOR SAVING LIFE ON LAND AND AT SEA.

ALBERT MEDAL

Instituted by Her late Majesty Queen Victoria—
For saving life at sea, on March 7, 1866;
For saving life on land, on April 30, 1877.

Extract from Consolidating Warrant, dated June 5, 1905:—

"**The Albert Medal of the First Class,** when conferred for gallantry in saving life at sea, shall consist of a gold oval-shaped Badge or Decoration, enamelled in dark blue, with a Monogram composed of the letters **V.** and **A.**, interlaced with an Anchor erect in gold, surrounded by a Garter in bronze, inscribed in raised letters of gold, 'For Gallantry in Saving Life at Sea,' and surmounted by a representation of the Crown of His Royal Highness the lamented Prince Consort, and suspended from a dark blue riband of an inch and three-eighths in width, with four white longitudinal stripes."

"**The Albert Medal of the Second Class,** when conferred for gallantry in saving life at sea, shall consist of the like-shaped enamelled Badge, save and except in this class it shall be entirely worked in bronze, instead of gold and bronze, and shall be suspended from a dark blue riband of an inch and three-eighths of an inch in width, and two white longitudinal stripes."

"**The Albert Medal of the First Class,** when conferred for gallantry in saving life on land, shall consist of a gold oval-shaped Badge or Decoration, enamelled in crimson, with a Monogram composed of the letters **V.** and **A.**, erect in gold, surrounded by a Garter in bronze, inscribed in raised letters of gold, 'For Gallantry in Saving Life on Land,' and surmounted by a representation of the Crown of His Royal Highness the lamented Prince Consort, and suspended from a crimson riband of an inch and three-eighths in width, with four white longitudinal stripes."

"**The Albert Medal of the Second Class,** when conferred for gallantry in saving life on land, shall consist of the like-shaped enamelled badge, save and except that it shall be entirely worked in bronze, instead of gold and bronze, and shall be suspended from a crimson riband of an inch and three-eighths of an inch in width, with two white longitudinal stripes."

THE KING'S POLICE MEDAL

(Not illustrated.)

Instituted by His Majesty King Edward VII., July 7, 1909.
Extract from Royal Warrant :—

"It is ordained that the King's Police Medal shall consist of a circular Medal of Silver with Our Effigy on the obverse, and on the reverse a design emblematic of Protection from danger, and shall bear on the rim the name of the person to whom the Medal is awarded.

"It is ordained that the Medal shall only be awarded to those of Our Faithful Subjects and others who, being members of a recognised Police Force or of a properly organised Fire Brigade within Our Dominions, or in Territories under Our Protection or Jurisdiction, have performed acts of exceptional courage and skill, or have exhibited conspicuous devotion to duty. . . . The riband, of an inch and three-eighths in width, shall be dark blue, with a narrow silver stripe on either side."

BOARD OF TRADE MEDAL

The Medal is granted only to British subjects, or persons serving on board British ships.

Obverse.—The head of King Edward VII., with the Legend, "For Gallantry in Saving Life at Sea," below E.R.I.

Reverse—The figure of a man holding on to a spar, in the water, and signalling to a lifeboat in the distance, a man supporting a rescued sailor, and a woman and child seated on a rock.

Ribbon.—Red, with white stripes at edge.

THE FOREIGN OFFICE MEDAL

In (1) Gold and (2) Silver, and of four classes bearing on the reverse the following inscriptions, respectively :—

"(1) For saving the life of a British subject," and within two oak branches, "Presented by the British Government," with crown above.

"(2) For assisting a British vessel in distress."

"(3) For saving the lives of British subjects."

"(4) For Gallantry and Humanity."

The obverse of these Medals is the same, viz. the head of King Edward VII., with legend, "Edwardus D. G. Britt. Omn. Rex F.D. Ind. Imp."

LLOYD'S MEDAL

Silver and Bronze

Medals are presented by the Committee of Lloyd's as an honorary acknowledgment to those who have by extraordinary exertions contributed to the saving of life at sea.

The subject of the Medal is taken from the *Odyssey*, where Ulysses, after various adventures during his return to his native Ithaca, subsequent to the fall of Troy, is described as being rescued from the perils of a storm by Leucothöe—

> "A mortal once,
> But now, an azure sister of the main."

The words addressed by Leucothöe to the shipwrecked hero represent the action of the obverse side—

> "This heavenly scarf beneath thy bosom bind,
> And live; give all thy terrors to the wind."

Obverse.—In the sea a man clinging to a floating mast, his left hand stretched upwards to grasp the mantle of Leucothöe, who hovers over him, in the act of rendering assistance. Above is the motto, "Leucothœ Naufrago Succurrit."

Reverse—Within two oak branches, "Ob Cives Servator"; above, "Presented by Lloyd's."

The reverse is taken from a medal of Augustus; a crown of oak being the reward given by the Romans to him who saved the life of a citizen. The Latin motto is derived from the same authority.

NEW ZEALAND CROSS

The Cross, which is of oxydised silver, is in the form of a Cross-pattée, with gold crown above; a gold ring and clasp for suspension; a laurel branch in relief on the bar.

Obverse.—A plain centre surrounded by a band, thereon "New Zealand" within a gold laurel chaplet, on each arm of the Cross a gold star of six points.

Reverse.—On the centre circle "1863," surrounded by the name of the recipient above, and the bottom "Defence."

Ribbon.—Crimson ribbed silk.

THE MEDAL OF THE ROYAL NATIONAL LIFE-BOAT INSTITUTION

Obverse—Bust of His Majesty King Edward VII., double legend, "Royal National Lifeboat Institution. Founded in 1824. Incorporated 1860. King Edward VII., Patron."

Reverse.—Figure of Hope assisting Coxswain-Superintendent of Lifeboat, to buckle on his life-belt, and wishing him and his crew "God-speed." Lifeboat manned in distance ready to launch, and awaiting the instructions of the Coxswain-Superintendent. "G. W. de Saulles."

The colour of the ribbon, which is corded silk, attached to the Medal is blue.

Since the establishment of the Royal National Lifeboat Institution on the 4th March 1824 to the 31st December 1908, the Committee of Management have awarded 101 Gold Medals and Clasps, and 1261 Silver Medals and Clasps, as well as £286,162 in money for the saving of 47,983 lives.

The Committee of Management earnestly appeal to the British public for funds to enable them to maintain their 281 lifeboats now on the coast and their crews in the most perfect state of efficiency.

ROYAL HUMANE SOCIETY

Was established in London for the recovery of persons in a state of suspended animation, 1774.

Highest award: **The Stanhope Gold Medal.**

Origin of the Medal.—On July 7, 1871, there died Captain C. S. S. Stanhope, R.N., an officer universally respected in his profession, and a Memorial Fund of about £400 was raised to commemorate his services. This was handed over in trust to the Royal Humane Society on condition that a Gold Medal, to be called the "Stanhope Medal," should be annually given to the best case brought to the Society's notice.

Note.—Captain Stanhope himself held the Society's Silver Medal for a very gallant rescue at sea, off the west coast of South America, on August 7, 1850, while serving as Lieutenant on H.M.S. *Asia.*

THE LIVERPOOL SHIPWRECK AND HUMANE SOCIETY

Was instituted January 9, 1839, and incorporated November 21, 1888. The Objects of the Society are:—

To save human life, particularly in cases of shipwreck in the neighbourhood of Liverpool.

To reward persons instrumental in rescuing human life from danger, and to relieve the widows and families of those who may perish in the attempt to save others.

To relieve the immediate necessities of those saved, and assist them in getting to their destination.

Generally to grant rewards and relief in deserving cases.

The Society is enabled by a special endowment to grant Medals and rewards for rescues from Fire and all other dangers.

MEDAL

Obverse.—Within two oak branches the crest of the city of Liverpool, viz., on a wreath ar., and sa., a cormorant with wings endorsed proper, holding in the beak a branch of laver inverted vert. Legend "Liverpool Shipwreck and Humane Society, 1839."

Reverse.—A man on a floating piece of wreck, rescuing a woman and child, sailors in a boat also rescuing a man, a ship in the distance. Motto, "Lord save us: we perish."

Ribbon.—Navy blue, one and a quarter inch broad.

THE GLASGOW HUMANE SOCIETY

Instituted 1790, and its Medal is given for intrepidity of conduct and success in rescuing from drowning.

THE LONDON FIRE BRIGADE

Established January 1, 1866; formerly known as the Metropolitan Fire Brigade.

The V.C. of the Fire Brigade is their Silver Medal, which is solely awarded in cases of extreme gallantry in saving life.

From October 7, 1871 to November 16, 1906 there have been only fifty-eight awards of this coveted Decoration.

THE GRAND PRIORY OF THE ORDER OF THE HOSPITAL OF ST. JOHN OF JERUSALEM IN ENGLAND

The Medal of the Order, originally instituted in 1874, is by the Charter allowed to be awarded, as heretofore, for gallantry in saving life on land. It is circular, either of silver or bronze; on the obverse is the Maltese Cross, embellished alternately at each of the principal angles with a lion guardant and a unicorn, both passant, surrounded by the inscription "For Service in the cause of humanity," and on the reverse, a sprig of the plant St. John's Wort, with which is entwined a scroll bearing the names "Jerusalem, England," the whole surrounded by the inscription "Awarded by the Grand Priory of the Order of the Hospital of St. John of Jerusalem in England." It is worn suspended from a black watered-silk ribbon. The Medal can only be awarded to those, who by a conspicuous act of gallantry, have endangered their own lives.

THE MEDAL OF THE CARNEGIE HERO FUND TRUST

For the British Isles was instituted by Mr. Andrew Carnegie of Skibo and New York, on September 21, 1908.

The Trust Funds amount approximately to £250,000, yielding an annual income of about £22,500. The Fund is applicable to the British Islands and the Territorial Waters thereof; and its administration has been committed to the Carnegie Dunfermline Trustees, who administer also a Trust created by Mr. Carnegie in 1903, for the benefit of the people of Dunfermline. Down to

September 7, 1909, seventy-nine Awards of Money and Medals have been made for cases of heroism submitted to the Committee.

So far the Trustees have decided to award Bronze Medals only, and the question as to whether it is desirable—in specially meritorious cases—to award a Medal of a more expensive material remains for consideration when the occasion arises.

"The obverse of the Medal shows two symbolical figures ; one that of a winged angel, a messenger of light to mankind, appearing from the great central source of light, holding aloft in one hand the ever-burning lamp which lights the way to higher attainment. The other figure represents man, who has received from the angel of light a spray of palm leaf, the emblem of peace. The angel inspires and guides him to heroic endeavour in the upward path of life. His feet are furnished with wings, emblems of that swiftness in the service of man which is the mark of true nobility."

CONTENTS

LIST OF ILLUSTRATIONS

JANUARY

" *This royal throne of kings, this sceptred isle,*
This earth of majesty, this seat of Mars,
This other Eden, demi-paradise,
This fortress built by Nature for herself,
Against infection and the hand of war;
This happy breed of men, this little world,
This precious stone set in the silver sea."

—Richard II.

CALENDAR OF HEROES

JANUARY 1

V.C. Lieutenant-Colonel Crimmin, C.I.E., **Bombay Medical Service.** Gazetted for distinguished gallantry in tending the wounded under fire at Lwekaw, and for saving the life of one patient by killing several ferocious Karens who attacked them. **Burmah. 1889.**

"Valour is the fountain of pity."—*Carlyle.*

Albert Medal of the Second Class to Lieutenant the Hon. Francis R. Sandilands, R.N., of H.M.S. *Audacious*, for risking his life in a gallant attempt to rescue a man who had fallen overboard. **1875.**

A Yorkshire Youth drowned after saving a Boy's Life. While a number of people were skating and sliding on Cross Pool, near Sheffield, the ice broke and several lads fell through. Frederick Dyson plunged into the hole and brought one lad to the bank, where others received him. The ice then cracked once more, and in spite of all attempts to save him the gallant young rescuer perished. **1869.**

Postman's Park Heroine and Martyr. Tablet 44. Eliza Coghlan, aged 26, of Stoke Newington, was terribly burned while carrying a blazing paraffin lamp to save the house in which her children were sleeping. It ignited her clothes, and the devoted mother died in hospital the same day. **1902.**

JANUARY 2

V.C. Field-Marshal Earl Roberts, K.G., K.P., G.C.B., O.M., G.C.S.I., G.C.I.E., D.C.L., LL.D., P.C., **Bengal Artillery.** "Virtute et Valore." (Born September 30, 1832.) Decorated for two acts on the same day, one of which was that of saving life.

Khodagunge, Mutiny. 1858.

Lord Roberts, who spent forty-one years of most arduous service in India, and has taken part in more engagements than any other officer, went out to South Africa—where his only son had laid down his life—in his sixty-eighth year. During the course of 1900 he defeated the Boers several times, relieved Kimberley and Mafeking, and annexed the two South African Republics. On his return to England he was appointed Commander-in-Chief of the British Army, succeeding Lord Wolseley, created Earl Roberts of Kandahar, Pretoria and Waterford, and was voted a grant of £100,000 by Parliament. He retired from the office of Commander-in-Chief in February 1904, upon which occasion His Majesty King Edward VII. issued an Army Order in recognition of his long and eminent services, thanking him for his "unswerving zeal and unfailing success," and expressing deep regret at his retirement.

V.C. Private H. Addison, **43rd Oxford Light Infantry.** Decorated for saving the life of a wounded officer, in the performance of which he lost a leg, and was otherwise terribly hurt at Kurrereah. **Mutiny. 1859.**

JANUARY 3

A gallant New Zealand Colonist. Mr. Henry Lawson, aged 25, son of Sir William Lawson of Brough Hall, near Catterick, Yorks, was drowned in New Zealand while making a bold attempt to save the life of one of his shepherds, who was carried away in the Waitanga river when engaged in sheep washing. **1857.**

A brave little Wiltshire Boy. Two lads were sliding on a pond near Swindon, when the ice gave way and one fell in. Thomas Lucas, aged 10, went to help his friend, but he also was drowned. **1890.**

A Cumberland Hero. As Mr. Charles Martin, artist and musician, and Miss Mabel Barker were skating at Edenhall, near Penrith, the ice broke and the young lady fell through. Her companion made a desperate effort to save her, but he too perished. **1895.**

JANUARY 4

V.C. Major-General D. Macintyre, **Bengal Staff Corps.** (Died 1903.) With a small party, under furious fire, sprang up a flaming stockade eight feet high, and successfully stormed the position.

Looshai, N.E. India. 1872.

Welsh Lifeboat Tragedy: Loss of the entire Crew of the Point of Ayr Lifeboat while trying to help a Wreck off Pensarn. Robert Beck, John Sherlock, John Bleddger, Joseph Davies, Thomas Roberts, Richard Davies, Robert Williams, John Ellis,

David Davies, Edward Phillips, Robert Roberts, Edward Roberts, and Thomas Owens were all drowned while trying to help the crew of a brigantine sunk off Pensarn, Abergele, who were afterwards saved by the Rhyl lifeboat. A fund of £500 was raised for the widows and orphans, all save four having been married men with families. **1857.**

Two little Cheshire Heroes. While John E. Hilton, aged 13, William Burgess, 12, and Eli Atkins, 14, were skating at Park Lane, Macclesfield, the latter boy fell through the ice. Hilton and Burgess stood on either side of the hole to help their friend, but unhappily the ice again broke, and the two brave boys fell into the water. All three were drowned. **1865.**

January 5

V.C. Major Sir J. P. Milbanke, Bart., **10th Hussars.** (Born 1872.) "Resolute and firm." After being severely wounded at Colesberg during a reconnaissance, rode back under galling fire to rescue a man whose pony was exhausted. **Boer War. 1900.**

"Bravery never goes out of fashion."—*Thackeray.*

Eight gallant Margate Seamen. William Emptage, John Emptage, Isaac Solly, George Smith, Abraham Bembridge, Henry Paramor, Charles Fuller, and Frederick Batt were on their way in a lugger to the assistance of the *Northern Belle* in a furious gale, when a tremendous sea broke over their boat and capsized her, her occupants being all drowned. The crew of the stranded *Northern Belle* were afterwards rescued by the Broadstairs boatmen. **1857.**

Norfolk Lifeboat Tragedy: Two Lives lost. James Stageman and James Haylett, of Bacton, lost their lives on this date while engaged on lifeboat service. **1880.**

Carnegie Hero Fund. The sum of £5 to Angus Mackenzie, of Stornoway, who, with his heavy sea-boots on, plunged from a fishing-boat to the rescue of his comrade who had fallen overboard. By means of a rope, which Mackenzie tied to the drowning man, both were hauled aboard. The Royal Humane Society also awarded their **Bronze Medal** and £1 to this plucky fisherman. **1909.**

JANUARY 6

V.C. Private B. McQuirt, **95th (Derbyshire).** Decorated for a dogged encounter with the mutineers at Rowa, of whom he killed one and wounded two, while he himself received six wounds. **Mutiny. 1858.**

V.C. Colonel O. E. P. Lloyd, **Army Med. Staff.** (Born 1854.) Was severely wounded while, under fierce fire, he was dressing the hurts of Captain Morton, whom he afterwards helped to remove to Sima Post Fort. **Burmah. 1893.**

V.C. Lieutenant R. J. T. Digby-Jones, **R.E.**
V.C. Trooper H. Albrecht, **Imperial Light Horse.**
Two heroes who lost their lives after displaying the greatest bravery in the defence and re-capture of Wagon Hill, Ladysmith.

V.C. Major J. E. I. Masterson, **Devonshire Regiment.** Born 1862. After leading a charge which captured a ridge was shot through both thighs while carrying a message under terrible cross-fire at Wagon Hill.

V.C. Lance-Corporal J. Pitts, **63rd (Manchester Regiment).**

V.C. Lance-Corporal R. Scott, **63rd (Manchester Regiment).** With indomitable perseverance defended a sangar at Cæsar's Camp for fifteen hours, without food or water, and under pitiless Boer fire. Scott, who was wounded, served throughout the entire siege, and was never once absent from duty.

The above five at or near Ladysmith, Boer War. 1900.

Albert Medal of the First Class to the Rev. C. Cobb.
Albert Medal of the Second Class to John Batist, R.N. These two medals were awarded for great gallantry in attempting to reach a wrecked French lugger. Mr. Cobb had a line attached to him, but Batist refused to have one. Both were natives of Dymchurch, Kent. **1867.**

The Royal National Lifeboat Institution Gold Medal to Mr. Charles E. Fish, coxswain of the Ramsgate lifeboat, for distinguished courage, skill, and determination in aiding the crew of the wrecked barque *Indian Chief*, when the lifeboat's crew were exposed unceasingly to a furious gale and heavy sea for twenty-six hours. **1881.**

London Fire Brigade Silver Medal to George Biscardine for rescuing a child from a burning house in Whitechapel. **1901.**

The Order of St. John of Jerusalem in England. Certificate of honour to a postman named Arthur E. Turner, who sustained serious injuries while trying to stop a runaway horse near the Savoy Hotel, London. **1906.**

JANUARY 7

V.C. Private J. Barry, **18th (Royal Irish).** "Although surrounded and threatened by the Boers at the time, smashed the breech of a Maxim gun, thus rendering it useless to its captors, and it was in doing this splendid act for his country that he met his death." (Official account.) **Boer War. 1901.**

Albert Medal of the Second Class to Able Seaman John Ramsay, R.N., for extreme promptitude and pluck in leaping from the platform at Temple Meads Station before an incoming train and saving the life of a man who had fallen on to the metals. The train was only about twenty yards distant. **1908.**

JANUARY 8

Royal Humane Society's Bronze Medal to R. Deelarkhan for rescuing a man who had fallen overboard from R.I.M.S. *Lawrence* in the Persian Gulf, in thirty feet of water, and holding him up until picked up by a boat. **1906.**

Splendid Lifeboat Rescue Work. Fine services were rendered by the *Star of Hope* lifeboat at Moelfra Bay, Anglesea, in a tremendous gale, to the *Walter Williams*, whose crew of five she brought off with great difficulty. Soon afterwards the *Star of Hope* was called to the assistance of another vessel in distress, and saved three men. A third appeal was made, and despite the fearful sea the gallant lifeboatmen took their craft to yet another imperilled vessel, from which they brought sixteen men and a stowaway by means of ropes. **1909.**

JANUARY 9

Three Yorkshire (North Riding) Fishermen of one Family drowned in trying to save Life near Redcar. Richard Picknett, aged 60, and his nephews, Edward and John Picknett, were drowned by the capsizing of a fishing coble, in which they were on their way to aid a trawler in distress at Marske. Several other fishermen of the rescue party, including the father of the two young men, were able to regain their coble when she righted herself, but the above gallant trio perished. **1901.**

Lieutenant Shackleton, M.V.O., the Hero of Farthest South. On this date, after incredible hardship and suffering and in a temperature 40 degrees below freezing-point, Lieutenant E. H. Shackleton planted the Union Jack, presented by Her Majesty Queen Alexandra to the expedition, at 88 degrees 23 minutes longitude 162 east.

This is the most southerly point ever reached by man, and only 111 miles from the Antarctic Pole, which is now known to be more than 10,000 feet above sea-level. The *Nimrod*, under Lieutenant Shackleton, left the Thames on August 7, 1907, and the intrepid explorer arrived in England on his return on June 12, 1909. The latter part of the perilous quest was made on sledges drawn by Manchurian ponies through an icy slough of soft snow full of dangerous crevasses, the explorers being frost-bitten in their sleeping-bags. But for a lack of provisions, Lieutenant Shackleton would have attained the goal of his ambition, the South Pole itself. **1909.**

"Fear death?—to feel the fog in my throat,
The mist in my face,

JANUARY

Jno. Crimmin.
Lt. Col. I.M.S.

Roberts, F.M.

J. Milbanke, Major
10th. Hussars.

R. J. T. Digby Jones

James Pitts (V.C.)

Robert F. Scott.

Ernest H. Shackleton

When the snows begin, and the blasts denote
I am nearing the place,
The power of the night, the press of the storm,
The post of the foe.

Yet the strong man must go :
For the journey is done and the summit attained."
—"Prospice," *Browning*.

JANUARY 10

V.C. Lieutenant C. L. Smith, **Cornwall's Light Infantry.** Gazetted for a desperately heroic but unhappily ineffectual attempt to rescue Dr. Welland, who had himself been wounded while trying to save life. Lieutenant Smith got the doctor on to a horse, and, when that was shot, on to a mule. This animal was also hit and its rider speared by the dervishes. The brave rescuer's life was miraculously preserved, he being literally hemmed in by the enemy.

Jidballi, Somaliland. 1904.

Lancashire Boy of 12 drowned in trying to save his Chums. While several boys were sliding at night on a frozen pond at Morecambe, Lancaster, James Curwen fell through the ice. Samuel Edmondson made a gallant effort to rescue his companion, and in doing so perished also. 1876.

Lifeboat Disaster at Whitby: Three Lives lost. Samuel Lacy, Richard Gatenley, and John Thompson were drowned through the capsizing of the lifeboat *Harriott Forteath*, while on her way to help the *Agenoria*. The crew and the master of the vessel were rescued by the coastguard by means of the rocket apparatus. 1877.

JANUARY 11

Wreck of the ss. *London*. When the ss. *London* foundered in the Bay of Biscay with 220 souls on board, nineteen only were saved in a boat picked up by an Italian vessel. A tragedian named Gustavus Brook and many others displayed great heroism, many of them working incessantly at the pumps as long as a chance of keeping the wreck afloat remained. Captain J. Bohun Martin refused to leave his vessel, and, when urged to do so, replied, "No, my men, I will not come into the boat. I will go with the ship, passengers, and crew. Good-bye! God speed you." The captain and Mr. Brook went down with the vessel. **1866.**

"My wonder . . . is always at the height which this human nature can attain. . . . The *nature* of it is in the nobleness. . . . Take the faith in its utmost terms. When the captain of the *London* shook hands with his mate, saying, 'God speed you! I will go down with my passengers,' *that* I believe to be 'human nature.' He does not do it from any religious motive,—from any hope of reward, or any fear of punishment; he does it because he is a man."—*John Ruskin.*

Postman's Park Railway Hero and Martyr. Tablet 29. Inspector A. Croft, aged 31, lost both legs and one arm while saving the life of an insane woman, who threw herself under a train at Woolwich Arsenal Station. Croft died in a few hours. He left a widow and two little children. **1878.**

Liverpool S. & H. Society's Gold General Medal to Mr. Walter Carey for a magnificent but unhappily unsuccessful attempt to save a poor fellow caught in some machinery in motion. Mr. Carey himself became entangled, had one leg broken in three places, and an arm badly injured, narrowly escaping the terrible fate from which he tried to save the other. **This is the only award of a Gold General Medal by the Society. 1894.**

JANUARY 12

Lifeboat Coxswain Hero. William Brown lost his life in a tremendous sea on "Old Harry Ledge" Hook Sands, near Poole, through the capsizing of the Swanage lifeboat, which was on its way to succour the crew of the Norwegian barque *Brilliant*. Brown had acted as coxswain for nineteen years, and one of his crew said of him, "When William Brown led us there was no turning back." His widow and seven children were provided for by the Royal National Lifeboat Institution and a subscription fund raised by the Rector of Swanage. **1895.**

Liverpool S. and H. Society's Silver Medals and Votes of Thanks to Nurses Janet Griffiths, Ruby Dalzell, and Jessie Elmsley for courageously extinguishing the burning clothing of a fellow-nurse, who was fatally burned at the Royal Infirmary, Liverpool. **1909.**

JANUARY 13

Albert Medal of the Second Class to Mr. William Hinton, of Halesowen, for extreme pluck in entering a burning house and removing a canister of blasting powder, which was actually blistered by the flames when the intrepid man brought it out, thus averting a terrible explosion. Mr. Hinton had previously removed a large quantity of explosive material from the premises. **1881.**

Splendid Heroism after a Fire at Edinburgh Theatre. George Lorimer, Dean of Guild, architect; John Taylor,

Bernard M'Vie, and George Sweeney lost their lives in a fine attempt to save a man from the ruins of the burned theatre. The victim, who lay on his back pinned under a great stone, called piteously for help. One of the walls threatened to collapse each moment, but the splendid quartette, though fully alive to the risk they ran, persevered in their efforts to extricate the suffering man. When these heroic souls at length tried to run into safety, it was too late; the wall fell upon them, and all perished in the ruins. **1865.**

Gorleston Lifeboat Tragedy: Thirteen Men drowned. Edward W. Woods, James Woods, Charles Woods, James Fleming, Christopher Parker, Christopher Wiley, William Darkins, Benjamin Harris, William Manthorpe, Robert Shillings, Edward Welton, Abel Neuson, and Robert Warner lost their lives on the harbour bar, owing to the rudder of the lifeboat *Rescuer* becoming unshipped. A heavy sea struck her, and she was at once capsized. Some of the crew were saved by the lifeboat *Friend of all Nations*, among them being Robert Warner, who died two days later. **1866.**

January 14

V.C. Surgeon J. F. M'Crea, **Cape Mounted Yeomanry.** (Died 1894.) Saved a disabled soldier, and was afterwards badly wounded himself, but in spite of this he ministered to the injured and bore them into shelter before attending to his own hurt. **Basutoland. 1881.**

Edward Medal of the First Class to Mr. John Jones. A native workman was overcome by fumes at the bottom of the Witwatersrand Gold Mine, Johannesburg, and two men, named Owen and Griffiths, went down to assist him. With the help of Jones, who followed, the native was drawn up, but Owen and Griffiths were then overcome, and fell to the bottom of the winze, and Jones became unconscious on reaching the surface. Others went down, and one of them was unable to return. On regaining consciousness, Jones insisted on again descending the mine, and succeeded in bringing up two of the men. He then descended a third time, and brought the remaining man to the surface. Unfortunately Griffiths, Owen, and the native workman succumbed to the effects of the gas. **1909.**

Albert Medal of the First Class to William Dodd, under manager, for heroism in saving many lives on the occasion of the flooding of the Diglake Mine, Audley Colliery, Staffs. **1895.**

"They challenged each 'gallery,' hasted along
Till they won where the 'pit boys' cowering stood,
Thrust them from hand to hand through the flood;
They cheered the aged, they led the strong.

. . . .

It is darker than night o'er the deep dark grave—
Grave of the living who fain would die—
Hope's sun has set, there are stars in the sky.
There are stars upon earth—Dodd's work was brave."
—"Ballads of Brave Deeds," *Canon Rawnsley.*

A little Denbighshire Lad's noble Death. While three brothers, Edward Jones, aged 14, Robert, aged 11, and Hugh, aged 9, were playing on a pool near Wrexham the two elder ones fell through the ice. The youngest boy pluckily went to their assistance, but he also fell in and sank. When the boys were got out two were dead, and the third expired soon afterwards. **1885.**

JANUARY 15

V.C. Private D. Millar, **Black Watch.**
V.C. Private W. Cook, **Black Watch.**
Awarded the decoration for taking command of a party when all their officers were killed or wounded in a fierce fight at Maylah Ghaut, and for displaying great courage, coolness, and discipline.

V.C. Captain H. M. Clogstoun, **Madras Native Infantry.** (Died 1861.) Charged and dispersed a large number of mutineers with only eight followers. He was terribly wounded, and lost all save one of his noble little band at Chickumbah. **Mutiny. 1859.**

"His Brother's Keeper." Thomas R. Smith, aged 11, went with his brother Charles, aged 7, sliding on a pond in the Pollokshaw Road, Glasgow. The younger boy fell through the ice, and the elder went to his rescue, but both were drowned. **1885.**

JANUARY 16

V.C. Sergeant J. Danaher, **Connaught Rangers.**
V.C. Lance-Corporal J. Murray, **Connaught Rangers.**
While making a desperate effort to save two wounded men under withering fire at Elandsfontein were taken prisoners. Murray was badly hit by a ball.
Boer Revolt. 1881.

Anglesea Lifeboatman lost while engaged in Rescue Service. During a storm of terrific violence at Holyhead, a schooner was seen to be drifting towards the rocks on the east side of the bay. The lifeboat, manned by a crew of fifteen, which put out to the rescue, left four of her men aboard, by whose help the schooner was run ashore on to Penrhos Sands in comparative safety. On returning to harbour the lifeboat capsized, but was quickly righted, so that seven of her crew were able to cling to her. The remaining four were mercilessly dashed about by the fearful waves for more than an hour. Three of the brave fellows were eventually picked up by a steam tug, but William Hughes had drifted away and was drowned. He left a widow and five children. **1865.**

" But, on my honour, I'd like to know if pluckier men in the world exist
Than those who buckle the life-belt on, when wives are left and the children kissed.
. . . Will you send a cheer from the friends on shore
To the men who go to their death at sea, and do their duty?—men can't do more.

. . . .

Ready to die is the motto of men—and this is the reason the Lifeboat's manned."—*Clement Scott.*

Royal Humane Society's Bronze Medal to Ernest Downing, seaman, who at great personal risk jumped from a barge into the canal at Stainforth, near Doncaster, and succeeded in rescuing Wilfred Hornsby. Downing had to swim seventy yards and then dive for Hornsby, who was in an unconscious state when rescued. **1904.**

Glasgow Heroic Life-saver. Everybody—or almost everybody—in Glasgow knows the name of Mr. George Geddes, who so frequently has saved persons from drowning in the river Clyde. He began his career at the age of 14 years, when he saved a girl from drowning, and during the past twenty years he has on no fewer than fifty-nine occasions plunged into the river. " On only four of these occasions," he added, "have I been unsuccessful." In 1901 he was awarded the Silver Medal of the Humane

Society for life-saving, and in 1900 he gained first place in the Paris International Life-saving Competition held on the Seine. Mr. Geddes is also an expert in restorative treatment, and where there has been a chance of setting aglow the dying embers of life he has never yet failed. **1909.**

January 17

V.C. Troop-Sergeant-Major D. Spence, **9th Lancers.** Another gallant soldier, who saved a life at imminent risk of his own. **Mutiny. 1858.**

V.C. Major-General Reginald W. Sartorius, C.M.G., **6th Bengal Cavalry.** (Died 1907.) Under heavy fire at Abogoo carried a dying Houssa into shelter. Brother of General E. H. Sartorius (see Oct. 24th). **Ashantee. 1874.**

V.C. Gunner Albert Smith, **R.A.** Made two noble attempts to save Lieutenant Guthrie in the square at Abu Klea from a Soudanese, who however inflicted a fatal wound upon that officer. **Nile. 1885.**

A French Tribute to British Heroism. In the year 1899 a beautiful monument was erected at Calais in memory of four English sailors, who had perished in a fine attempt to save the crew of a French vessel thirty-two years earlier. The inscription on one side is as follows:—

"A la mémoire des Sauveteurs, Victimes
de leur Dévouement.

Wilson, William Henderson, James Lumsden, John Hopkinson, Matthew	Sujets Anglais.	Sauvetage du navire *Trois Sœurs* 17 Janvier 1867."

1867.

JANUARY

James Murray V C

J. Danagher

Reg W Sartorius

A Smith V C

Teignmouth Melvill

Nevill: J: A. Coghill

J. H. Reynolds

H. Hook. V.C.

Postman's Park Railway Hero and Martyr. Tablet 48. Daniel Pemberton, aged 61, foreman at Twickenham Station, was surprised by a train while ganging the line with another man. Pemberton hurled his mate out of the track, thus saving his life, but he himself was crushed to death. **1903.**

JANUARY 18

A brave Sutherland Pair. Thomas Fleming, butler in the family of Mr. Bonar, was drowned in Duddingston Loch while making a gallant effort to save life. A large number of people were skating when the ice broke, and many of them fell into the water. Fleming, after doing all he could to save a woman, sank, and a young man named Dewar, who tried to rescue him, was pulled ashore with great difficulty. **1839.**

A Lifeboat Tragedy at Yarmouth: Six Lives lost. Robert Symonds, James Ditcham, John Sherwood, Charles Beckett, Henry Masterson, and one other were drowned by the capsizing of the lifeboat after rendering assistance to a schooner ashore. Mr. J. Abram, of 1 Middle Temple Lane, wrote: "I know five of the poor fellows well. They were all steady, honest, hardworking men, **ready, as the Yarmouth boatmen always are, to risk their lives to save others."** **1881.**

JANUARY 19

Albert Medal of the First Class to Captain William J. Nutman of the ss. *Aidar.* When his vessel was sinking, and his crew with one exception had been rescued by that of the ss. *Staffordshire,* he absolutely refused to abandon an injured fireman. When the *Aidar* had gone down, Captain Nutman, with his charge clasped in his arms, was seen on the bottom of an upturned boat. Half-an-hour later a boat from the *Staffordshire* succeeded in picking them up. **1896.**

We had passed Messina's Straits
And the Whirlpool at the gates,
When suddenly in Adria we saw the rockets leap ;
And we heard our Captain say
As we lowered the boats away,
"She cannot last much longer for her hull is lying deep."

And we toiled through all that night,
And by grey of morning light,
Though the Master still stood by her, we had rescued twenty-nine.
But he cried from off the wreck,
"With a wounded man on deck,
What Master would forsake a man ? His fate shall sure be mine."

And our hearts were sorely tried
As we pulled off from her side,
For his courage seemed to shame us, as from death and doom we fled.
Then the *Aidar* rolled in pain,
Foundered head-first in the main,
And we felt the whirlpool surges as we plied our oars in dread.

. . . .

But we saw a dark thing float.
God be praised ! The *Aidar's* boat—
Bottom up ! with men upon her ! fireman ! master ! how we cheered !
How we rowed across the swirl !
Heedless all of water-whirl !
How the sea-foam sprang right over, as our rescue straight we steered.

. . . .

So with skill of hand and oar
Very gently then we bore
The fireman, nigh to swooning for the bitter cold and pain.

But no word of praise would come
As full-hearted we went home,
With the truest master-mariner that ever sailed the main.

—"Ballads of Brave Deeds," *Canon H. D. Rawnsley.*

JANUARY 20

Albert Medal of the Second Class to James Dee, a constable of the Swansea police force, for conspicuous bravery in endeavouring to save life at a fire which occurred at Swansea. **1883.**

London Fire Brigade Silver Medals to James Pearce and Geo. W. Burgess. For splendid courage and self-sacrifice in saving two children, who were in an unconscious state, from the upper floor of a burning house in Houndsditch. **1888.**

Four Northumberland Men sacrifice their Lives in trying to save their Comrades. W. M'Guire, C. English, W. Vickers, and J. Taws perished while trying to rescue a comrade from a retort house at Lynemouth Gas Works, the man having been overcome by sulphuretted hydrogen. Of the other workmen who made gallant attempts to save the victims and narrowly escaped the same fate, all but those named above, and the man they tried to save, were restored by artificial respiration. **1896.**

Two gallant East Riding Men. Tom Boyton, chief engineer of the steam trawler *Molope*, of Hull, lost his life while trying to swim ashore with a line to rescue the crew of his vessel wrecked off the Iceland coast. A seaman named Thomas North afterwards managed the perilous task, and the crew of nine landed in safety. **1903.**

JANUARY 21

Fifeshire Doctor drowned while trying to save his Wife and Child. On the occasion of the wreck of the emigrant steamer *John Tayleur*, on the rocks off Lanbay Island, Dublin Bay, in a terrific gale, Dr. Robert H. Cunningham, of Pitarthie, aged 27, made a splendid effort to save his child by swimming ashore. When half-way, the rope fastened to the wreck was dragged from the hands of those on the rocks. The gallant doctor, who was carrying his child, was precipitated into the boiling surf, but swam back to the ship. He endeavoured to save a woman, but the furious waves washed her away. He then tried to get his wife ashore. His efforts, however, were useless, and both perished, with their two little boys. Over 400 lives were lost in all, and about 230 were saved, among the latter being the captain, who was the last to leave the doomed vessel. **1854.**

Twenty-six Lives saved by the Portpatrick Lifeboat. While bound from Glasgow to the River Plate the ss. *Baron Glamis*, of Ardrossan, stranded on the "Ebbstone" in thick weather. The Portpatrick lifeboat at once proceeded to the scene, though at the time the weather was not so bad as to cause any alarm. From the position of the vessel, however, it was seen that if the wind veered round to the westward it would be necessary to take off those on board, and, therefore, the lifeboat decided to remain alongside. Towards midnight the weather got worse, but it was not till nearly daybreak that they were able to commence the work of rescue. Eventually all the crew were landed in safety at Loch Ryan, while the vessel became a total wreck. In appreciation of this excellent service, resulting in the saving of 26 lives, the committee conferred on the coxswain the thanks of the Institution inscribed on vellum and framed. **1904.**

JANUARY 22

HEROES OF ISANDLWANA AND RORKE'S DRIFT

The tragic story of Isandlwana's Camp of Death and the superb defence of Rorke's Drift are too deeply rooted in England's memory, and the facts have been too often set down in print to need repetition at any length. Their countrymen will never forget Melvill and Coghill, immortal heroes of the "Colours"; brave Wassall, the only V.C. hero of Isandlwana who lived to wear the small brown cross "For Valour"; or the little force of 100 white men behind their pathetic defence of mealie bags and biscuit boxes, who for fifteen terrible hours defended the sick, fought the flames, and kept 4000 ferocious Zulus at bay by sheer obstinate pluck. The various acts of heroism, which were acknowledged by the First Decoration in the Empire, touched the high-water mark of self-sacrifice. Nothing finer has occurred in our national service annals.

V.C. Lieutenant T. Melvill, **24th (S. Wales Borderers).** (Born 1842.) "Quod potui, perfeci."

V.C. Lieutenant N. J. A. Coghill, **24th (S. Wales Borderers).** (Born 1852.) "Non dormit qui custodit."

Killed by overwhelming hosts of Zulus outside the camp at Isandlwana, after the one hero (Coghill) had saved the other from drowning in the river. The "Colour" they died to save sank below the water, and was found by Major Black on February 16th.

"But we who feel what wealth of hope for ever there was lost,
What bitter sorrow burns for them, how dear those Colours cost,
Can but recall the sad old truth, so often said and sung,
That brightest lives fade first,—that those whom the gods love die young."

—"The Saving of the Colours," *Sir F. H. Doyle.*

V.C. Private S. Wassall, **S. Staffordshire Regiment.** In the presence of many Zulus saved a comrade from drowning in the river, both escaping death almost by a miracle.

The Eleven V.C.'s of Rorke's Drift, of whom seven belonged to the "Noble 24th," which claims sixteen recipients of the decoration—the highest number awarded to any regiment.

V.C. Colonel J. R. M. Chard, **R.E.** (Died 1897.) In command of the besieged post, aided by

V.C. Major G. S. Bromhead, **24th.** (Died 1891.) (Then both holding the rank of lieutenant.)

V.C. Lieutenant-Colonel J. H. Reynolds, **A.M.D.** Said "to have earned his Cross repeatedly."

V.C. Private John Williams, **24th.** His brother—not gazetted—and a man named Horrigan defended the make-shift hospital while the patients were carried into the other part of the building.

V.C. Private Henry Hook, **24th.** (Died 1905.) Who fetched water for the sufferers under fierce fire, and defended the hospital until all but one delirious man—who refused to go and was stabbed as he lay—had been removed.

V.C. Private William Jones, **24th.**

V.C. Private Robert Jones, **24th.**

V.C. Sergeant W. Allen, **24th.**

JANUARY

Frederick Hitch. V.C

John Williams V.C

Samuel Wassall V.C.

Alan Hill-Walker
Major
Col
Northampton
Regt.

John Doogan V.C

Reg Hart

V.C. Private F. Hitch, **24th.** Rescued six men from the hospital.

V.C. Corporal F. C. Schiess, **Natal Native Contingent,** who sprang on a wall and despatched several Zulus while suffering from a bad wound in his foot.

V.C. Mr. James L. Dalton, **Commissariat Staff Corps.** One of the four civilians awarded the honour, who did fine service in holding off the savages, and saved a soldier's life. **Zululand. 1879.**

"Flushed with victory then the Zulus made a sudden rush
For the hospital where our wounded lay, right in the heart of the bush;
And the sequel came to England—in the gloom a sudden rift—
When we knew of the deeds of the heroes who fought for us at Rorke's Drift.

. . . .

There were only four to defend it, and two of the number fell,
But Williams and Hook—both privates—were left in that scene of hell.
They kept their heads, and they kept the place, though the odds were hundreds to one,
Nobody knew of the task they faced till after the work was done."

—*Madge St. Maury.*

A Red Cross Heroine of the Connaught Rangers. Annie Fox, wife of Quartermaster Fox, of the 94th Regiment, was one of three women with a convoy escorted by a detachment of the Connaughts, which was attacked and cruelly massacred under a flag of truce by the Boers at Bronkspruit on December 20, 1880. Mrs. Fox was severely wounded, but, seeing that the "Colours" were in danger, allowed two sergeants to conceal them under her bed. She and other survivors were prisoners of war for three months. As the doctors were unable to extract the bullet, Mrs. Fox endured great agony, but notwithstanding this she amazed all about her by her energy and activity. Without a thought of self, this brave woman devoted herself to the sick and wounded, doing her utmost to cheer and succour her fellow-prisoners. On the conclusion of peace she came home, the terrible ordeal of her wound, privation, and captivity having utterly shattered her health. She lived eight years, dying on the anniversary of Rorke's Drift, and was buried with full military honours (the same as would be given to a captain) in Portsmouth Cemetery. On her monument it is recorded that "For her heroic and unselfish conduct on that occasion in nursing the wounded, desperately wounded though she was herself, she was decorated by Her Majesty with the Order of the Royal Red Cross. This monument is erected to her memory as a token of affection and esteem by officers (past and present), non-commissioned officers and men of the 2nd Connaught Rangers." **1888.**

January 23

A Norfolk Mother's heroic Death. On discovering an outbreak of fire in their house, over a shop in Market Place, Great Yarmouth, Mrs. Pigg, with her infant in her arms, ran upstairs to her other children, although the flames were spreading with fearful rapidity. She refused to leave her children, and immediately afterwards the roof fell in, and she with her three babies was buried beneath the burning mass. Her husband, one other child, and the servant escaped. **1868.**

Two Lancashire Miner Heroes. Daniel Walker and James H. Shorrocks were two of eighteen whose lives were sacrificed at the Stonehill Colliery, Farnworth, near Bolton. A large wall of cannel, 100 yards long, was in flames, and Walker rushed forward to warn the men of their danger. Shorrocks, who could have escaped, turned back to help his son, who was afterwards found clasped in his father's arms. **1877.**

Wreck of the *Republic*. Splendid heroism was displayed by Jack Binns, aged 22, wireless telegraphy operator, who stuck to his key and called for help in all directions when the liner was thought to be sinking after being rammed by the *Florida*. Binns remained at his post until the engine-room was flooded, the storage batteries exhausted, and the apparatus thereby put out of commission. The *Republic* eventually sank, but not before 2000 people had been rescued by vessels summoned to the spot through the steady devotion to duty of the young fellow, whom Peterborough is proud to claim as one of her noblest sons. **1909.**

BINNS OF THE *REPUBLIC*

(Mr. Jack Binns, of the White Star liner *Republic*, declined the offer of an engagement at a New York music-hall at £200 a week in the following terms: "I can't act. I'm a wireless operator, and I don't want to be made a tin god.")

Binns, wireless operator, by fear of death undashed,
When his liner with another in mid-Atlantic clashed,
Stuck to his job, and did it for fourteen hours or more,
And proved the means of bringing several hundreds safe to
 shore.

Binns, wireless operator, on touching Yankee soil,
The wiles of lion-hunters found it precious hard to foil;
For if he went to see a play they brought him on the stage,
And the practice of embracing him in public was the rage.

Binns, wireless operator, continually threw
Cold water on his worshippers ; but still the frenzy grew,
Till a music-hall proprietor, considering him a freak,
Came and offered an engagement at two hundred pounds
a week.

Binns, wireless operator, is not a millionaire,
But the loss of self-respect involved was more than he
could bear ;
So in spite of all the blandishments of Barnum and his
tribe,
He firmly but politely refused the tempting bribe.

Binns, wireless operator, you simple British soul,
Whose name is worthy to be inscribed on Valour's golden
scroll,
Most truly may your countrymen of your achievements say,
" *Tu saltem bene meruisti de Republica!* "

—*Punch*, Feb. 10, 1909. Reprinted by permission of the proprietors.

Carnegie Hero Fund. The Tottenham outrage was the occasion of a number of instances of heroism. Two foreign desperadoes, armed with revolvers, robbed a clerk, and to escape capture ruthlessly shot down all who barred their progress. A little boy named Ralph J. Joselyn and Police Constable W. F. Tyler were killed, the latter losing his life in the execution of his duty. A fund was raised for his widow, and also for those wounded while trying to stop the assassins, both of whom finally shot themselves. The Committee contributed £100, and presented bronze medals to Police Constables Nicod, Eagles, Dixon, Cater, Newman, Ziething, and Dewhurst. **1909.**

JANUARY 24

V.C. Major-General H. Shaw, C.B., **18th (Royal Irish).** "Per castra ad astra." With the help of four privates, whose names cannot be ascertained, saved the life of a wounded soldier under heavy fire at Nukumaru.

New Zealand. 1865.

Albert Medal of the Second Class to Alexander Christie for great courage in remaining in ice-cold water after his vessel, the *Expert*, had been run down by the *Countess of Durham* off Dunnottar Castle, and waiting until the only surviving member of his crew had been picked up. **1879.**

Albert Medal of the First Class to William Cole, of the Metropolitan Police Force, for conspicuous bravery at an explosion in Westminster Hall. **1885.**

Yorkshire Miner killed in attempting to rescue his Two Sons. After two explosions, followed by a fire, at Victoria Colliery, Rothwell Haigh, near Leeds, Samuel North went to that part of the pit to which his two sons and three other boys had gone to fetch "chocks." This was the spot where the first explosion occurred. The brave father's heroism was unhappily of no avail, as he, another miner, and the five lads perished from burns and after-damp. **1840.**

January 25

Postman's Park Actress, Heroine, and Martyr. Tablet 21. Sarah Smith, a pantomime artiste, was burned to death whilst extinguishing the flaming flimsy apparel of a companion at the Princess' Theatre, London. The heroic girl lingered for three days, when death mercifully released her. **1863.**

Postman's Park Labourer, Hero, and Martyr. Tablet 34. Thomas Simpson, aged 45, after saving many lives from beneath the broken ice on Highgate Ponds, was stooping to rescue another victim when the ice upon which he was standing broke once more, and the brave fellow perished. **1885.**

Royal Humane Society's Bronze Medal to P.-C. Watkins, who at great risk plunged into Prince's Dock—20 feet deep—at Hull, on a very dark morning, and kept afloat an old man who had fallen in until both were picked up by a boat. **1906.**

JANUARY 26

General Charles G. Gordon killed while defending Khartoum against the forces of the Mahdi in the Soudan. **1885.**

Always known as "the Good General Gordon."

Seven noble Beachmen of Yarmouth drowned while trying to save Life. James Boulton, William Warner, James Shreeve, James George, George Barney, Abraham Wetherell, and Gannam Hilling, in a furious storm accompanied by snow and intense cold, put off in a yawl to the assistance of a large brig in distress on Scroby Sands. A terrible sea caused the brig and the yawl to collide, and the latter was dashed to pieces. The lifeboat put off to their assistance. Eventually the beachmen and some of the crew of the brig were drowned, and the brig was also lost. The lifeboat saved eight. **1845.**

JANUARY 27

Swansea Lifeboat Disaster: Four of her Crew drowned. William Rogers, William Malk, John Jenkins, and William Jenkins were drowned in trying to aid a wreck at Mumbles Head. Their boat was stove in and her crew thrown into the water, the survivors being terribly knocked about. The Silver Medal of the Royal

The Lifeboat Medal.

The Metropolitan Fire Brigade's Medal.

National Lifeboat Institution was given to the coxswain, and monetary rewards to the members of the crew. **1883.**

Glamorganshire Albert Medalist and Two Men perish in Rescue Work. Daniel Thomas (see Albert Medal, April 11), manager and proprietor of the Dinas Colliery, Thomas Lewis and Edward Watkins lost their lives while attempting the rescue of the entombed miners after a serious explosion. Others engaged in this noble work narrowly escaped the same fate. **1884.**

"A noble deed, a splendid piece of self-sacrifice, have the same constraining attractiveness for the highest souls that beauty has for the artist; they are all messages from some distant fortress of God."—*Arthur C. Benson.*

Postman's Park Clergyman, Hero, and Martyr. Tablet 19. The Rev. G. Garnish, a young curate just ordained, lost his life while trying to save another in a boating disaster at Putney. **1885.**

London Fire Brigade Silver Medal to H. T. Harbour, who ascended a fire-escape at 72 Wigmore Street, London, W., and with the utmost difficulty, owing to the heat and smoke, rescued a man from the third floor. Harbour was in hospital a month in consequence of the severe burns he received in accomplishing this heroic deed. **1906.**

January 28

V.C. Major A. R. Hill-Walker, **58th (Northampton).** "Ready and faithful." While carrying a wounded officer out of action, a second ball killed the latter in his rescuer's arms. Later on, Major Hill-Walker saved two men, who were lying badly hit, under heavy fire.

V.C. Private J. Doogan, **First Dragoon Guards.** Although severely wounded himself, offered his horse to his dismounted officer, Major Brownlow, and was again shot while performing this act of self-sacrifice.

Laing's Nek, Boer Revolt. 1881.

V.C. Lieutenant W. J. Hardham, **New Zealand Contingent.** Was gazetted for a similar act to the above at Naauwpoort, twenty years later. **Boer War. 1901.**

"Heroism feels, and never reasons, and, therefore, is always right."—*Emerson.*

Edward Medal of the Second Class awarded to the widows of Robert Pattinson and Matthew Hilliard, who sacrificed their lives at the Roachburn Colliery, Cumberland. A heavy fall of roof had taken place, and a miner named Wharton having failed to escape, Pattinson and Hilliard descended the mine to his rescue but did not return. **1908.**

January 29

A Yorkshire Heroine (East Riding). Clara Robinson gave her life in a splendid attempt to save her father and mother from the blazing farmhouse of Sproatley Grange. She and her sister had escaped from the building, but on hearing that her parents were still upstairs, Clara rushed back, and was never again seen alive. This brave girl was to have been married a fortnight later. **1867.**

An Aberdeen Man drowned in trying to save his Child. George Watt, aged 30, an employé at Messrs. Pirie's paper mills at Aberdeen, seeing his little son of 8 fall through the ice on a dam at the Cutter paper works, near Aberdeen, went to his assistance. His own weight again broke the ice, and he sank in deep water and was drowned with his child. **1870.**

JANUARY 30

Edward Medals of the First Class to Arthur Torr Blakemore, Benjamin Kelly, James Brack Barnes, Thomas Menzies, Alfred Francis, and Joseph Graham Richardson; and

Edward Medals of the Second Class to Martinus, Coco, Thomas, Elias, Aaron, and Isaac, all miners employed at the Kimberley Diamond Mine, who after most arduous labour succeeded in rescuing six natives who had been cut off by a mud rush at the mine. An attempt was made to clear the mud away, when a second rush took place. The only possible way of reaching the entombed men was by working over the top of the mud and handing it back in small quantities—a further rush, which would have overwhelmed the workers, threatening all the time; but they stuck to their task and succeeded in rescuing the six natives, who had been entombed forty hours. **1909.**

Kentish Schoolboy's Death while trying to save a Companion. On or about this day at New Romney, Frank Allen, aged 12, and Charles Pearce, aged 14, were skating on a pond, when the ice broke and the latter fell through. Allen went to his assistance, but he too fell in. At length Allen obtained a slight hold upon the broken ice. Just as he did so, Pearce rose to the surface, and in his desperation gripped his friend's arm so tightly that the latter let go his hold, and both sank. **1870.**

A gallant Norfolk Rescue. Mr. William Wright, of the smack *Wildflower*, saved twenty lives off Lowestoft when the German steamer *Elbe* went down. The captain of the *Elbe* and three hundred and thirty-three others perished in this disaster. **1895.**

JANUARY 31

V.C. Sergeant S. M'Gaw, **Black Watch.** (Died 1878.) Led a party through hard fighting the whole day, being at the same time severely wounded.

Amoaful, Ashantee. 1874.

V.C. Lieut.-General Sir Reginald C. Hart, K.C.B., **R.E.** (Born 1848.) "Celer atque fidelis." Ran 1200 yards across rocky ground at Dakkah and brought into safety a wounded native soldier. The Victoria Cross is one of five decorations this gallant soldier has received for saving life. **Afghanistan. 1879.**

"Tragedy warms the soul, elevates the heart, can, and ought to create heroes."—*Napoleon.*

Albert Medal of the Second Class to Lieutenant Alfred Carpenter, R.N., of H.M.S. *Challenger*, for attempting to save a seaman who had fallen overboard. **1876.**

A Naval Lieutenant's heroic Death from Cold and Exposure. Lieutenant Michael Breen, R.N., while serving with the fleet at Salamis Bay, was with a number of others thrown from a pinnace into the sea during a gale near the island of Lypso. Several reached the island, but the cold became so severe that the clothes of the wrecked men froze upon them. One of them suffered so intensely that Lieutenant Breen generously took off his own coat, and laid it over the poor fellow. Some of the party took refuge in a cave, and were found three days later in a torpid condition. Mr. Breen wandered away alone, and was found dead. Ten men were missing.

1850.

Splendid Lifeboat Work. When the German steamer *Eider* struck the rocks off the Isle of Wight in a dense fog, nearly 800 lives, the mails, and a quantity of silver bars were saved by the noble exertions of the lifeboat men. The German Emperor subsequently presented £200 to the Royal National Lifeboat Institution, and gold watches, &c., to some of the masters of the boats which rendered such fine service on the occasion. **1892.**

FEBRUARY

England's heart! Oh, never fear
The sturdy good old stock;
Nothing's false or hollow here,
But solid as a rock."

—MARTIN F. TUPPER.

FEBRUARY

FEBRUARY 1

V.C. Major Lord E. F. Gifford, **24th (S. Wales Borderers).** (Born 1849.) "Non sine numine." Distinguished himself on many occasions as a scout, going alone repeatedly where no other white man would venture. His finest act was at the taking of Becquah on this date. **Ashantee. 1874.**

"I am just going to leap into the dark."—*Rabelais.*

Stanhope Medal to Alexander C. Henderson, who in a fearful storm in the Bay of Biscay went from the ss. *City of Corinth*, of which he was third officer, to a wrecked brig, and brought back by means of a line a man who was hanging on to some wreckage. **1902.**

Some splendid Attempts to save Life in Glamorganshire. Loss of Six of the Crew of the Mumbles Lifeboat. Tom Rogers, Daniel Claypit, George Michael, David John Morgan, Tom Gammon, and Bob Smith, all middle-aged men, were drowned by the capsizing of the lifeboat *George Stephenson VII.*, when going to the assistance of the ss. *Christiana* off Port Talbot in a fearful sea. The survivors, aided by three French sailors and an Irishman, did all that was possible to rescue their ill-fated comrades. Captain Jones, harbour master of Port Talbot, seeing a poor fellow struggling with one leg caught between two boulders, succeeded in reaching the man, when a furious wave dashed him thirty yards away and flung him against the concrete wall, which hurt and partly disabled him. The brave captain, however, again reached the drowning man, but, owing to the injuries he had received, was unable to retain his hold. One of the saddest circumstances in connection with the tragedy was that, owing to some misunderstanding, the lifeboat had been called out, when her services were not really required. **1903.**

Carnegie Hero Fund. The sum of £25 awarded to the parents of Alexander Macfarlane, a labourer at Greenlaw, who lost his life while attempting to save a friend who had fallen through the ice into water eleven feet deep. **1909.**

FEBRUARY 2

Royal Humane Society's Bronze Medal to George Tremayne, chief officer of the training ship *Clio*, who in very cold weather dived from a boat and saved the life of a boy who had fallen from the vessel. **1907.**

Liverpool S. & H. Society's Clasp to Gold Medal (see April 28) and binoculars to Mr. Stephen H. Hobbs, chief officer of the ss. *St. Cuthbert*, for the ability, courage, and devotion displayed on the occasion of that steamer being on fire on a voyage from Antwerp to New York. The master being incapacitated, the command of the vessel and all responsibility in connection with the rescue of the crew devolved on Mr. Hobbs, who so carried out these duties as to win the encomiums of the naval court, the owners, and all concerned. **1908.**

FEBRUARY 3

From His Majesty King Edward VII., Eight Silver Medals to the crew who manned the *Cymric's* lifeboat; also

From the Board of Trade, a Silver Cup to Lieutenant W. Finch, R.N.R., the commander, and a binocular glass to Lieutenant John Stivey, R.N.R., in charge of the lifeboat; and

The Liverpool S. & H. Society's Gold Medals to each of the above officers for great gallantry in rescuing forty-one survivors of the ss. *St. Cuthbert*, abandoned on fire in the North Atlantic Ocean. **1908.**

A Glasgow Stableman drowned while saving an old Man. While a large number of people were skating on a pond near Rutherford Bridge, the ice broke and several men were drowned. An old man who had saved two lives became exhausted, and Robert Park, aged 20, went to his assistance and held him up until he was drawn ashore by a rope. The gallant young fellow himself became exhausted and perished. **1878.**

February 4

V.C. Colonel Mark S. Bell, C.B., **R.E.** (Died 1906.) "Perseverantia." For intrepid coolness and courage in remaining with and encouraging a party of Fantee labourers who were working under double fire without a covering party—an almost unprecedented occurrence in British warfare. **Ordashu, Ashantee. 1874.**

A Wiltshire Hero. Jacob Isley, of Trowbridge, lost his life in attempting to save that of a workman who had become unconscious from the fumes in a beer vat. The man's father had been trying to pull his son out, and, when the rope broke, Mr. Isley ventured into the vat, and both perished in the noxious gas. **1869.**

A noble Daughter. Royal Humane Society's Bronze Medal to Miss Nora K. Wilson. While skating on the canal at Tiverton, Lady Wilson fell through the ice in six feet of water seven yards from the bank. Her daughter Nora crawled to the hole, and managed to support her mother till she ultimately brought her within reach of the bank, where both were pulled out. **1907.**

FEBRUARY 5

Albert Medal of the Second Class to Thomas Chapman for gallantry in saving life in a colliery at Calstock, Cornwall, after an accident. **1889.**

Postman's Park Hero and Martyr. Tablet 39. Edward Blake lost his life while attempting to save two drowning girls at Welsh Harp pools, Hendon. The ice had broken and Blake went down in sight of his brother, who eventually succeeded in saving the drowning girls. **1895.**

Three Heroes of Yorkshire. Carnegie Hero Fund. Awards of £3 per month to the father of Melchior Chadwick, and a similar allowance to his widow; £3 per month to the father of George Gibbon; and a donation of £20 to the father of Thomas Leng Major. Chadwick, Gibbon, and Major were drowned at North Landing, Flamborough, while making an heroic effort to save the lives of three men whose coble was sinking near the rocks. The men were got aboard the rescuing coble *The Two Brothers*, but this was struck by a terrific wave and overwhelmed in the raging sea. None of the six men emerged alive. **1909.**

FEBRUARY 6

V.C. Sergeant W. B. Traynor, **W. Yorks Regiment.** (Born 1870.) After risking his life to save a wounded man at Bothwell Camp, an act in which he was nobly seconded by Corporal Lintott, and in the performance of which he was badly hit, he remained in command of his section throughout the action. Lintott received the medal for "Distinguished Conduct."

Boer War. 1901.

Two heroic Miners of Monmouthshire. James Thomas and William Reed sacrificed their lives at Llanerch Colliery, near Pontypool, the former in rescuing a comrade, and the latter in waiting after the explosion in the mine to search for his son. Father and son were afterwards found in each other's arms. **1890.**

London Fire Brigade Silver Medals to William J. Drain and Samuel Maystone, who saved three lives from a room on the second floor of a house in Banner Street, St. Luke's. The gallant men brought down their charges by means of a fire-escape. **1894.**

FEBRUARY 7

Stanhope Medal to Captain the Hon. E. B. Fremantle, C.B., R.N., who sprang from H.M.S. *Invincible* between Aboukir Bay and Alexandria after a man who had fallen overboard, and kept him afloat in a shark-ridden sea until they were picked up by the ship's cutter. **1880.**

"**Fletcher's Fight.**" Mr. William Fletcher, a non-commissioned officer of Royal Engineers, with a handful of men, held a half-finished stockade at Malemya's Town, Nyassaland against 1500 warriors. After a stubborn fight of four hours, when their ammunition was exhausted, they charged their enemies and put them to flight. **1895.**

"We were eighteen men all told that day,
Inside a half-built wooden pen,
When the king Kawinga came our way
With his fifteen hundred fighting men.

. . . .

'Now fix your bayonets,' loud I cried,
'Let us give them a cheer and charge, my men.
It is better by far to fall outside
Than die like beasts in a cattle pen.'

. . . . . .

And the cheer we gave as beneath the smoke
Of our own fierce volley we charged like flame,
It bred such panic, the foemen broke,
For they deemed that devils to fight them came."

—"Ballads of Brave Deeds," *Canon Rawnsley.*

FEBRUARY 8

V.C. Major-General A. T. Moore, C.B., **3rd Bombay Light Cavalry.** (Born 1830.) "Fortis cadere, cedere non potest."

V.C. Captain J. G. Malcolmson, **3rd Bombay Light Cavalry.** (Died 1902.) Associated in one of the most thrilling episodes in Victoria Cross annals, wherein one V.C. hero saved the other's life. At Khoosh-ab, General Moore achieved a feat almost unparalleled in warfare. Charging an infantry square of 500 Persians, he leaped clean over the bristling bayonets into their midst, where he stood with shattered sabre astride his dead charger, when his brother-officer fought his way through the enemy, gave a stirrup to his comrade at bay, and bore him triumphantly out of the very jaws of death.

Persia. 1857.

V.C. Surgeon Captain A. Martin Leake, **South African Constabulary.** "Parti animo." This gallant surgeon, while tending the wounded under heavy fire from 40 Boers at 100 yards range at Vlakfontein, was shot three times; but although so grievously hurt, he refused water to relieve his own thirst until all the others (eight) had had some. **Boer War. 1900.**

Royal Humane Society's Bronze Medals to Harold B. Wright and C. F. Atkinson. At Orange River Colony a cart containing four persons was swept away while crossing Groenvlie Spruit, and three of them were rescued at great personal risk by the above-named. **1906.**

FEBRUARY 9

Whitby Lifeboat Tragedy: Twelve Lives sacrificed. John Dickson, Robert Leadley, Matthew Leadley, Robert Harland, William Walker, Isaac Dobson, John Philpot, William Storr, William Tyreman, George Martin, John Storr, and Christopher Collins lost their lives in rescue work in a terrific storm, which strewed the beach with seven wrecks. Five times the lifeboat, manned by the finest picked seamen of Whitby, braved the furious sea, and five times returned with crews saved from vessels in distress. A sixth vessel in peril was discovered; and, though they were exhausted by their splendid achievements, these noble fellows again put forth. Fifty yards from shore a huge wave capsized their craft, and almost within a stone's-throw of safety these gallant men were buffeted until all save one sank. They were watched by thousands on the beach, powerless to help those who had laid down their lives for others. **1861.**

"By such means as these we shall make the name of Englishman as great as that of Roman was in Rome's most palmy days."—*Oliver Cromwell.*

Stanhope Medal to Major H. W. J. Senior, **Bengal Infantry,** who, at great risk of being pulled under water by the drowning men, swam out on the Barrack River (India) six times to some coolies in a boat wrecked on hidden rocks, each journey rescuing one. **1881.**

FEBRUARY

A. E. Ind

W.B. Traynor Sergt.

A. G. H. Moore
Major General C.B.-V.C.-

A. Martin-Leake

Sergt. A. Atkinson

James Osborne

J. J. McLeod Innes

Sergeant Albert Edward Curtis V.C.

Royal Humane Society's "In Memoriam" Certificate to the parents of James Mather, aged 10, who lost his life in attempting to rescue a child who was drowning at Unsworth. **1907.**

FEBRUARY 10

V.C. Colonel J. A. Tytler, C.B., **Bengal Native Infantry.** "Occultus non extinctus." Decorated for a magnificent dash, single-handed, to the defence of the guns at Choorpoorah, during which he was shot in the arm, received a spear wound in the chest, and a bullet through the sleeve of his uninjured arm.

Mutiny. 1858.

Fearful Gale on Yorkshire Coast: Six Lifeboatmen lost. During the most disastrous storm within living memory at Bridlington, in which over sixteen vessels were wrecked, the lifeboat *Harbinger* capsized after doing splendid rescue work. David Purdon, Richard Atkin, John Clappison, Robert Pickering, William Cobb, and James Watson—six out of a crew of nine—were unable to regain the boat after she righted herself, and were drowned. **1871.**

A Waterford Girl drowned in trying to save her Sweetheart. Bridget Tracey, a servant, seeing a young man to whom she was engaged fall from the hulks into the water, jumped in to save him and was drowned. The man was rescued. **1901.**

FEBRUARY 11

V.C. Major C. Heaphy, **Auckland Militia.** While defending a wounded soldier from a swarm of Maoris, and staying with him the entire day, this humane and courageous officer had his clothes riddled by bullets, three of which seriously wounded him.

Mangapiko River, New Zealand. 1864.

A brave old Lancashire Wife. Catherine Garsden, the wife of an old farmer at Oswaldtwistle, near Accrington, who had herself escaped from their blazing home, went upstairs again to rouse her husband. Smoke and fire cut off their retreat, and both were suffocated. **1880.**

Carnegie Hero Fund. Award of £5 and **Royal Humane Society's Bronze Medal** to William Wilson, who in his oilskins and sea-boots waded through a terrific sea, carrying a rope from a coble in peril of sinking near Anstruther harbour. Wilson reached the shore in safety, and the rest of the crew were rescued by means of the rope. **1909.**

February 12

London Fire Brigade Silver Medals to Frederick Bishop and William J. Tizard. At a fire in Kensington Court, Tizard entered a room where two children were in bed, passing them through the window to Bishop, who carried them safely down. Tizard then resumed his search, but the terrible heat and smoke forced him to retire. **1895.**

A Life given for a Friend (Gloucestershire). Stephen Adams, aged 57, a collier, near Coleford in the Forest of Dean, died from injuries received in the rescue of his mate, upon whom a heavy weight (about 6 cwt. of marl) had fallen. Adams removed the débris and saved his friend, but the tremendous effort strained his heart irremediably, and he passed away the same day. **1903.**

FEBRUARY 13

Edward Medals of the First Class to John Jones, William Dickson, and T. Teasdale; also to the widow of the late William Nicol Muir the medal which would have been awarded to her husband. These four men showed conspicuous gallantry in descending the shaft of the Glencoe Colliery, Natal, with various rescue parties after a series of destructive explosions. It was while thus endeavouring to save the lives of others that William Nicol Muir died. **1908.**

Death of a Sussex Coastguardsman. Horace Terry, of Rye, was drowned when returning in a galley from the rescue of a fisherman, being swept overboard by the heavy surf. The man who was saved had been robbed and abandoned by his crew, and had crossed the Channel from Dieppe to Newhaven alone. His smack foundered, owing to his having mistaken the Fairlight Cliffs for Beachy Head, where there was deep water close inshore. He was in a state of extreme exhaustion when rescued. **1864.**

Carnegie Hero Fund. Award of a suitably inscribed silver watch to Angus Fraser, of Alvah, Banff, for a most gallant attempt to catch a bolting horse attached to a gig, from which the occupant was hanging by one foot, and was being dragged along the road. Fraser went in pursuit on his bicycle and stopped the horse, but the unfortunate driver died from his terrible injuries. **1909.**

FEBRUARY 14

Board of Trade Bronze Medal to Alfred G. Cheshire, coastguardsman, Jury's Gap, Dungeness, for saving two lives from a wreck. **1905**

Royal Humane Society's Bronze Medal to Lieutenant A. R. G. Willcock, R.I.M., who plunged, fully clothed, from the R.I.M.S. *Irrawaddy* in the Manbin Creek, Burmah, and rescued William Smith, who had fallen overboard. **1908.**

February 15

Relief of Kimberley. On February 15th, Rimington's Scouts, at the head of General French's column, entered Kimberley, and the siege, which had lasted 124 days, was raised. For his valiant and skilful defence of the town, Lieutenant-Colonel Kekewich was promoted to full Colonel. The defence of Kimberley, with only a handful of trained soldiers, occupies an honourable place in the history of the **Boer War.** **1900.**

Stanhope Medal. While the body of a native woman was being taken to a ghaut on the banks of the Ganges for cremation, signs of returning animation appeared. Under the impression that evil spirits had taken possession of her, she was thrown into the river where there was a whirlpool twenty-five feet deep. Kristo C. Chuckerbutty plunged in at the peril of his life and rescued her. In addition to the bodily danger, Mr. Chuckerbutty ran the risk of losing caste in touching what might have been a dead body. **1878.**

A Staffordshire Gentleman drowned in trying to save his two Brothers. While the three sons—Ernest, Benjamin, and Samuel—of Mr. Green, of Hart's Hill, were skating at Brierley Hill the ice broke and the two latter fell through. Ernest went to the rescue, but he too perished. **1901.**

Royal Humane Society's Silver Medal to James Gater for conspicuous gallantry in rescuing his comrade, a youth aged 18, from a flooded mine in the Coppice Pit at the Brereton Collieries, Staffs. **1908.**

FEBRUARY 16

Albert Medal of the Second Class to George Oatley, R.N., who was the means of rescuing the crew—five in number—of a vessel which had foundered on the rocks near Boddam, south of Peterhead. **1880.**

Six gallant Children of Kirkcudbrightshire. James Campbell; Mary Campbell, aged 10; Catherine Smith, 13; Elizabeth Faulds, 12; Jane Faulds, 8; and William Faulds, 14, with four other children, were walking by a loch near Springholm when the first-named went on to the ice and was precipitated into ten feet of water. In trying to rescue their companion all the others perished. **1873.**

A gallant Ayrshire Boy. George Quigley, aged 13, lost his life while trying to save that of another lad who had fallen through the ice at Kilburnie Loch. At great personal risk a policeman tried to save the unfortunate pair, but both were drowned. **1901.**

FEBRUARY 17

Albert Medal of the Second Class. After a terrible fire on the barque *Arracan* on this date the crew took to the boats, one of which was not picked up for thirty-one days. In this boat was David Webster, second mate, who by his heroic self-sacrifice and control of those with him ultimately saved their lives. The sufferings they endured from hunger and thirst deprived some of them of their reason, and it was with great difficulty that Webster saved the life of a boy whom the maddened men wished to kill in order to eat. **1874.**

Two Glamorganshire Miner Heroes. William Rosser, son of the manager of Pentire Colliery, Upstrad, Rhondda, and Joseph Thomas, collier, were suffocated by sulphuretted hydrogen while going with a rescue party in search of entombed miners after an explosion. The other members of the party turned back, finding the air unbreathable, but these two noble fellows sacrificed themselves in the hope of saving others. **1871.**

February 18

PAARDEBURG'S TWO SILENT HEROES

V.C. Lieutenant F. N. Parsons, **44th (Essex)**. (Born 1875.) "Pro Deo et Rege." After going out and dressing the wounds of a man of his battalion and bringing him back, Lieutenant Parsons went down twice to the river to fetch water under a hail of bullets. The gallant young officer escaped unhurt on this occasion, but was killed a month later at Dreifontein.

V.C. Sergeant A. Atkinson **(Yorkshire Regiment)** carried Lieutenant Hammick of the Oxford Light Infantry, who was wounded, out of danger, and then with splendid self-sacrifice went six times under severe fire to fetch water for his wounded comrades, but on the seventh errand of mercy was mortally wounded. The Victoria Cross, so nobly won, was sent after his death to the hero's father, Farrier-Major J. Atkinson, H. Battery, R.A., one of the party who helped to capture the Russian cannon from which the Victoria Crosses are now cast.

Boer War. 1900.

London Fire Brigade Martyr to Duty. Sydney H. H. Crowe, aged 22, while at work with other men at a fire in

Westminster Bridge Road, was buried beneath a fallen wall. All the others were more or less injured, but Crowe was killed. **1890.**

FEBRUARY 19

A Cornish Hero. Nicholas Jacobs, of St. Ives, went out in a rowing gig to the assistance of a schooner aground on Porthminster Beach. Two other gigs went also, followed by the lifeboat, and the five men aboard the sinking craft were rescued. The gig which contained Jacobs was capsized. All, however, were picked up, with the exception of Jacobs, who sank before his comrades could reach him. **1868.**

A Somersetshire Man dies in trying to save his Father. Edward Dunthorne, aged 31 years, a tailor of Glastonbury, was killed in a gallant attempt to save his father, who had, in a fit of temporary insanity, thrown himself in front of a train on a level crossing. **1903.**

FEBRUARY 20

A Flintshire Governess dies in trying to save her Pupils' Lives. Miss Mattie Garrett, governess in the family of Sir William G. Williams, Bart., Pengwern Hall, Rhudlan, N. Wales, was drowned while making a splendid attempt to save two little girls who had fallen through the ice. **1902.**

Splendid Lifeboat Work at Hartlepool. During a blinding snowstorm, with a strong northerly gale, the ketch *Myrtle*, of Yarmouth, with three men on board, was driven ashore near West Hartlepool harbour, lost her rudder, and became unmanageable. A tug got into communication with her, but after an hour's work had to abandon her, and the No. 2 lifeboat, *Charles Ingleby*, was launched to the rescue. Heavy seas were washing right over the doomed vessel, but with skilful management the three hands were saved. **1906.**

FEBRUARY 21

A Yorkshire Mother's Self-sacrifice. Eliza Gittings, whose little child had strayed on to the line near the Decoy Crossing, a mile from Doncaster, rushed to save it, but the buffer of the engine killed the little one, and the mother was terribly injured and died the same day. **1856.**

Fine Lifeboat Work in Norfolk. After a collision between the ss. *Martello* and another vessel in a heavy sea, in which the former was badly damaged, her crew were saved by the magnificent services of the Winterton lifeboats, whose crews were occupied for six days in salving operations. **1904.**

FEBRUARY 22

V.C. Private J. Osborne, **58th (Northamptonshire).** At Wesselstroom, under heavy fire from 42 Boers, Private Osborne rode into the open, bringing back on his horse a man who lay wounded and unable to move.

Boer Revolt. 1881.

London Fire Brigade Silver Medals to Frederick Tiplady and Charles Tennuci, who saved five lives at a fire in Warren Street, Fitzroy Square. **1881.**

Royal National Lifeboat Institution Gold Medal to Mr. William Owen, who by his intrepid and skilful management of the Holyhead lifeboat, *Duke of Northumberland*, of which he was coxswain, was the means

FEBRUARY

E. T. Inkson

Capt [illegible]

James Firth V.C.

Hugh George

Wallace Wright

Joseph J Farmer

[illegible]

W. T. Marshall

of rescuing the crew of the wrecked steamer *Harold.* Mr. Owen had previously received the Silver Medal of the Institution, as well as a similar decoration from the Royal Humane Society. The rescue was accomplished during a gale of unusual severity, and the lifeboat was at times in imminent peril of being driven against the disabled ship. A number of Silver Medals were also awarded in connection with this fine piece of heroism.

1908.

FEBRUARY 23

V.C. Lieut.-General J. J. M'Leod-Innes, **R. (Bengal) E.** (Died 1907.) "Pro patriæ." At Sultanpore, under fire from a hundred matchlocks, General M'Leod-Innes rode alone at a gun in possession of the mutineers, shot the gunner, and kept the enemy at bay until help arrived.

Mutiny. 1858.

V.C. Sergeant A. E. Curtis, **E. Surrey Regt.** Associated with Private Morton (not gazetted) in the gallant rescue of Colonel R. H. W. H. Harris, C.B., who had lain all day exposed to Boer fire. Despite the officer's repeated requests not to imperil their own lives, the gallant pair, after giving the wounded Colonel drink from their flasks, carried him into safety. **Boer War. 1900.**

A West Riding Man and Boy drowned in attempting to save the Brother of the latter. While crossing the frozen canal at Hoyle Hill, near Barnsley, Harry Williams, aged 14, fell through the ice. A labourer named Uriah Green, and the boy's brother John, aged 9, tried to save the drowning lad, but all three perished.

1895.

Carnegie Hero Fund. £20 awarded to James Priestly, a ploughman of Ballyroney, Banbridge, Co. Down, who was severely burned while extinguishing the flames enveloping a little girl who had thrown over a lamp. By his prompt and courageous deed the house and its occupants —a mother and seven children—were saved. **1909.**

FEBRUARY 24

V.C. Captain E. T. Inkson, **R.A.M.C.** (Born 1872.) Under a tornado of lead carried Lieutenant Devenish, sorely wounded, 400 yards into safety at Hart's Hill, Colenso.

V.C. Corporal J. J. Clements, **Rimington's Guides.** Although lying shot through the lungs and called upon by five Boers to surrender, he sprang up, shot three of his assailants, and compelled the others to surrender to a couple of his comrades, who came on the scene at Colenso.

"The star of an unconquered will."—*Longfellow.*

V.C. Sergeant W. Firth, **W. Riding Regt.** Carried one wounded man into shelter from heavy fire; then returned for Lieutenant J. H. B. Wilson, who was in the same plight. While engaged on this second deed of mercy, the gallant sergeant was shot through the eye and nose.—ARUNDEL. **All above during Boer War. 1900.**

Royal Humane Society's Bronze Medal to J. R. Denton, who slid down a rope from the ss. *Arzila* off Mogador, coast of Morocco, in a high sea and strong gale, and made a gallant but unsuccessful attempt to rescue a man who had jumped overboard. **1908.**

FEBRUARY 25

V.C. General Sir Hugh H. Gough, G.C.B., **1st European Light Cavalry.** (Died 1909.) "Faugh a' Ballagh." Distinguished himself on two separate occasions, upon each of which he captured a couple of the mutineers' guns. On this date had two horses killed under him, received a bullet through his helmet, another through his scabbard, while a third found a billet in his leg.

Mutiny. 1858.

Postman's Park Hero and Martyr. Tablet 37. Samuel Lowdell, a bargeman, was drowned after rescuing a boy from the Thames at Blackfriars. This was the third life this humble hero had saved. **1887.**

FEBRUARY 26

V.C. Captain W. D. Wright, **R. W. Surrey Regiment.** (Born 1875.) "Mens sibi conscia recti." With one other officer and about forty men charged and drove back a force of 1000 cavalry and 2000 infantry at Kano Sokoto, Nigeria. **1903.**

H.M.S. Troopship, "Birkenhead," was wrecked off St. Simon's Bay, South Africa, and sank within thirty minutes. There were nearly 500 aboard, of whom 454 perished, her commander Robert Salmon being among them. Splendid coolness and heroism were shown by the troops of various regiments. **1852.**

"All was silence. All was sleep. Night lay pillowed on the Deep,
'Neath cold stars that watched unwinking in a cloudless sky,
And these whispered to the Wave, 'Tell us stories of the brave.
We would see this night thy pageant, How the English die.'

. . . .

Then the sullen ocean played round the ambush Death had laid,
Rocking soft the gallant vessel where she rode its treacherous tide.
Till she touched the hidden rock, and night echoed to the shock
Of her rending, whilst the waters stormed the breaches in her side.

. . . .

The names may yet exist in some old war-office list
Of five hundred men that perished, heroes all. But tears might trace
With diamonds, not gold, such a tale as here is told,
How Death met young lads and veterans, and they stared him in the face."

—"The 'Birkenhead,'" *Dr. John A. Goodchild.*

Carnegie Memorial Medallion and £3 per month to the widow of Duncan Macgregor, who gave his life at Methil New docks to save that of another workman. The man was right in front of an approaching engine and had completely lost his presence of mind, when Macgregor sprang on to the metals and dragged him clear of the engine, but was struck himself, and died within a few minutes. **1909.**

FEBRUARY 27

V.C. Corporal J. J. Farmer, **Army Hospital Corps**. (Born 1854.) The tragic fiasco of Majuba Hill was relieved by one of the most courageous deeds of mercy recorded of our V.C. heroes. Under fire from the Boers, who totally ignored a white bandage held up as a flag of truce, Farmer was shot in the hand while tending the wounded. In spite of his hurt, he continued his work, but was shortly afterwards struck by a second bullet in the other hand, and rendered powerless to continue.

Boer Revolt. 1881.

V.C. Captain C. Mansel-Jones, **W. Yorks Regiment.** (Born 1871.) "Quod vult valde vult." While severely wounded, Major Mansel-Jones rallied his men, and "by his self-sacrificing devotion to duty at a critical moment" saved a position from the enemy.

Terrace Hill, Boer War. 1900.

MAJUBA, 1881

CRONJE CAPTURED, 1900

By Field-Marshal Earl Roberts, V.C., K.G.

Kincardine Lifeboat Disaster: Four Men lost. Samuel Leiper, cox, J. Brown, A. Main, and J. Lees, of the Stonehaven lifeboat crew of twelve, lost their lives through the capsizing of their craft on the bar of Aberdeen harbour while on her way to the assistance of a wrecked barque, of whose crew of sixteen only one was saved by the Aberdeen lifeboat. **1874.**

February 28

Ladysmith Relieved by the **Natal Carbineers and Imperial Horse,** under Lord Dundonald, after being isolated and besieged by the enemy since November 2, 1899. Magnificent defence by General (now Field-Marshal) Sir George White's forces and the Naval Brigade, under Captain (now Rear-Admiral) Lambton. **1900.**

Two gallant Cadets of the Merchant Service. While a party of twenty-two cadets of the training ship *Worcester*, under the charge of the boatswain, John Cashman, were out on "boat exercise" in a sailing barge on Erith Reach, a sudden squall capsized their craft. Cashman made determined efforts to save life, and succeeded in holding up several of the boys until help arrived, being much exhausted when picked up himself. A lad named Evington Ord Denton was bringing two of his comrades, who were unable to swim, ashore, but apparently another drowning victim seized him and pulled all under water. Another fine young fellow, Charles R. Johnstone, called to Cashman to save all he could, and that he himself, being a good swimmer, would do the same. Johnstone then seems to have been struck by the falling mast of the overturned boat, and he too sank. In all ten lives were lost. **1865.**

Postman's Park Railway Hero and Martyr. Tablet 10. William Goodrum, aged 60, a flagman, saved the life of a workman on the line at Kingsland Bridge Road by flinging him out of the way of an approaching train which the other had not noticed. The buffer of the engine, however, caught the brave old man, who was instantly killed. **1880.**

> "Whoe'er amidst the sons
> Of reason, valour, liberty, and virtue,
> Displays distinguished merit, is a noble
> Of Nature's own creating."
>
> —*Thomson.*

Surrey Youth of 16 drowned while trying to save a Man. While a man named Chapman was on thin ice on the lake near Cumberland Lodge, Windsor Great Park, he fell into deep water. William Howe at once went to his rescue, but the ice again splitting, he also fell in. Both were drowned, the efforts of another young fellow, who gallantly tried to save them, proving of no avail. **1886.**

February 29

V.C. Admiral Sir Arthur Wilson, K.C.B., K.C.V.O., **R.N.,** (Born 1842.) Commander of the Channel Squadron. "Res non verba." In a desperate encounter with a force of Arabs at El Teb, in which his sword was broken, Admiral Sir Arthur Wilson gave them a practical lesson in the British art of fisticuffs, fighting with his naked fists until help arrived. Afterwards, although wounded, he continued in action throughout the day.

V.C. Major W. T. Marshall, **19th Hussars.** (Born 1854.) On the occasion mentioned above, Major Marshall saved Colonel Barrow, who was lying wounded, from the enemy, by whom he was surrounded, dragging him through their ranks to a place of safety.

Red Sea Littoral, Soudan. 1884.

Royal Humane Society's Bronze Medal to William Saunders, hauler, who at Ebbw Vale, Mon., saved a youth who had fallen through broken ice on a pond into twelve feet of water. **1904.**

MARCH

"Lives of great men all remind us
We can make our lives sublime,
And, departing, leave behind us
Footprints on the sands of time."

—LONGFELLOW.

MARCH

MARCH 1

V.C. Lieut.-Colonel F. R. Aikman, **4th Bengal Native Infantry.** (Died 1888.) Received a terrible gash in his face from a sabre while, with only 100 men, attacking a rebel force of 500 infantry, 200 horse and two guns. Despite his wound, the young officer defeated the force and took the guns. This fine act was accomplished under heavy flanking fire on broken ground near Lucknow. **Mutiny. 1858.**

Albert Medal of the Second Class to J. W. Smith, master of a fishing boat, who contracted a serious illness in consequence of most heroic conduct in swimming 100 yards from shore in twenty feet of water during a fierce gale at Scarsferry, Scotland, to save life. **1891.**

MARCH 2

Three Heroes of Northumberland. On the occasion of an explosion at Usworth Colliery, near Newcastle, Richard Slee and Elijah Donnelly, with Mr. Lindsay, assistant viewer, went down the mine to the rescue of the imprisoned miners. Donnelly became stupefied by the deadly after-damp, and the others had to hold him up, when Slee also succumbed and fell. Mr. Lindsay made a splendid attempt to rescue the men, whom he dragged a distance of forty yards, but was found utterly exhausted and narrowly escaped death. Forty-two lives were lost through the accident. **1885.**

Seven Lives saved by the Berwick Lifeboat. The brig *Traen*, of Christiania, was wrecked during a north-easterly gale on the Goswick Sands, and the Berwick lifeboat *Matthew Simpson* went to her assistance. She was found fast ashore, with her cargo of telegraph poles floating about, which rendered the task of reaching her all the more difficult and dangerous, the lifeboat sustaining some damage. The crew of seven were eventually taken off, and within two hours of the rescue the vessel had disappeared. **1906.**

MARCH 3

V.C. Surgeon-Major H. F. Whitchurch, **Indian Medical Service.** (Died 1907.) While four Gurkhas were carrying Captain Baird, mortally wounded, in a dhoolie, three were killed and one wounded. Dr. Whitchurch picked up the stricken officer and carried him three miles through fierce fire, having continually to put down his burden to fight the enemy. Captain Baird was again hit before reaching the fort, and died next day.

Chitral Fort. 1895.

"The ravines might smoke and the rock spit fire,
But there on the heights was a wounded man!
If a hundred bugles had bade retire,
Would Whitchurch be baulked of his soul's desire
To save from the clutches of Umra Khan?

. . . . .

The Fort is won! they are safe inside!
Safe from the clutches of Umra Khan!
In the arms of his fellows the Captain died;
But the Doctor's daring—a nation's pride—
Shall live as long as we honour a man."

—"Ballads of Brave Deeds," *Canon H. D. Rawnsley.*

V.C. Lieutenant F. B. Dugdale, **5th Lancers.** Killed in the hunting field, 1902. "Pestis patriæ pigrities." Gazetted for giving up his horse to a wounded man, and afterwards finding another horse and bringing in a second wounded trooper in safety. **Boer War. 1901.**

Edward Medal of the Second Class to Morgan Howells. On the occasion of an explosion at the Neath Colliery, by which five men were killed, Morgan Howells and a boy, whose lamps were extinguished, began to make their way out, but the boy became almost insensible, and was dragged and carried by Howells five hundred yards into a place of safety. **1908.**

Albert Medal of the Second Class to Captain J. B. Willoughby, R.N., for a most heroic rescue of a soldier, who had fallen between a steamer and the pier into the shark-infested waters of Alexandra harbour. **1869.**

Stanhope Medal to E. A. Hatton, seaman of the *Dunbar Castle*, who, at dark, with a high sea and the steamer going ten knots an hour, rescued the carpenter, who had been swept from the deck into a sea full of sharks. **1895.**

> "What tho' Leviathan with mouth of hell
> Watched if his prey should overboard be cast?
> What tho' his ship thro' darkness to her goal
> Stood on with ever undiminished speed,
> He leapt to rescue, felt a brother's need
> Could claim life's offering whole,
> And plunged for God and Heaven."
> —"Ballads of Brave Deeds," *Canon H. D. Rawnsley.*

March 4

Edward Medals of the First Class to James Hopwood, James Whittingham, James Cranswick, John H. Thorne, and Walter Clifford; and

Edward Medal of the Second Class to Joseph Outram. On the occasion of the terrible disaster at the Hamstead Colliery, Birmingham, when, in consequence of a fire, twenty-four miners were entombed, the above-named men, together with John Welsby, who succumbed, descended the mine at various times at great personal risk to rescue their imprisoned comrades. They were unable to reach the victims. His Majesty was graciously pleased to allow the widow of John Welsby to receive the Medal which would have been granted to her husband. **1908.**

Two Cheshire Lads drowned in trying to save their Brothers. While William T. Day, aged 11, and his brother George, aged 7, were sliding on a small pit at Puddington they fell into the water. Charles Day, aged 17, and John E. Day, aged 15, rushed to the pit, and the poor mother, who had followed the boys, saw all her sons drowned together. The elder boys fully realised their risk in trying to rescue the little ones, as Charles had discovered a few days previously the great depth of the water, and begged his mother not to let the children go near it. **1888.**

A Derbyshire Heroine. Miss Monica Turnbull was fatally burned in attempting to save the life of her sister Dorothea, who was enveloped in flames through the explosion of a paraffin lamp, on February 9th. She died on this date, and her sister succumbed on April 29th. **1901.**

March 5

The Order of St. John of Jerusalem in England. Silver Medal to Mr. John Beynon, under-manager at Genwen Colliery, Cwyfelin, for gallant conduct and presence of mind in leading a rescue-party after an explosion. Mr. Beynon, who was in great peril from after-damp and gas, remained in the pit nearly all night. **1907.**

Royal Humane Society's Bronze Medal to Captain A. A. Sanders, who, when thrown into the sea at Karachi, India, with Lieutenant F. M. James, through the capsizing of their boat 220 yards from the shore, kept his companion afloat until they were picked up. **1908.**

MARCH 6

V.C. Corporal W. Goate, **9th Lancers (Queen's Royal).** For a double attempt to save an officer's life at Lucknow. Goate's Cross was sold in 1902 for £85.

Mutiny. 1858.

Albert Medal of the Second Class to G. Williams, coastguardsman, who, while saving several lives from a wrecked brig by means of a rope, was seriously injured. **1881.**

A tiny Salopian's gallant Death. While Percy Madden, aged 7, and his younger brother were playing by the Severn at Shrewsbury, the little one fell in. The river was in strong flood at the time, but Percy pluckily jumped in to help his brother. Both children perished before help could reach them. **1901.**

Stanhope Medal to John Stockton. While some men were cleaning a sewer at Warrington, the first man to go down the manhole was rendered unconscious by foul gas. Two fellow-workmen tried to save him, but were also overcome. John Stockton, a baker's carter, who knew nothing whatever of sewer work, at great risk went down three times and brought up all the men, one of them being dead. **1905.**

MARCH 7

Liverpool S. & H. Society award of 15s. to Horatio Horn for rescuing a woman from the canal near Bankhall Bridge. **1905.**

Splendid Lifeboat Service at Rosslare. The schooner *Yarra Yarra*, of Skerries, bound from Newport to Wexford with a large cargo of coal, was driven ashore during the night near the Rosslare Lighthouse in a strong gale and very rough sea. The lifeboat and life-saving apparatus immediately responded to their signals of distress. When the lifeboat succeeded in getting near the stranded vessel, the crew of three were in a position of great peril, owing to the darkness, the fierce gale, and the heavy seas, which were dashing right over them, but were eventually dragged one by one by a line to the lifeboat and landed in safety. **1905.**

MARCH 8

Ten Heroes of the R.N. Sub-Lieutenants William A. Jukes and William J. Talbot; Richard H. Thomas, William Renouf, Richard Bailey, John S. Squires, James G. Hewson, Frederick Holland, Samuel Blackburn, and William Heaney, seamen of H.M.S. *Ariadne*, lost their lives between Oporto and Lisbon in a gallant attempt to save a man who had fallen overboard. Nine of the above ten put off in a cutter, which was recalled after a long and fruitless search, but on her return journey was capsized and completely swamped. The starboard cutter sent to her rescue was also swamped, and one of her crew, Willam Heaney, was drowned; but the other occupants were picked up. All in the first boat were drowned, with the man they tried to save. Sub-Lieutenant Talbot had previously been the means of saving many lives.

1872.

> "God mend his heart who cannot feel
> The impulse of the holy zeal,
> And sees not with his sordid eyes
> The beauty of self-sacrifice."
> —*Whittier.*

MARCH 9

V.C. Colonel T. A. Butler, **1st Bengal European Fusiliers.** Born 1836. Died 1901. Under heavy fire swam across the river Goomtee to find the whereabouts of the rebels, staying alone on the other side until the position was captured. This officer had a miraculous escape from death at Delhi twelve months previously, when he was pinned between the bayonets of a couple of Sepoys to a screen. Neither of the deadly points, however, touched his body, and he promptly despatched both his assailants with his revolver.

Lucknow, Mutiny. 1858.

V.C. Lieutenant F. E. H. Farquharson, **42nd (Black Watch).** Spiked two guns, stormed a bastion, and secured a position. He was severely wounded the following day. **Lucknow, Mutiny. 1858.**

> "Danger, the spurre of all great mindes."—*Herbert.*

Gallant Rescue Work. While a gale was blowing from the S.E., accompanied by a cross sea, intense darkness and rain, the ss. *Malta*, of North Shields, went aground on the Bulmer South Rocks. The lifeboat *Miliscent* was launched at 1.20 A.M., and found the vessel lying in a bad position and leaking. Her crew of nineteen men were taken in safety to Bulmer. **1900.**

MARCH

[illegible]

Percy S. Marling

W. J. Gordon. V.C

H. Wm. Englehart

Redvers Buller

Edmund Fowler

MARCH 10

Three Coxswains of Isle of Man Lifeboats drowned. Moses Munt and Cotton, the two coxswains of the Brightstone lifeboat, and R. Cooper, coxswain of the Brook lifeboat, lost their lives in the sea off Atherfield, near the scene of a previous disaster. Munt and Cotton had already saved several lives, and it was on their return from the second journey to the ship *Serenia* that their boat twice capsized in what Munt, who has been in the Service since 1860, described as "the worst sea he had ever faced." All save the two coxswains were able to regain the lifeboat as she righted herself. Reuben Cooper of the Brook lifeboat also lost his life. **1888.**

Splendid Heroism in a Glamorganshire Coal-mine. Daniel Brounsell, aged 30, lost his life after a fearful explosion at the Morfa Colliery, when eighty-seven men were killed. Brounsell and two men, named Williams and Handford, had previously rescued five miners from the terrible choke-damp, and were themselves brought out of the mine insensible. When Brounsell regained consciousness he returned to the pit, and was again overpowered by the noxious fumes; but, though brought out alive a second time, he succumbed to heart failure. **1890.**

A Kentish Lifeboat Disaster: Three Men lost. During a terrific storm of snow and wind the Dungeness lifeboat put off to the assistance of a stranded vessel. So tremendous was the force of the waves that Daniel Ryan was washed out of the boat soon after she was launched. The boat capsized, but righted herself, and her crew made another effort to reach the distressed vessel, when their craft again capsized against the Faggot Groin. The poor fellows were washed about for some time, but eventually landed. Thomas Sullivan and Samuel Hart, however, died from exposure and exhaustion.

1891.

MARCH 11

V.C. Colonel Sir Henry Wilmot, K.C.B., **Rifle Brigade.** (Died 1901.) "Quod vult valde vult."

V.C. Corporal W. Nash, **Rifle Brigade.**

V.C. Private D. Hawkes, **Rifle Brigade.** (Died 1859.)

Associated in the gallant rescue of a fourth man in a narrow street near the Iron Bridge, while they were surrounded by a large force of rebels. Hawkes, although severely wounded, helped Nash to carry their comrade, while their officer fought the enemy single-handed, and succeeded in piloting them all into shelter.

Lucknow, Mutiny. 1858.

"The fire is biting bitterly; onward the battle rolls;
And Death is glaring at them from ten thousand hiding holes.
. . . .
Death everywhere, Death in all sounds, and, thro' its smoke of breath,
Victory beckons at the end of long dark lanes of death."

—*Gerald Massey.*

V.C. Major-General W. McBean, **Sutherland Highlanders.** Ploughman; private soldier; Major-General. In these few words is comprised the history of a soldier who achieved a deed seldom equalled in warfare. Meeting a party of eleven mutineers at a gate of the Begum Bagh, he despatched the entire number single-handed.

Lucknow, Mutiny. 1858.

Albert Medal of the Second Class to Mr. H. Hood, coxswain of the Royal National Lifeboat Institution at Seaton Carew, for saving life at imminent risk to his own on the occasion of the wreck of the schooner *Atlas* on Long Scar Rocks. **1883.**

Liverpool S. & H. Society's Gold Medals to Captain A. Schau and Captain J. Parry, and several Silver Medals and other awards to the crews of the ss. *Bostonian* and *Manheim*, for a magnificent rescue of eighteen lives from the *British King*, which foundered 120 miles southward of Sable Island. **1905.**

MARCH 12

V.C. Colour-Sergeant A. Booth, **80th (Staffs)**. With a few men covered the retreat of a party for three miles, thereby saving them all from a large force of Zulus.

Zulu War. 1879.

Stanhope Medal to Sub-Lieutenant D. J. D. Noble, who, when a man fell overboard from H.M.S. *Leviathan* in the Gulf of Lyons, at once went after him, but failed to save him. **1906.**

Royal Humane Society's Bronze Medal to A. Parkinson, who plunged into forty feet of water in Park Lake, Blackburn, and succeeded in rescuing a woman who was bent on suicide. **1908.**

MARCH 13

V.C. Seaman E. Robinson, R.N. (Died 1896.) For magnificent pluck in beating out the flames of a battery which had become ignited. Was severely wounded while accomplishing this act under a hail of bullets.

Lucknow, Mutiny. 1858.

V.C. Colonel P. S. Marling, C.B., **King's Royal Rifles.** (Born 1861.) "Nulli præda sumus." Gazetted for the brave and humane rescue of a wounded soldier, whom he carried eighty yards under fierce fire into shelter.

V.C. Private T. Edwards, **Black Watch.** For the fine defence of a gun, during which he was badly wounded by an Arab's spear. **Tamaai, Soudan. 1884.**

V.C. Lance-Sergeant W. J. Gordon, **W. India Regiment.** One of the three men of colour who have been awarded the Cross "For Valour," which he won for shielding his officer from being shot, receiving the charge through his own lungs. **River Gambia, W. Africa. 1892.**

V.C. Sergeant H. Engleheart, **10th Hussars.** (Born 1864.) While in great danger of capture and under heavy fire, rescued a dismounted man in a deep spruit near Bloemfontein. Was one of the last batch of men personally decorated by Her late Majesty Queen Victoria. **Boer War. 1900.**

A Daughter's Self-sacrifice in W. Riding. While engaged in rescuing her mother from a burning house at Hartshead, near Brighouse, Ada L. Crowther, aged 19, lost her own life. The mother was helped through a window by the girl and saved, but Ada was cut off by the flames and perished. **1903.**

Carnegie Hero Fund. A watch suitably inscribed and £1 per month for his benefit for one year awarded to George Bragly, 10 years of age, who rescued a younger sister and brother from a burning bed at Canonmills, Edinburgh. The curtains had caught fire, and this plucky little chap took the others out of the bed, which was totally destroyed. **1909.**

MARCH 14

V.C. Private D. Dempsey, **10th (N. Lincoln)**. Carried a bag of powder through a burning village near Lucknow, under fierce fire, to mine a passage in the enemy's rear. Dempsey had previously saved an officer's life.

Mutiny. 1858.

Royal Humane Society's Bronze Medal to Private J. W. Bradley, 3rd Battalion East Lancashire Regiment, who plunged into a dam at Karree, Orange River Colony, and rescued Private Turner, who had got out of his depth while bathing. On two previous occasions Private Bradley had performed similar deeds of bravery in the same place. **1901.**

MARCH 15

Stanhope Medal to William Allen. A fitter who entered a tar-still at Sunderland to do some repairs was rendered unconscious by foul gas, and two men who tried to save him were also overcome. William Allen then went into the still three times with a rope round him, each time rescuing a man. **1900.**

Liverpool S. & H. Society's Silver Medal and Vote of Thanks to Captain Achilles Andrea of the steamer *Scholar* for the rescue of the crew (twenty-five in number) of the German steamer *Licata* in the Bay of Biscay; also **Silver Medal and Vote of Thanks** to Mr. John Abernethy, chief officer in charge of lifeboat, and £2 to each of the boat's crew of four men.

The *Licata* was sighted about 200 miles north of Cape Finisterre in a sinking condition, flying signals of distress. The *Scholar* stood by for twenty-four hours in a heavy gale, after which, "urgent" signals being hoisted, volunteers were called for the lifeboat. Two trips were made, and the whole of the crew were safely brought on board. The sea was so rough that the lifeboat had to be abandoned. **1905.**

MARCH 16

Liverpool S. & H. Society's Silver Medal to Charles Lyons, who was seriously injured while pluckily attempting to stop a runaway horse attached to a brougham in Hope Street; also

Vote of Thanks and £1 to Charles Gardner for eventually stopping the horse. The Society made a grant of £1 a week to Lyon's wife for the fourteen weeks he was detained in the Royal Infirmary, and 10s. a week for three months afterwards. **1904.**

Royal Humane Society's Bronze Medal to H. M. Scantlebury, Customs officer, who, when two men were thrown into the sea at Queenstown harbour by the capsizing of their boat, immediately jumped from his launch, and with the aid of a lifebuoy kept them both afloat until they were picked up. **1907.**

MARCH 17

V.C. General R. H. Keatinge, C.S.I., **R. (Bombay) A.** (Died 1904.) Having with his servant the night before found a small path across a ditch into Chandairee, led his column into the stronghold under heavy cross-fire, by which he was twice severely wounded.

Mutiny. 1858.

V.C. Lieutenant-General Sir E. P. Leach, K.C.B., K.C.V.O., **R.E.** (Born 1847.) With a handful of Sikhs at Maidanah overcame a large force of tribesmen, being severely wounded by an Afghan in a personal encounter.

Afghanistan. 1879.

Albert Medal of the Second Class to Theophilus Jones.

Albert Medal of the Second Class to James Hudson, aged 17.

For a noble rescue by means of life-lines of seven men from a vessel stranded on the Cornish coast in a strong squall. **1867.**

Albert Medal of the Second Class to Corporal W. McQue.

Albert Medal of the Second Class to William Seed.

Together with other gallant fellows went on an intensely dark night over a breakwater of jagged rocks with ropes, and, although repeatedly dashed back by the furious waves, reached a wrecked launch 80 yards off shore at Gibraltar, and saved many lives. **1891.**

Carnegie Hero Fund. Ten shillings weekly for three months to Hugh Wilson, a quarryman at Newtownards, Co. Down, whose hand was terribly injured while pushing aside a large piece of rock, which would otherwise have crushed a comrade to death. Also £5 to a miner named James Thomson, for saving a man who had been rendered unconscious by bad air in a pit at Leven Collieries. **1909.**

March 18

V.C. Sergeant-Major J. Lucas, **40th (S. Lancashire).** (Died 1893.) For assisting Lieutenant Rees, who was lying severely wounded, under heavy fire in the Huirangi Bush, and remaining with him until help arrived. **New Zealand. 1861.**

Royal Humane Society's Bronze Medal to Samuel Ansett, who plunged into the Thames at North Woolwich (where the water was ten feet deep and there were no means of landing) to the assistance of a boy who had fallen in, and supporting him until they were both picked up. **1904.**

March 19

V.C. Cornet W. G. H. Bankes, **7th Hussars (Queen's Own).** (Born 1836.) "Velle vult quod Deus." Died after most heroic endurance of prolonged and fearful agony from shocking mutilation of all his limbs, received while charging the mutineers near Moosa Bagh.

> "To every man upon this earth
> Death cometh soon or late;
> And how can man die better
> Than by facing fearful odds,
> For the ashes of his fathers,
> And the temples of his gods?"
>
> —*Macaulay.*

V.C. Troop-Sergeant-Major D. Rushe, **9th Lancers.**
V.C. Private R. Newell, **9th Lancers.**

The former showed conspicuous bravery in attacking a number of mutineers, and the latter helped a dismounted comrade from the rebels at Lucknow. **Mutiny. 1858.**

Albert Medal of the Second Class to Mr. Frank Hughes for extreme courage and self-sacrifice in diving operations in a flooded mine at Bonnievale, Western Australia, to save a man imprisoned on a rock-drill. Mr. Hughes made four descents, but was then so exhausted that he was obliged to rest, after which he again entered the mine and took food to the imprisoned miner. Descents were then made daily, but it was not until March 28th that the water fell sufficiently for the poor fellow (then too weak to walk) to be carried into safety. **1907.**

MARCH

A. D. Cameron

John McNeill

C. E. Parker V.C.
Sergt Major

E. J. Phipps Hornby
(Colonel)

Isaac Lodge V.C.

H H Glasock

MARCH 20

Two Kentish Boatmen drowned in giving aid to a Schooner. In a strong wind and a heavy sea a schooner was experiencing great difficulty in making Ramsgate harbour for shelter, and a boat went to her assistance. When they got alongside the vessel and a man had jumped on board, a heavy swell filled the boat, and her four occupants were thrown into the water. Alfred Clanis and John Rigden were carried round the East Pier by the tide and both perished, while the others in a very exhausted state were dragged ashore by a rope. **1859.**

A brave Battersea Girl. Seeing that P.-C. Heal was being murderously assaulted by a powerful ruffian, Miss Florence Smith—a girl of 19—was the only one out of a large crowd who made any effort to save the policeman's life. Making her way through the cowardly crew, this brave maiden seized the constable's whistle and blew it. The policeman's ferocious assailant snatched it from her and threw it amongst the onlookers, but, finding it, she again blew it shrilly, thus bringing aid and saving Heal's life. He was, however, so fearfully injured as to be permanently incapacitated for duty. **1909.**

"A plague on all cowards, I say."
—*King Henry IV.*

MARCH 21

Royal Humane Society's Bronze Medal to Robert Hogg, and Vellum Testimonial to Thomas Fenwick, two schoolboys who jumped into the river Tyne at Gateshead and made heroic efforts to save four drowning children. One of the victims clutched Hogg so fast that he nearly lost his own life. Two of the children were saved by a man. **1905.**

Royal Humane Society's Medal to R. Barrett, a toll collector at Margate Pier, who plunged into the sea and rescued a boy who had fallen in. **1909.**

MARCH 22

V.C. Colour-Sergeant G. Gardiner, **57th (W. Middlesex).** For great courage on two occasions under terrible fire, upon one of which he aimed at the enemy from behind a parapet formed of dead bodies of his comrades.

V.C. Private A. Wright, **77th (E. Middlesex).** Throughout the campaign showed absolute fearlessness. On one occasion, while holding a position under terrific fire, was severely wounded. **Sevastopol, Crimea. 1855.**

Three Heroes of the Merchant Service. William Cawsey, chief officer, W. Hutchinson, second engineer, and C. Hansen, carpenter, lost their lives by going out in the lifeboat of the *Wilhelmina* (their vessel), to assist the *Taber*, wrecked in the Mauritius harbour. Their boat and another which ventured out capsized under the lee of the wreck, and when men, boats, and wreckage were washed ashore, the above-named three were dead. **1901.**

MARCH 23

First Albert Medallist: Albert Medal of the First Class to S. Popplestone for great courage in going out alone, over jagged rocks in a strong gale and dangerous sea, to the assistance of the crew of a wrecked barque off Start Point, Devon. Mr. Popplestone was repeatedly washed off the rocks, but he ultimately succeeded in bringing two men ashore. **1866.**

Postman's Park Heroine and Martyr. Tablet 11. Mrs. Jarman, a labourer's wife at Bermondsey, while making a third attempt to ascend a burning staircase to save her mother's life, was so terribly injured that she died three days later. **1900.**

A Lancashire Man's splendid Self-sacrifice. While John Barlow was in bed with a chill at Marsh Road, Little Lever, near Bolton, he heard screams from some boys skating near by. He got a rope and hurried to the rescue, cutting his arms with the ice, which he broke to reach the drowning boys. He developed pneumonia and died. **1901.**

London Fire Brigade Silver Medals to William J. May and Laurence A. B. Peile. At a fire in Whitechapel eleven people had been safely brought down the escape, but a child was missing, which May and Peile succeeded, at imminent risk to their own lives, in bringing out of the blazing house. **1903.**

March 24

Rescue Work on the Suffolk Coast. During a strong wind and with a heavy sea running, flares were seen from a vessel on the South Newcombe Sands. The Pakefield lifeboat crew proceeded at once to her assistance. On reaching the Sands they found the steam trawler *Frobisher*, with her rudder broken, but with the assistance of a tug they succeeded in saving the vessel and her crew of nine hands. **1905.**

March 25

Gallant East Riding Man dies in helping the Bridlington Lifeboat Crew. A man named Brown was drowned while trying to rescue the crew of the lifeboat *Seagull*, which had been dashed against the sea-wall. Ropes were thrown to the men, who were all got up in safety, but Brown was washed out to sea. **1898.**

Royal Humane Society's Bronze Medal to Thomas Harrison, who at great personal risk entered a lime-kiln at Dacre, Cumberland, and brought out a man who had fallen in and was unable to move, his feet having become fast in the contents of the kiln. **1905.**

March 26

An Exeter Hero. Henry Smith, seaman, of the *Uzziah*, of Salcomb, was drowned in an attempt to save life from the wrecked steamship *Pelton*, of Newcastle. The entire crew, with one exception, went down with the foundered vessel. **1882.**

Royal Humane Society's Bronze Medal to P.-C. Conrad Scott, who jumped into the Surrey Canal at Rotherhithe fully clothed, and saved a woman who had been thrown into the water by her sweetheart. **1907.**

March 27

Royal Humane Society's Bronze Medal to Patrick Dooley, who, despite the fact that he could only use one hand, plunged into the river Barrow at New Ross, Co. Wexford, swam forty yards, and, with great difficulty and risk to himself, rescued a drowning man from water twenty-five feet deep. **1907.**

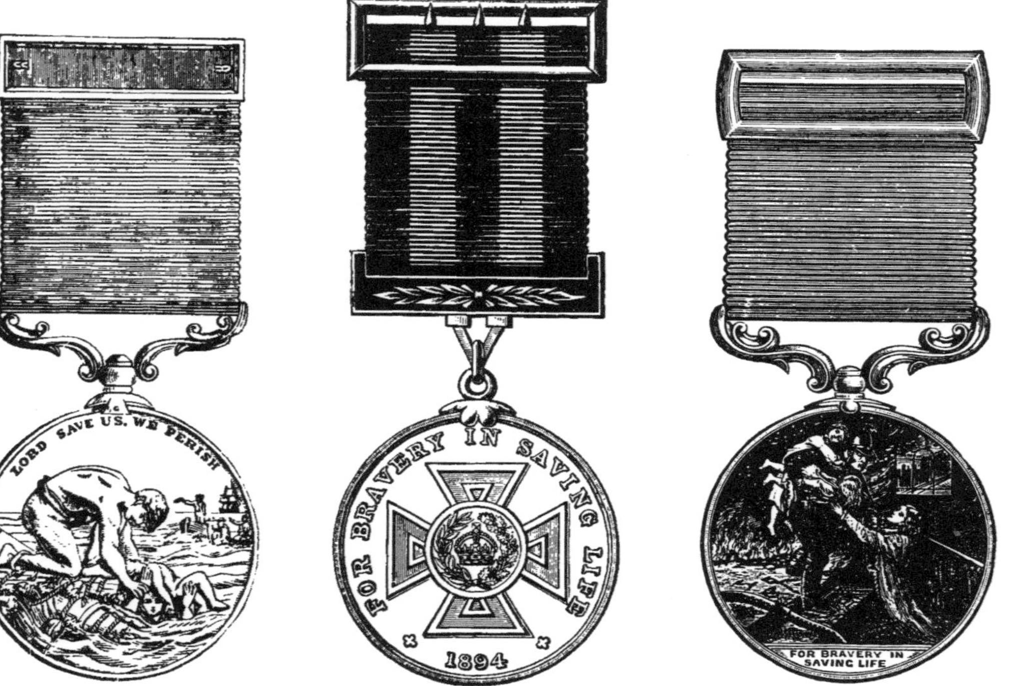

The Liverpool Shipwreck and Humane Society's Medal.

Liverpool S. & H. Society's Silver Medal and Vote of Thanks to Captain Thomas Jones, of the ss. *Turcoman*;

Silver Medal, Vote of Thanks, and binoculars to Mr. P. Phelps Williams, chief officer; and £2 each to the lifeboat's crew (four men) for the rescue of the crew of the barquentine *Bearne et Bretagne*. The vessel was sighted in mid-Atlantic, dismasted and flying signals of distress for her crew to be taken off. The lifeboat from the *Turcoman* in three trips succeeded in bringing away thirty men, while five of the crew came aboard in their own boat. **1908.**

MARCH 28

V.C. Leading Seaman W. Odgers, R.N. (Died 1873.) Victoria Cross, together with the New Zealand Cross, sold for £110 in 1904. Gazetted for gallantry in storming a position and capturing a "Colour" at Taranaki.

New Zealand. 1860.

V.C. General the Right Honourable Sir Redvers Henry Buller, C.B., G.C.B., G.C.M.G., P.C., **60th Rifles (King's Royal Rifle Corps).** (Died 1908.) "Aquila non capit muscas." The name of this officer will always be remembered for the dogged persistence with which its owner broke through well-nigh impregnable barriers, and eventually relieved the sorely beset garrison at Ladysmith on March 1, 1900. General Buller went through nine campaigns, including China, 1860, and Zululand, 1879, where he won the V.C. By sheer pluck he saved many lives—six at the very least—from a large force of Zulus, who cut up a raiding party on this date.

Zululand. 1879.

V.C. Major-General the Hon. W. Knox-Leet, C.B., **13th (Somerset).** (Died 1898.) Saved the life of Lieutenant Smith under heavy fire at Inhlobane Mountain.

V.C. Lieutenant-Colonel H. Lysons, **Scottish Rifles.** (Born 1858.) "Valebit."

V.C. Sergeant E. Fowler, **Scottish Rifles.** Cross sold in 1906 for £42.

These two rushed upon a number of Zulus in a narrow passage leading to a cave, where only one man could pass at a time, and by their dashing gallantry drove the enemy from their stronghold. **Zululand. 1879.**

London Fire Brigade Silver Medal to Robert Kington, who after vainly endeavouring to save a man's life nearly lost his own, the escape having caught fire as he began to descend it. **1892.**

March 29

V.C. Private W. Coffey, **34th (Border Regiment).** One of eight Crimean heroes decorated for the splendid feat of picking up a live shell and throwing it out of the range of danger. **Sevastopol, Crimea. 1855.**

V.C. Brigadier-General E. S. Browne, C.B., **24th.** (Died 1907.) "Tout jour." Decorated for riding back twice under hot fire, in face of a host of pursuing Zulus, and helping a dismounted soldier into safety.

Zululand. 1879.

The Order of St. John of Jerusalem in England. Bronze Medal to Lily M. Wood, aged 15, who, at terrible risk to herself, sprang in front of an electric tram-car, which the driver was unable to stop, and snatched out of danger a little child on the track. **1907.**

MARCH 30

V.C. Colonel A. S. Cameron, C.B., **Seaforth Highlanders.** "Perseverance." (Died 1909.) With a small party attacked a loop-holed house full of armed rebels, three of whom he despatched, losing half of one hand by a tulwar slash in the encounter. Colonel Cameron's four brothers and five sons are, or have been, in the Service.

Gwalior, Mutiny. 1858.

"This hand for my country."

V.C. Major-General Sir John McNeill, K.C.B., K.C.M.G., G.C.V.O., **107th Bengal Infantry**. (Died 1904.) "Vincere aut mori." Under heavy fire from a pursuing host of the enemy, rode back and rescued a dismounted soldier near Ohanpu. **New Zealand. 1860.**

V.C. Trooper H. S. Henderson, **Buluwayo Field Force.** (Born 1875.) This gallant soldier, whose comrade, named Cellier, was shot and dismounted, both being cut off from their party, put his companion on his own horse and supported the wounded man for four days and three nights, leading him at last into safety. Throughout this time the only food he had was a few plums.

Matabeleland. 1896.

Postman's Park Heroine and Martyr. Tablet 3. Wreck of the ss. *Stella*. While going full speed through a fog, the *Stella* struck on the Black Rock, near the Casquets, off Alderney, and sank in eight minutes. Mary Rogers, stewardess, after helping many of the ladies to put on lifebelts, at the last moment gave up her own place in the boats leaving the doomed vessel. Lifting up her hands she called out, "Good-bye! Good-bye! Lord, have me," and a moment later went down with the sinking ship. **1899.**

"Such souls,
Whose sudden visitations daze the world,
Vanish like lightning, but they leave behind
A voice that in the distance far away
Wakens the slumbering ages."

—*Henry Taylor.*

MARCH 31

V.C. Colonel E. J. Phipps-Hornby, **"Q" Battery R.H.A.** (Born 1857.) "Crede cornu."

V.C. Sergeant C. Parker, **"Q" Battery R.H.A.**

V.C. Bombardier J. Lodge, **"Q" Battery R.H.A.** (Born 1866.)

V.C. Driver H. H. Glasock, **"Q" Battery R.H.A.**

V.C. Major F. A. Maxwell, D.S.O., **Indian Staff Corps.**

All the above, with the exception of Major Maxwell, were elected, under Rule XIII. of the Victoria Cross Warrant, for an achievement unsurpassed in all the Royal Artillery's glowing records. The English batteries were caught in a death-trap, under an appalling deluge of lead, while the bullets rattled like hail on the jeopardised guns, of which nearly all the gunners were disabled or slain. The "U" Battery was captured, and the historic "Q" only escaped by sheer dogged pluck. Every man who took part deserved the little brown medal. Rule XIII. was, however, specially framed to meet cases like the above.

"Exigui numero, sed bello vivada virtus."
(Small in number, but their valour tried in war and glowing.)

Korn Spruit, Boer War. 1900.

Albert Medal of the Second Class to Seaman W. Carter, R.N., for gallantry in saving many lives on a voyage from Monte Video to Penascola. **1889.**

A gallant little Northamptonshire Lad. Dennis Petchell, aged 7, was drowned in the river Nene while trying to rescue a boy, named Dadford, who had slipped into the water. Another lad, named Osborne, fell in also while trying to help the others, and he and Dadford were eventually rescued by a man named Atkins, who pluckily sprang into the water from the farther bank. **1902.**

APRIL

" *The brave man is not he who feels no fear,*
For that were stupid and irrational;
But he, whose noble soul its fear subdues,
And bravely dares the danger nature shrinks from."

—JOANNA BAILLIE.

APRIL

April 1

V.C. Colonel H. S. Cochrane, **86th (Royal Irish Rifles).** "Virtute et labore." For capturing a gun at Jhansi, where he had three horses shot under him. **Mutiny. 1858.**

V.C. Major J. Leith, **14th Hussars.** For a brilliant rescue, single-handed, of another officer from several Sepoys at Betwah. **Mutiny. 1858.**

Seven heroic Officers of the Merchant Service. Commander E. C. Kemp; A. H. Tongue, 1st; F. Luce, 3rd; R. G. Atherley, 4th; and Henry Whitrow, purser; J. Marshall, boatswain; and A. Jones, quartermaster, of the Royal Mail Steamer *Douro*, in saving lives after a collision with the *Yrurac* off Finisterre, lost their own. Forty out of seventy lives of the latter were lost. One hundred and twelve of those on the *Douro* were saved, including all the women and children, except one. **1882.**

Brave Attempt at a Rescue by an Irishman. While playing on the bank of a dam near Dewsbury, a lad fell into deep water. Patrick Muldoon, although unable to swim, plunged in to save the boy, but both were drowned. **1900.**

Carnegie Hero Fund. An allowance of £3 per month awarded to the widow and child of William Galloway, of

Airdrie, who was killed by a lorry, the runaway horse of which he had gallantly stopped in Graham Street, which was at the time crowded with school children. **1909.**

APRIL 2

V.C. Lieutenant W. R. P. Hamilton, **Bengal Staff Corps.** For a brilliant and successful charge against a superior force at Futtehabad, where he also saved a life. This fine young soldier was killed at Cabul five months later.

Afghan War. 1879

Postman's Park Hero and Martyr. Tablet 15. William Drake was mortally injured while stopping the runaway horse of a brougham at Stanhope Gate, Hyde Park, whereby two ladies were saved from imminent peril. One lady was Madame Tietjens, the famous contralto, who promised to provide for her rescuer's family.

1869.

APRIL 3

V.C. Major-General H. E. Jerome, **86th (Royal Irish Rifles).** (Died 1901.)

V.C. Private James Byrne, **86th (Royal Irish Rifles.)** Cross sold for £35.

With great gallantry rescued Lieutenant Sewell, who was lying severely wounded in an exposed spot under terrific fire. Captain Jerome specially distinguished himself, and was shockingly wounded.

V.C. Private F. Whirlpool, **3rd Bombay European Regiment.** (Died 1899.) A splendid fellow, who rescued several wounded under fierce fire. Received seventeen fearful wounds himself while defending an officer later on in the Mutiny.

V.C. Bombardier J. Brennan, **R.A.** } Both decorated for fine service with the guns under fierce fire.
V.C. Corporal M. Sleavon, **R.E.**

V.C. Private J. Pearson, **86th.** For carrying a wounded comrade out of action under galling fire.

All above at Jhansi Fort, Mutiny. 1858.

Albert Medal of the Second Class to Sapper William Borland, who received terrible injuries from an accidental explosion of a 100 lb. gun-cotton mine on a boat engaged in submarine mining operations in Sydney. Finding the boat sinking, Borland jumped overboard, and, despite his hurts, supported two wounded comrades, one after another, until a boat came up. **1892.**

A brave London Girl. Beatrice A. Dunton, aged 18, was severely burned while, with great difficulty and at imminent peril of her life, rescuing two children from a blazing house in South Lambeth Road. A third child was fatally burned. **1909.**

April 4

Albert Medal of the Second Class to Edward C. Thompson, Esq., M.B., for devoted courage in endeavouring to save the life of a child dying of diphtheria at Tyrone County Infirmary by sucking the poison from his throat. **1885.**

Cambridge Undergraduate's Heroism. Temple Freere, Esq., of Trinity College, was drowned while trying to save a friend's life in the river Cam. His friend was rescued. This sad occurrence bereaved Mr. Freere's father (a clergyman of Roydon) of his only surviving son, the younger having been burned to death in a school near Harrow a year earlier. **1840.**

Liverpool S. & H. Society. Illuminated Vote of Thanks to Captain G. C. Apfeld for gallantry in extinguishing a fire on board the ss. *Friesland* in mid-Atlantic. **1903.**

April 5

Two Sailor Martyrs. Philip Hughes, of Llanelly, and Frank Martin, a Maltese, gave their lives in an attempt to save those of their drowning comrades of the barque *Gleam*, which struck on a reef at Port Nolloth, 250 miles from Cape Town. **1882.**

Liverpool S. & H. Society's Silver Medal to Mr. J. Walker, and illuminated Vote of Thanks to Captain B. Hayes, of the *Majestic*, and £1 to each of the life-boat's crew for great gallantry in rescuing the crew of the Norwegian steamer *Helios* during a gale with a heavy sea running. **1908.**

April 6

V.C. Sergeant W. Napier, **13th Somerset L.I.**

V.C. Private P. Carlin, **13th Somerset L.I.** Cross sold in 1907 for £63.

Both gazetted for great devotion in saving wounded comrades from the Sepoys.

Azionghar, Mutiny. 1858.

Albert Medal of the Second Class and **Stanhope Medal** to Sub-Lieutenant R. A. F. Montgomerie, afterwards Admiral R.N., who died 1908. For jumping from the bridge of H.M.S. *Immortalité*, into a sea abounding in sharks on a dark night, in an unsuccessful endeavour to save a man who had fallen overboard. The gallant young officer was himself picked up, greatly exhausted, by a boat twenty-one minutes later. **1877.**

Only Award of a Gold Fire Medal by the Liverpool S. & H. Society to Mr. H. B. Haughton, engineer of the steamer *Blackrock*, then in Prince's Dock, who, when the ship had caught fire while he was off duty, made his way through the flames into the engine-room, where he opened the cocks, allowing the pent-up steam to escape, and thus helped the Fire Brigade. By his superb coolness and courage a terrible calamity was averted. **1894.**

APRIL 7

Her Life for her Brother's (Staffordshire). Annie Grace Bell, aged 11, was killed at Lougton station while crossing the line with her younger brother in front of a train. The brave little maiden pushed her brother off the track, but in doing so was herself caught by the buffer of the engine, which hurled her some distance down the line. **1895.**

Carnegie Hero Fund. A grant of £5 to Mr. Thomas Dow, also Royal Humane Society's testimonial, for plunging into the Tay and bringing ashore, in an unconscious condition, a boy who had slipped from a rock and drifted into water 15 feet deep. **1909.**

APRIL 8

V.C. Lieut.-Colonel R. G. Scott, D.S.O., **Cape Mounted Rifles.** "Fidus et fortis." Had a hand shattered, and was otherwise badly hurt, by the bursting of a shell which he was throwing over the enemy's defences at a critical juncture during the attack on Moirosi's Mountain.

V.C. Trooper Peter Brown, **Cape Mounted Rifles,** hearing the screams of three sorely wounded men, went alone under a tornado of bullets to carry water to the sufferers, was himself terribly injured. After his death Trooper Brown's Victoria Cross and several war medals were sold for only 25s. They were afterwards presented to the officer in command of the C.M.R.

Basutoland. 1879.

Albert Medal of the Second Class, also **Stanhope Medal** to Mr. Alfred J. Cooper, fourth officer on the P. & O. ss. *Masselia.* When the ship was in the shark-infested Gulf of Aden, Mr. Cooper plunged overboard to the help of a lascar who had fallen into the sea, and supported him until they were both picked up by a boat.

1890.

A gallant Bristol Foreman. Two men having been overcome by foul gas in a sewer at St. Philips, James Smith made a plucky dash and succeeded in dragging them through the manhole. The brave man narrowly escaped with his life, himself collapsing as soon as he had accomplished his task, but recovered. **1909.**

APRIL 9

V.C. "The Hero of Manipur." Lieut.-Colonel Charles J. W. Grant, **Madras Staff Corps.** (Born 1861.) This dauntless young soldier's nine days defence of Thobal with only eighty natives against the whole Manipuri army is one of the most brilliant achievements in Victoria Cross records. Lieut. Grant was wounded in the neck in a fight with a Sepoy. **N.-E. India. 1881.**

Death of Three Dublin Men in trying to aid a distressed Vessel. John Bell, Lloyd's Agent, John Reece, coastguard, and Captain R. Bailey, of the schooner *Franklin*, were drowned while making a gallant attempt to save the crew of the smack *Boaz*, which sank off

Roddens Head at the entrance to Belfast Lough in the early hours of the morning. **1877.**

Order of St. John of Jerusalem in England. Medals to Herbert Attwood, John Simms, and William Gould for splendid rescue work after an explosion at Norton Hill Colliery, Somerset. Attwood descended a few minutes after the catastrophe; and as the cage could not reach the landing, 100 yards above the shaft bottom, slid down the greasy iron guides. He went some distance alone towards the scene of the explosion, and was afterwards joined by Gould and Simms. The noble trio found two of their comrades dead, and soon themselves succumbed to the deadly fumes of choke-damp, being found later on by another relief party. A large number of doctors, ex-soldiers, and others received certificates for heroic services on this occasion. **1908.**

Splendid Devotion of a London Well-sinker. Five men, while sinking an artesian well at the Savoy Hotel, became overpowered by foul gas. Four were rescued. John Perrin, discovering that his mate had been left behind, then insisted on going down again to his assistance. Both men were unconscious when drawn to the surface, but eventually recovered. **1909.**

April 10

V.C. Bo'sun's Mate J. Sullivan, **R.N.**, under terrific fire planted a flag on a mound near a Russian battery, in order to guide our men to the spot. **Crimea. 1855.**

New Zealand Cross awarded to Sergeant R. Hill, **Armed Constabulary,** for bravery at the relief of Jerusalem, Pa. Mohak, and other places. He also holds two Royal Humane Society's Medals. **1869.**

APRIL

Sergt Major W. Napier V.C. 1st Battn 13th Light Infantry Somersetts.

C J Grant Lt Col
92nd Punjabis

W.H.S. Nickerson Capt.
R.A.M.C.

O'M Creagh Lieut-General
Indian Army

Frank Baxter

A Northumberland Son dies in saving his Father. While Samuel D. Johnston, aged 26, and his father were in charge of a water boat near Northumberland dock, the latter fell overboard. The gallant young fellow leaped into the water and held his father up until help arrived, but sank himself from exhaustion as the old man was taken into the boat. **1874.**

APRIL 11

V.C. Quartermaster Sergeant Lendrim, **R.E.**, extinguished a fire in a magazine, also volunteered to destroy rifle pits before Sevastopol. **Crimea. 1855.**

Albert Medals of the First Class to Daniel Thomas, William Beith, Isaac Pride, and John W. Howell; also **Albert Medals of the Second Class** to David Davies, George Ablett, Thomas Jones, Charles Baynham, Edmund Thomas, Richard Hopkins, Thomas Thomas, Richard Howells, Thomas G. Davies, Charles Oatridge, David Evans, John Williams, David Jones, Robert Williams, Henry Lewis, Edward David, Isaiah Thomas, William Morgan, William Thomas, David Rees, and Rees Thomas, for splendid heroism in rescuing five men who were imprisoned nine days in a flooded colliery near Porth in Rhondda Valley, South Wales. **1877.**

Four grand old Heroes of Glamorganshire. P. Jones, C. Cavel, W. Williams, and L. Williams, all elderly men, after an accident at the G. W. Colliery, Rhondda Valley, each in turn gave up a place in the cage going up the shaft, so that a young man might be saved. When the cage came down again the four heroes were found to have been suffocated. **1893.**

"Out spake one of the four: 'My head is greyer than thine.
Leap to the cage, lad, leap, and say, if we fall in the smother,
Life had learned to forego love's best in the Rhondda Mine,
Was stronger to give than to get, was willing to die for a brother.

Up speeds the cage into light, with a shout, 'There are four left behind.'
Round roars the drum, and the sparks fly, as the cables outrun.
Slow, may the cables coil back, and the drum with a groan may rewind!
There are four brought back to the day who shall never behold the sun!"

—"Ballads of Brave Deeds," *Canon H. D. Rawnsley.*

Cornish Lifeboat Tragedy: Eight Lives lost. John S. Martin, James B. Old, Joseph Stevens, Sidney E. East, David Grubb, James Grubb, Edward Kane, and John Bate, jun., were drowned in Hell Bay, off Padstow, by the capsizing of a steam lifeboat on its way to assist a Lowestoft fishing-boat. The first-named four were battened down in the engine-room, and were either scalded to death or crushed by the machinery. **1900.**

London Fire Brigade Silver Medals to T. J. Lloyd and Evan George, who, by means of a fire-escape, and at imminent risk of their lives, rescued two women from the third and fourth floors of a blazing house at Egerton Terrace, Brompton. **1904.**

April 12

Gallant Act of a Cheshire Station-master. Noel Pitchford, station-master of Willaston, lost his life while trying to avert an accident to a train travelling at 40 miles an hour. An arm of a crane, which had been left near the line, was overhanging the metals over which the express would pass. Pitchford, too late, tried to swing the arm round, but dislodged the steel plate on the crane, and the falling mass, weighing 2 cwt., killed him instantly. As the train rushed by, the crane struck the funnel of the engine and one of the rear coaches. Several passengers were shaken and two injured. **1893.**

Postman's Park Hero and Martyr. Tablet 1. Tom Griffin was scalded to death at a sugar refinery at Battersea in a noble effort to save his mate from a room in which a terrible explosion had occurred. This sad sacrifice turned out to have been unnecessary, as his "mate" had already escaped when Griffin gave his own life for him. **1899.**

"A friend is worth all hazards we can run."—*Young.*

Brother lays down his Life to save his Sister (Devonshire). While on her way to take her brother his dinner near Bickleigh Station, an elderly woman, who was very deaf, failed to hear an approaching train. Seeing her danger, William Gregory, aged 59, rushed forward to intercept her, but was himself struck by the engine and killed instantly. The woman was also seriously hurt, but recovered. **1902.**

April 13

V.C. Private S. Evans, **19th (Yorks).** (Died 1901.) This man was one of the 62 who were personally decorated by Queen Victoria in Hyde Park on June 26, 1857. He repaired an embrasure under terrible fire before Sevastopol. **Crimea. 1855.**

V.C. Private J. Bergin, **33rd (W. Riding).**
V.C. Drummer M. Magner, **33rd (W. Riding).**

For great intrepidity in forcing the enemy's defences, being the first two men to enter the city of Magdala. **Abyssinia. 1868.**

Drummer Magner was 14 years old when he won the V.C., being the youngest soldier gazetted.

Her Life for her Child's: Rhondda Valley. At a terrible fire, in which five lives were lost, Mrs. Hemmings, a collier's wife, went upstairs to fetch her baby. The ceiling crashed down upon the devoted mother, who was found the next day with her little one clasped in her arms. **1909.**

APRIL 14

Heroic Cheshire Miner. Charles Jones was suffocated by gas at Astley Deep Pit, Dunkufeld, Cheshire, while engaged in rescue work after a bad explosion followed by a fire lasting thirty hours. He had ventured alone into one of the workings, and was not missed until his wife made inquiries for him. **1874.**

Gallant Deed in the Isle of Man. Mr. Alfred Rudd and Mr. J. M. E. Kermode were walking on the cliffs at the Abbey Lands of Lonan, and the latter, in trying to reach a bird's nest, fell into shallow water and hurt his foot. Mr. Rudd went to his assistance, lent the injured man some of his own clothes, and, after helping him on to the rocks, re-ascended the cliff. In taking a short cut at a very dangerous spot, he fell to the bottom, sustaining fatal injuries. Mr. Kermode, after a perilous and painful effort, managed to crawl up the cliff and reach a farmhouse. **1876.**

APRIL 15

V.C. Lieut.-General W. M. Cafe, **56th Bengal Native Infantry.** (Born 1826. Died 1906.)

V.C. Lance-Corporal A. Thompson, **42nd (Black Watch).**

V.C. Private E. Spence, **42nd (Black Watch).**

During the attack by the Black Watch on the Fort of Ruhya the above trio, with Private Cook, V.C. (see January 15), and a man named Crowie, not gazetted, went out under heavy fire and carried in Lieut. Willoughby, who was mortally wounded. Spence was also fatally hurt, and was carried by Captain Cafe into shelter.

VC. Private James Davis, **Black Watch.**
V.C. Quartermaster J. Simpson, **Black Watch.**

Decorated for similar gallant deeds on the same occasion.

V.C. Private M. Murphy, **Military Train.**
V.C. Private S. Morley, **Military Train.**

Associated in saving the life of Lieut. Hamilton, who was wounded and surrounded by the mutineers near Azimghur.

All above at Indian Mutiny. 1858.

London Fireman Martyr to Duty. Frederick G. Baldock, 34, was suffocated upon entering the area of a house on fire in Brixton Road. **1901.**

April 16

The oldest Hero in the Book (Suffolk). On April 15th Robert Watts, aged 78, went with others to the aid of a vessel in distress on Shipwash Sands, Felixstowe. Their boat was out ten hours in a rough and bitterly cold wind. The gallant old man died on this day from the effects of the long exposure. **1890.**

Liverpool S. & H. Society's Silver Medal to Captain A. M. Pope; and
Liverpool S. & H. Society's Silver "In Memoriam" Medallion to the parents of David Belsham.

In a heavy gale in the South Pacific Ocean the above men, captain and second officer of the barque *Dee*, together with their crew, at great peril to their own lives, saved fifteen people in their lifeboats from the wrecked barque *Cambrian Chieftain*. After accomplishing this, there was a second attempt to save the eleven men still on board. The one lifeboat was dashed to pieces while being launched, and the second, manned by Mr. Belsham and four others, was swamped in the darkness, nothing more being seen of her or her occupants. **1894.**

APRIL 17

V.C. Major-General M. C. Dixon, C.B., **Royal Artillery.** (Died 1905.) "Quod dixi dixi." After five guns of his battery had been disabled by a shell, which also killed and wounded ten men, gallantly opened fire with the remaining gun, which he continued to work with his own hands for seven hours under heavy concentrated fire from the enemy's line. **Sevastopol, Crimea. 1855.**

Albert Medal of the Second Class to Lieutenant C. W. Robinson, R.N.R. While the *Teutonic* was steaming at 21 knots an hour a passenger flung himself into the sea. Fully dressed, Mr. Robinson sprang from a height of 25 feet, and only about 30 feet forward of the propellers, towards which he was in great danger of being drawn. The suicide, after a violent struggle with his would-be rescuer, wrenched himself free and was drowned. The gallant young officer was picked up in a very exhausted condition. **1895.**

London Fire Brigade Silver Medal to Philip Renby, who saved eight lives by his great bravery at a fire in High Holborn. **1880.**

Father starves himself to feed his Children. Mark H. Vaal, aged 52, a dock labourer, whose wife was in an asylum, and who was unable to get work, fell down dead in London. It was proved that the man had deliberately starved himself in order to give what little food he could obtain to his children. "Feed my lambs." **1890.**

A Forfar Teacher gives his Life in trying to save a Boy. Mr. Thomas Millar, a Dundee teacher, in company with a friend and his son, had gone to Deil's Head, where the latter fell into the water. Millar plunged after him and succeeded in seizing the boy, but, owing to the slippery state of the rocks, was unable to land. The father of the drowning boy went to his assistance, and both were eventually rescued, but Millar perished. **1897.**

APRIL 18

Albert Medal of the Second Class to Mr. Edward Nicholls for great courage after a terrible explosion in rescuing his comrade from a mine at Kalgoorlie, Western Australia. When another explosion occurred shortly afterwards, Nicholls escaped without injury, but the man he tried to save was fatally hurt. **1905.**

A Lanarkshire Engineer loses his Life in saving the Stewardess of his Vessel. The ss. *State of Florida* having collided with the barque *Ponema* both vessels sank. Mr. John Bain, chief engineer of the former, made a fine effort to save the stewardess of his ship, and, against her will, had forced her into a boat, when the vessel careened over and he went down with her. The survivors were rescued by the barque *Theresa*. **1884.**

APRIL 19

V.C. Sergeant J. Park, **77th (E. Middlesex)**, displayed great gallantry on three occasions, upon one of which he was severely wounded.

V.C. Captain H. McDonald, **Royal Engineers.** (Died 1893.) For distinguished service at the Rifle Pits. **Sevastopol, Crimea. 1855.**

London Fire Brigade Silver Medal to Samuel J. Pipe for gallantry in saving a life at a fire in Great Prescott Street. **1881.**

A Worcestershire Mother's Self-sacrifice. Sarah Harris was drowned in the Severn at Worcester in trying to save her little girl, who had fallen into the river. **1897.**

Noble Death of two Leicestershire Colliery Lads. On the occasion of a disastrous fire at Whitwick Colliery the deputy-manager, J. Clamp, sent his son William and Albert Gee to warn the miners of their peril. They started, but never were seen again alive. Gee's body was not found until January 1899. It was then disclosed that the noble lads had performed their dangerous mission with the utmost bravery. Gee was found over a mile from the place he started from, and all this distance must have gone through a very narrow way in pitch darkness, facing smoke and foul air. His lifeless body was found beside those of the men whose lives he had tried to save. **1898.**

April 20

V.C. Captain W. H. Nickerson, **R.A.M.C.** Went out under heavy rifle and shell fire at Wakkerstroom to minister to a wounded man, with whom he stayed until he was able to place him in shelter. **Boer War. 1900.**

Postman's Park Hero and Heroine. Tablet 45. Arthur Regelous, carman ("Little Peter"), and Alice M. Denman perished while trying to save the children of the latter from a burning house in Bethnal Green. To reach the house Regelous had to go through a narrow passage between two walls of flame. "'Little Peter' has now become 'Peter the Great,'" said one who knew him well. **1902.**

APRIL

APRIL 21

V.C. General Sir O'Moore Creagh, K.C.B., **Bengal Staff Corps.** "Thournib' crev'th." Gazetted for conspicuous courage in defending for many hours with only 150 men the village of Kam Dakka against a force of about 1500. **Afghanistan. 1879.**

London Fire Brigade Silver Medal to Isaac Gooch, who saved three lives from a burning house in Somers Town. **1880.**

Postman's Park Hero and Martyr. Tablet 6. Herbert P. Cazaly, 30, a clerk, while attempting to save the life of a man in the Thames, near Kew, was dragged under by him and both perished. **1889.**

APRIL 22

V.C. Private R. McGregor, **Rifle Brigade.**
V.C. Private J. Bradshaw, **Rifle Brigade.**
V.C. Private R. Humpston, **Rifle Brigade.**
For exceptional bravery at the rifle pits.
Sevastopol, Crimea. 1855.

V.C. Trooper F. W. Baxter, **Bulawayo Field Force,** gave up his own horse to a wounded comrade, and was himself assagaied and slain by the Matabele. This gallant young fellow's Victoria Cross was sold in March 1909 for £45. **Matabeleland. 1896.**

"All honour to Trooper Baxter, who lies in an African grave,
Who gave his own life freely his comrade's life to save.
What better reward for a soldier, when he reaches his journey's end,
Than to have this epitaph written: 'He laid down his life for a friend'?

What prouder record could he bear above his soldier's
grave
Than this: 'Here lies a hero, who died his friend to
save'?

O noble soldier spirit, that deed of thine shall last,
When wars and all their pomps and pride are buried in the
past;
For thou hast proved to English hearts that deep within
them set
The grand old martyr of the past is living yet.

The old heroic spirit has never wholly gone,
Whose light at Crecy, Agincourt, and Balaklava shone;
It lived, that old-time chivalry, in every place and age,
Nor does the hero-martyr live alone in olden page."

V.C. Sergeant H. Beet, **Derbyshire Regiment.** (Born 1873.) Under heavy fire attended to the injuries of a wounded Yeoman and stayed with him until help came. **Wakkerstroom, Boer War. 1900.**

V.C. Colonel J. E. Gough, **Rifle Brigade.** (Born 1871.) Son of one and nephew of another recipient of the Cross "For Valour." The only family possessing three of these coveted trophies. "Faugh-a-ballagh."

V.C. Lieutenant-Colonel W. G. Walker, **Indian Army.** (Born 1863.)

V.C. Major G. M. Rolland, **Indian Army.**

Decorated for the splendid rescue of Lieut. Bruce, R.A., mortally wounded during the retreat of 200 men, who were short of ammunition and exhausted by want of food and water, before a large force of Somali. With four native soldiers those named rode back through a splashing hail of bullets, and, being cut off from the retreating column, fought through the enemy and succeeded in mounting their dying comrade on a camel. They eventually brought him and Captain Godfrey, also mortally hurt, into camp. **Daratoleh, Somaliland. 1903.**

Stanhope Medal. First award to "Captain Webb" (of Niagara fame) for jumping overboard from the ss. *Russia* in mid-Atlantic, in an attempt to save a sailor who had fallen from the ship. **1873.**

April 23

A little Heroine and Martyr of Yorkshire. Eliza Lockwood, aged 13, was caught in some machinery, from which she was trying to extricate her little sister, and died from the injuries she received. The mother of the children narrowly escaped the same fate, she also having become entangled in her efforts to save her children.

New Mill, near Huddersfield. 1888.

A Cheshire Platelayer's heroic Death. Robert Watson, of Northwich, who was unable to swim, plunged into the river Dane to the assistance of a drowning boy. Both, however, were washed over a broken weir and drowned. **1901.**

April 24

Eight Waterford Heroes drowned while trying to save a Vessel's Crew. T. McNamara, M. Duggan, M. Mulcahy, J. Maher, T. Crawford, J. Crawford, M. Raher, Lawrence Linahan, and Patrick McNamara went out in a boat in answer to signals of distress from a dismasted brigantine drifting towards the Gaynor Rocks in Dungarvon Bay. Their help was refused, and on their return journey the boat was swamped by a heavy sea, and all her crew, excepting Patrick McNamara, who reached land on a broken oar, perished. There were four widows and twenty orphans left desolate. **1852.**

London Fire Brigade Silver Medals to Charles H. Dye and John E. Watson for great pluck in saving two lives from a burning house in Mile End Road. **1895.**

Carnegie Hero Fund. £3 awarded to William Tasker, blacksmith, Gateside, Fife, seriously burned while rescuing a comrade on the brink of a precipice, where he had been thrown by an explosion. **1909.**

APRIL 25

Wreck of H.M.S. *Gladiator* off the Isle of Wight. The gig of the ill-fated cruiser and a silver salver presented to Captain Walker and other officers, and a number of Royal Humane Society's medals and certificates to non-commissioned officers and men of the 22nd Company of the Royal Engineers for magnificent rescue work in connection with above catastrophe. Corporal Stenning—recipient of a Silver Medal—was specially complimented by Admiral Sir Arthur Fanshaw (who presented the honours) on his bravery in swimming out, when already exhausted by his splendid efforts, and saving seven more lives. **1908.**

APRIL 26

Postman's Park Heroine and Martyr. Alice Ayres, 26, a domestic servant, by an act of sublime self-sacrifice, laid down her life after saving those of her master's children from a blazing house in Union Street, Borough. **1885.**

"One by one,
Nobly done—
Seeks the children through the smoke,
Though the red flame break the door,
Though the white fumes through the floor
Curl, to stifle and to choke.

. . . . . .

Somewhere still
Work and will,
Tried by fire can stand the test.
Still we think in Red Cross Hall
Of 'our Alice,' hear her call,
'Die for others! Do your best!'"

—"Ballads of Brave Deeds," *Canon Rawnsley.*

Fire Brigade Silver Medal to Arthur Whaley, who, after being twice obliged by the fierce heat of a burning house to retreat, made a third attempt and succeeded in entering a room, where he found two boys, whom he saved from a terrible death. **1897.**

APRIL 27

V.C. Private George Richardson, **34th (Border Regiment).** Captured and disarmed a rebel while himself severely wounded at Kewanie. **Mutiny. 1859.**

Albert Medal of the Second Class, also
Stanhope Medal to Captain S. W. Scrase-Dickins, **Highland L.I.,** who jumped from the deck of ss. *Peshawar* after a lascar who had fallen overboard, and supported him for seventeen minutes until they were both picked up. This gallant act took place between Aden and Suez, where the sea is infested with sharks. **1893.**

APRIL 28

Albert Medal of the Second Class to Seaman Robert Gray, R.N., for saving, at great risk of his own life, a comrade who had fallen from H.M.S. *Eclipse*, the sea being intensely cold and strewn with ice blocks at the time. **1888.**

Albert Medal of the Second Class to Robert Munro for a splendid attempt to save a man from being crushed by a train at Brodie Burn, on the Highland Railway. This unhappily resulted in Munro's being maimed for life. **1906.**

Liverpool Shipwreck and Humane Society's Gold Medals to Captain E. D. Fitzgerald, of the ss. *St. Andrew*, and to Mr. S. H. Hobbs, first officer; also other rewards to the men who assisted in rescuing the passengers and crew (sixty-five in number) from a sinking brig near Newfoundland. The lifeboat of the *St. Andrew* made three trips in a heavy sea and tempestuous weather. All on the brig save five, who were washed overboard or killed by falling spars, were saved. **1903.**

APRIL 29

V.C. Surgeon-General W. G. N. Manley, C.B., **R.A.** (Died 1901.)

V.C. Captain of the Fore-top S. Mitchell, **R.N.** (Died 1894.) Associated in a splendid attempt to save the life of Commander Hay (mortally wounded at Tauranga), in spite of that officer's orders to leave him and save themselves. Surgeon Manley was one of the last to leave the stronghold. **1864.**

A Gloucestershire Wife Martyr. When their house caught fire, Sarah Robbins, wife of a Bristol labourer, believing her husband to be asleep upstairs, went to warn him of his danger. The man had, however, escaped, and his devoted wife was fatally burned. **1901.**

Carnegie Hero Fund. The sum of £10 to John Butters, shunter, Central Station, Newcastle-on-Tyne, for great courage and humanity in rescuing a man from a subway where an explosion of gas had occurred. Seeing smoke and fumes issuing from a manhole, Butters went down twice, and was driven back by the heat and poisonous fumes. The brave fellow would not give in, but, having covered his mouth and nose with wet cloths, descended a third time, and, although himself nearly overcome, succeeded in bringing the man out in safety. **1909.**

April 30

V.C. Major-General W. S. Trevor, **Bengal Engineers.** (Died 1907.) "Quid verum atque deceus."

V.C. Captain J. Dundas, **Bengal Engineers.** Killed 1879, in Afghanistan. "Essayez."

Associated in a thrilling deed of superb pluck. Climbing over a wall 14 feet high, they stormed a blockhouse containing 200 ferocious Bhootees. The only available entrance was an aperture 2 feet wide near the roof. Through this narrow space the intrepid pair forced an entrance for their followers amid the massed swords of those within. The escape of the dauntless two from instant annihilation is one of the miracles of warfare.

Bhootan, N.-E. India, 1865.

V.C. The blind Hero of Magersfontein. Captain E. B. B. Towse, **Gordon Highlanders.** (Born 1864.) Having on a former occasion made a desperate attempt to save the life of Colonel Downman, on this date, while with twelve men who refused to surrender to 150 Boers, was shot through both eyes, his sight being utterly destroyed. Captain Towse received the hardly-won Victoria Cross from the hands of the august and beloved lady by whom it was instituted. **Boer War. 1900.**

London Fire Brigade Martyr. Patrick Fitzgerald, while working at a fire in Somers Town, was killed by a falling wall from the burning building. **1880.**

Postman's Park Policeman Martyr. Tablet 22. P.-C. Robert Wright, 27, was suffocated while searching for a woman supposed to be in a burning house at North End, Croydon. This deed of heroism was in vain, the premises being unoccupied. **1893**

Grace Darling II.: Burmah. This namesake of a famous heroine proved her right to her name by the following gallant act, which cost her her life. Miss Darling, who was head-mistress of the Diocesan School at Rangoon, was staying at Amherst. One of her pupils while bathing was seized by a shark or alligator, and was being carried out by the tide. The girl's sister and Miss Darling rushed in after the victim, and the latter had caught her by the hair, when she herself was attacked by the shark, and disappeared under the water still clinging to the child. Some native sailors came to the rescue and succeeded in dragging all three ashore, but the head-mistress and the favourite pupil she had nobly tried to save were dead. The exact date of this splendid deed cannot be ascertained, but the story came from the Rev. T. Ellis, of St. Gabriel's, Rangoon, and appeared in the *Times* of May 25, 1894, so that it probably occurred on or about this date in **1894.**

Carnegie Hero Fund. An award of £3, also £1 from the Glasgow Humane Society, to William Anderson, engine-fitter of Glasgow, who was unable to swim, but placing a life-buoy under his arms jumped into the Clyde and rescued a drowning woman. **1909.**

MAY

" Men of England! who inherit
Rights that cost your sires their blood!
Men whose undegenerate spirit
Has been proved on field and flood:

By the foes ye've fought uncounted,
By the glorious deeds ye've done,
Trophies captured—breaches mounted,
Navies conquer'd—kingdoms won!"

—T. Campbell.

MAY

May 1

Royal Humane Society's Bronze Medal. A native named Sarbag, seeing another named Gobina Rai fall from a bridge of boats into the Cabul River, which was in flood at Mowshera, India, plunged in at great personal risk and saved the drowning man. **1907.**

Liverpool S. & H. Society's Vote of Thanks to Nurse Lily Wright for rescue and first aid to a baby whose cradle was on fire in Paget Street, Liverpool; also 15s. to Elizabeth Gregory for assistance rendered on this occasion. **1907.**

May 2

Albert Medals of the First Class to Reuben Smallman, Arthur Stokes, Charles Day, Charles Chetwynd.

Albert Medals of the Second Class to Joseph Chetwynd, William Morris, Thomas H. Mottram, William Pickering, Frederick S. Marsh, Samuel Spruce.

For splendid rescue work after a terrible explosion and fire at Baxterley Colliery, Atherstone, Warwickshire, where thirty-two lives were lost. **1882.**

A Sutherland Man dies as the Result of saving a Child from Drowning. As Charles M'Intire was walking in Kensington Gardens on Good Friday, a child fell into the Serpentine. M'Intire plunged in and rescued the drowning child, but contracted a chill which was followed by erysipelas and terminated fatally in the Middlesex Hospital on this day. **1860.**

Deaf and Dumb London Hero. Robert Cox, 69, a porter in Bishopsgate Street, was suffocated in the upper floor of a burning house while trying to save the life of the little daughter of Mr. Nix, his employer. **1866.**

MAY 3

A gallant Gardener of Lancashire. Thomas Gibbons, aged 48, head gardener at Peel Park, Salford, while endeavouring to save the life of a woman who had thrown herself into the river Irwell, sank from exhaustion. The woman was saved by others. **1852.**

A Derbyshire Railway Hero. William Hull, a porter at Derby station (M.R.), seeing a man trying to enter a moving train, the doors of which were all locked on that side, sprang to his assistance, intending to pull him on to the platform, but slipped, and, falling over the buffers at the end of the carriages, he was killed instantaneously. The other man escaped unhurt. **1861.**

MAY 4

V.C. Lieutenant-Colonel F. S. Le Quesne, **A.M.S.** (Born 1863.) For devoted ministrations to the wounded under severe fire at Tartan, during which the gallant doctor was severely hit himself. **Burmah. 1889.**

An aged Heroine of Somersetshire. Mary Gibbons, aged 78, was fatally burned at Frome while endeavouring to save a friend of her own age whose clothing had caught fire. Both died of their injuries. **1860.**

Order of St. John of Jerusalem in England. Certificates of Honour to Charles Painter, Frank Smith, Hugh P. Logue, and George Humphreys. A man having succumbed to carbonic acid gas in a shaft at the sewage farm, Willesden, Painter went down to his aid, but returned, becoming unconscious when he reached the fresh air. Smith then descended, tied a rope round the unconscious man, and fell senseless. Logue followed, and, after placing a rope round Smith, also lost consciousness. Humphreys, in turn, descended, and eventually all the men were drawn up. The man they imperilled their lives to save was dead, and the four brave fellows suffered severely, Smith not regaining consciousness for six hours. **1908.**

Carnegie Hero Fund. An allowance of 21s. per week during total disablement to William Hutchison of Hebburn-on-Tyne, who rushed to save a child which had run in front of a horse and waggonette at the corner of a street. Both were knocked down; the child was killed, while Hutchison's right foot was crushed. **1909.**

May 5

V.C. Quartermaster Sergeant W. Gardner, **42nd (Black Watch).** (Died 1897.) Gazetted for saving Colonel Cameron's life from three savage mutineers, two of whom he despatched, at Bareilly. **Mutiny. 1858.**

A Boyish Hero and Martyr. Charles Hawker, aged 14, hearing his elder brother call out from the Surrey Canal, "Charlie, help me!" at once jumped into the water to his assistance, but unfortunately both perished. **1870.**

Postman's Park Lighterman Hero and Martyr. Tablet 24. Joseph W. Onslow was seized with cramp and drowned while trying to save a boy's life off Wapping Stairs. The boy was saved by means of a boathook from a barge. **1885.**

Carnegie Hero Fund. While engaged in driving a mine in the Saline Collieries of the West Fife Coal Company, a volume of water broke in upon three miners, two of whom escaped. The third man's retreat was cut off by the rising water. A rescue party was organised, who made a tunnel 20 feet long through a mass of fallen rock blocking the passage to the imprisoned miner. After four hours' perilous work the imprisoned man was liberated. Awards as follows from the above fund were made:—

A Medallion and £25 to Mr. John Clemenson, manager, who organised the rescue and took the most dangerous part of the work.

Medallion and £15 to James Scott.

Medallion and £10 to William Taylor, junior, who assisted in opening the tunnel.

£5 each to Henry Baxter, George Fraser, and Charles White.

£3 each to James White, senior, P. Kelly, William Taylor, senior, and Fleming Easton. **1909.**

May 6

V.C. Private V. Bambrick, **60th (King's Royal Rifles),** for gallantry in a desperate encounter with three mutineers, in which he was seriously wounded, at Bareilly. **Mutiny. 1858.**

A Salopian workaday Hero. Thomas Evans, a bricklayer, lost his life at Broseley while trying to save that of his son, who had fallen down a disused coal-working, 18 feet deep, and was overcome by choke-damp. Father and son were both poisoned by the noxious fumes.

1889.

Royal Humane Society's "In Memoriam" Certificate and Medal to two Kentish Heroes. While Harold T. and Alexander Farbrother, together with two lads named Dickson, were sailing at Leysdown, Isle of Sheppey, a sudden change of wind capsized their boat, 200 yards from shore. The Farbrothers each took a boy on his shoulders, and tried to make for land. Harold, with the elder Dickson, sank and was drowned. Alexander Farbrother was picked up in an exhausted condition by a boat, and the boy he tried to save perished. Alexander received the Royal Humane Society's Silver Medal, and the parents of the gallant dead man were presented with an "In Memoriam" Certificate of the same Society.

1890.

Carnegie Hero Fund. While stopping a runaway horse attached to a van, in which a little girl had been left, a cabman named John Shaw, of Edinburgh, was knocked down and dragged thirty yards along the ground. His right foot was crushed by the wheel of the van, and he was incapacitated for some time. A donation of £5 was awarded. **1909.**

May 7

V.C. Brig.-Surgeon C. M. Douglas, M.D., **24th (South Wales Borderers).** "Amo."

V.C. Private D. Bell, **24th (South Wales Borderers).**

V.C. Private T. Murphy, **24th (South Wales Borderers).**

V.C. Private W. Griffiths, **24th (South Wales Borderers).** Massacred at Isandlwana, Zululand, January 22, 1879.

V.C. Private J. Cooper, **24th (South Wales Borderers).** The above five, at the greatest personal risk, saved seventeen men of their regiment from a terrible death at the hands of the natives. In a small boat, which narrowly escaped being swamped in a furious gale, they made three journeys to the island from the mainland, rescuing the whole of their comrades who had ventured into so perilous a position. **Little Andaman Island. 1867.**

New Zealand Cross (see March 10). Private Thomas Adamson, **Colonial Forces.** For hazardous services as guide and scout, and for special gallantry in unmasking an ambuscade in advance of the column at Ahikeru, when he was wounded. **1869.**

May 8

The Martinique Disaster: Lloyd's Meritorious Service Medal to Captain Edward W. Freeman, of the tramp steamer *Roddam*, for gallantry in bringing his ship safely out of port when Mount Pelée was in violent eruption. The Captain was at the wheel, and, though terribly burnt by the falling cinders and ashes, stuck to his post and saved the vessel. After escaping from her fiery ordeal in the West Indies, the *Roddam* was finally wrecked on the frozen wastes of Northern Siberia. Captain Freeman was appointed examiner of candidates for master's and mate's certificates. **1902.**

Royal Humane Society's Bronze Medal. P.-C. J. T. Carruthers, at great risk to his own life, jumped into 14 feet of water in the river Tyne at S. Shields; and although a strong tide was running at the time, he kept afloat a boy who had fallen in, until they were both picked up by a boat. **1906.**

May 9

Albert Medals of the Second Class to John Mitchell, William Stewart, and Charles Wilson, for great gallantry in saving life from several vessels wrecked by fearful tidal waves off Huanillo, following an earthquake. **1877.**

Liverpool S. & H. Society's Silver Medal to Police-Sergeant W. J. Burden, for stopping a runaway horse attached to a cab in Mossley Hill. **1907.**

Liverpool S. & H. Society's Vote of Thanks to P.-C. Joseph Nolan for gallantry in stopping a runaway horse attached to a lorry in Blundell Street. **1907.**

May 10

A gallant Liverpool Carman. John Hare, seeing a poor cripple in imminent danger of being run over by his vehicle, jumped down and rescued him, but in doing so he himself met the fate from which he had saved the cripple. **1862.**

A Devonshire Hero. George Hancock, aged 24, seeing a boy in difficulties in the river Tam at Barnstaple, sprang in and brought him safely ashore, but himself fell back into the water and was drowned. He was said to have been suffering from heart disease. **1896.**

May 11

V.C. Major-General T. de Courcy Hamilton, **68th (Durham Light Infantry).** (Died 1908.) "Qualis ab incepto." For distinguished bravery in a night sortie from Sevastopol, in which he charged the enemy with a small force and saved the guns from being captured. **Crimea. 1855.**

MAY

C. M. Douglas.

David Bell V.C.

T de Courcy Hamilton

G. H. Coulson

H. H. Lyster

F. F. Mackall
Capt Hampshire Regt.

DELHI'S NOBLE NINE

V.C. Lieutenant George Forrest, **Bengal Army.** "Vivunt dum virent."

V.C. Lieutenant William Raynor, **Bengal Army.**

V.C. Conductor John Buckley, **Bengal Ordnance.**

Lieutenant George D. Willoughby (in command), **Bengal Artillery.**

Conductor John Scully.

Conductor G. W. Shaw.

Sub-Conductor William Crow.

Sergeant Bryan Edwards.

Sergeant Peter Stewart.

This splendid band of whom five perished and only three were gazetted, after a desperate struggle with overwhelming hosts of ferocious mutineers, finally blew up the great powder magazine at Delhi to prevent its capture by the Sepoys. **Mutiny. 1857.**

Albert Medal of the Second Class to Sir William MacGregor, M.D., for saving many lives from a vessel wrecked in a terrible storm on a reef near the Fiji Islands. By means of a rope the gallant doctor and others drew to shore many coolies, of whom there were nearly 500 aboard. Only 49 were drowned. **1884.**

A young Sussex Lady's heroic Deed. Miss Katherine Sergison, aged 17, daughter of Prebendary Sergison of Slanghan, was burnt to death while trying to save her sister's life. Both girls were attired in light dresses; and, the elder one's taking fire, her sister tried to put out the flames, but instantly shared the same fate. Both were fatally burned, and the tragedy also involved a third death—that of the father of the victims—who died a month later from shock and grief. **1874.**

MAY 12

An Engine-Room Artificer of the R.N. dies in trying to save his Comrades. Frederick Platt, after being frightfully scalded and burnt by a boiler explosion aboard a torpedo boat, did all he could to save his comrades and the boat. He would not allow the surgeon to attend to his terrible injuries until all the rest had been cared for. The brave fellow expired after six hours intense agony borne without a murmur. **1887.**

Liverpool S. & H. Society's Vote of Thanks to John T. Kelly for the gallant rescue of a drowning boy. **1908.**

MAY 13

An heroic Nursemaid of Hampshire. Elizabeth Hayward gave her life in a brave attempt to save a little boy who had fallen into a pool in some gravel pits near Hythe, Southampton. The mother of the child—Mrs Falk—attempted to save the two in the water, and was herself rescued with great difficulty. **1867.**

Royal Humane Society's Bronze Medal. A woman accidentally fell into the Shannon at Limerick, the depth being 13 feet, and the water 15 feet below the level of the quay. Timothy Kelly, night-constable, plunged in and caught her. They were both safely landed. **1908.**

MAY 14

Royal Humane Society's Bronze Medal to D. C. Beadon, who, in a strong wind and heavy sea, went over the side of a ship at the mouth of the Tyne and saved W. C. Mason, who had been knocked overboard. **1906.**

Liverpool S. & H. Society's Vote of Thanks to P.-C. C. Heeley, for bravery in stopping a runaway horse attached to a lorry in Sandhills Lane. **1908.**

MAY 15

Four Essex Workmen Heroes and Martyrs. Daniel Mansfield, John Wailing, John Brooks, and Richard Williams perished while making a splendid attempt to rescue two of their comrades, who were overpowered by foul air, in a well at the gas-works at Becton, near Barking. **1870.**

Death of Two Lincolnshire Coastguardsmen on Volunteer Rescue Work. While a north-east gale, accompanied by tempestuous seas, was blowing, a brig was stranded at Donna Nook. Some of her crew reached shore in the ship's boat, and Dan Brooks, and Alfred A. Richards, two coastguards, with one other man, a civilian, went back in the boat to fetch the remainder. After accomplishing their noble task, a fearful sea capsized the boat. Two out of the three rescuing party were drowned, as well as two of the men they died in trying to save. The third man swam back to the brig, and was saved by means of the rocket apparatus. **1886.**

MAY 16

V.C. Lieutenant F. W. Bell, **W. Australian, M.I.,** took a dismounted man on to his own horse under heavy fire, but, finding the animal unequal to the double burden, gave it up to the other man.

Brakpan, Boer War. 1901.

Albert Medals of the Second Class to—
Lieutenant Ranald H. Macdonald, **R.E.**

Lance Naik Habib Khan, **Bengal Sappers and Miners.**

Sapper S. Shekh Abdul Samand, **Bengal Sappers and Miners.**

Sapper Kallan Khan.

For great gallantry in saving an officer and men of their regiment from a terrible avalanche near the summit of Lowarai Pass. **1898.**

Two brave young Inverness Men. George M'Kay was boating with a friend off the sea lochs at Clachnaharry, when the boat suddenly lurched, throwing the latter overboard. M'Kay jumped after him, but unhappily both sank. James M'Kay swam out from the pier and brought George M'Kay ashore, but all efforts to restore animation failed. **1896.**

Order of St. John of Jerusalem in England, Silver Medal to Albert B. Stevens, and **Bronze Medal** to Richard Grantham, for great self-sacrifice in attempting to rescue a foreman overcome by foul gas in a sewer manhole 24 feet deep at Burnham. Stevens descended four times and brought up Grantham, who had lost consciousness, as well as the foreman. The latter, however, was dead. **1907.**

May 17

Albert Medal of the Second Class to David Davis, **16th (Queen's) Lancers,** for gallantry in attempting to save life at Aldershot. **1890.**

Terrible Death of two Lancashire Colliers while trying to save a Third. A furnaceman on duty at midnight in the Wet Earth Pit, near Bolton, found that the free passage of air was stopped, and an explosion shortly occurred. The man was badly burned, and signalled for help. William and John Ivell—father and son—at once began to descend the mine, but when within a hundred yards of the bottom they were met by the fatal choke-damp, which so overpowered them that they fell out of the cage and were dashed to pieces. The pit afterwards took fire. **1874.**

A Liverpool Clerk gives his Blood to a dying Man. William Robert Williams, aged 32, a shipping clerk, allowed the local doctors to take from him six ounces of blood for transfusion to the body of a man whose life was trembling in the balance. Williams' action cost him his life, and was unavailing, as the patient died also. **1877.**

London Fire Brigade Silver Medal to Alfred Wylde, who, after having saved one woman from a burning house in Seymour Street, Euston Square, by means of a fire-escape, hearing that another woman was in a back room, made his way there from an adjoining house, only to find the room empty. **1881.**

MAY 18

V.C. Lieutenant G. H. B. Coulson, D.S.O., **25th (King's Own Scottish Borderers).** (Born 1879.) "Je mourrai pour ceux que j'aime." After having given up his own horse to a dismounted man, was himself taken up by Corporal Shaw of the Lincolns. A moment later both were hit, Lieutenant Coulson fatally. This young officer, who was noted for great coolness and gallantry under fire, was an only son. **Boer War. 1901.**

"A noble life crowned with heroic death rises above and outlives the pride, and pomp, and glory of the mightiest empire on earth."—*President Garfield.*

Relief of Mafeking, gallantly defended by General Sir R. S. Baden-Powell and all under him from October 13, 1899. Colonel Mahon with a flying column entered the besieged city at 4 A.M. on this date. **1900.**

Albert Medal of the Second Class to John Smith for a gallant attempt to save the life of Benjamin Hamley at Norfolk Works, Sheffield. **1889.**

Heroic London Policeman. Jesse Richardson, seeing a woman in the Thames about 50 yards from the Embankment, flung off his tunic, plunged into the river, and succeeded in bringing the would-be suicide ashore. The gallant fellow was wearing thick boots at the time. The woman died two days later in hospital. **1909.**

May 19

London Fire Brigade Silver Medal to Philip W. Benest, for a gallant search through a burning house in the Old Kent Road, to see if any one had been left there, during which he was severely burned. **1901.**

Liverpool S. & H. Society's Vote of Thanks to Harry Flarrit, for stopping a runaway horse in Smithdown Road. **1908.**

May 20

Postman's Park Hero and Martyr. Tablet 13. Richard Farris, a labourer, seeing a girl jump into the Surrey Canal between Peckham and Camberwell, lost his life in a brave attempt to save the suicide. **1878.**

Seven gallant Yorkshiremen. While a number of boys were bathing in a pond near Normanton, one of them fell into deep and icy-cold water. Seven men from an adjoining brickyard—all non-swimmers—made a gallant but unsuccessful attempt to rescue the drowning boy. John Miles, aged 31, caught a chill from his long immersion, which developed into pneumonia and proved fatal on July 19th. The Royal Humane Society presented certificates to the men who had shown gallantry on this occasion, and gold medals were subscribed for by the inhabitants of Normanton, that of the dead hero being given to his sister, Mrs. Brown. **1902.**

MAY 21

A little Essex Hero. As the driver of a train to Harwich was approaching Ramsey Bay crossing he saw a little girl between the metals and blew his whistle. The child's brother, James Ransom, aged nine, ran to help his sister, but before he could reach the spot the train had killed her. The gallant little fellow was also struck down, and injured so terribly that he died later. **1876.**

A devoted Mother and Aunt (Lanarkshire). Mrs. Donnelly, proprietress of a laundry at Glasgow, when a fire broke out in her house, made a most heroic attempt to save her little daughter and nephew. Mrs. Donnelly and her child died, but the boy recovered. **1898.**

"Earth's noblest thing: a woman perfected."—*J. R. Lowell.*

MAY 22

Heroism of a Welsh Stationmaster. William Anwgl, stationmaster of Bangor, was killed at Griffith's Crossing in trying to save a woman who had slipped in front of an oncoming express. Both were killed, and Anwgl's wife witnessed the terrible tragedy. **1859.**

Royal Humane Society's Medal to Mr. Allan McFarquhar of Aberdeen. A boy had fallen into the river Dee, and the rising tide carried him up a sewer. McFarquhar swam up the sewer after him, and at great peril of his own life brought the drowning boy safely ashore. **1909.**

MAY 23

V.C. Lieut.-General H. H. Lyster, C.B., **72nd Bengal Native Infantry.** (Born 1830.) "Retinens vestigia famæ." At Calpee, charged a square of rebels quite alone, broke it, and killed several Sepoys as they retreated. **Mutiny. 1858.**

London Fire Brigade Silver Medals to David J. Rice, who, although a small man, went up to the second floor of a burning house at Albert Gate, Knightsbridge, and brought down by means of a fire-escape an unconscious man who weighed 19 stone. **1881.**

Also to George W. Byne, who rescued a woman from a third-floor window in Egerton Gardens, Brompton, remaining with her until the fire from the lower windows had been checked. Afterwards he made a second attempt for a further search, but was beaten back by the flames. **1891.**

Warwickshire Nursemaid's gallant Deed. Emma Finch, aged 18, lost her life at Coleshill while trying to save a little boy named Thomson, who fell into the river Cole. The girl plunged into the stream, but the depth and tenacity of the mud proved too strong, and she was powerless to help either the child or herself. A miller, who saw the accident, made a brave attempt to save them, but he also stuck fast and narrowly escaped the same sad fate. **1882.**

Essex Lifeboat Tragedy: Two Lives lost. While engaged on rescue work at Clacton-on-Sea, James Cross and Thomas Cattermole lost their lives through the capsizing of the lifeboat in a succession of heavy seas.

1884.

MAY 24

Albert Medal of the Second Class to A.B. John Rickett, R.N., who sprang from H.M.S. *Clio* off the coast of Mexico into a sea infested with sharks, and supported a boy who had fallen overboard and sunk three times. The two were picked up by the ship's boat after being in the water fifteen minutes. This fine naval hero was suffering from the effects of coast fever when he accomplished his gallant deed. 1866.

Postman's Park Boy Hero and Martyr. Tablet 30. After having himself been rescued from a pond at Kilburn, Harry Sisley, aged 10 years, was drowned while making an heroic effort to save his brother's life. 1878.

London Fire Brigade Silver Medals to William Joussing for a gallant rescue of five lives at a fire in Cannon Street Road, E. 1880.

Also to James Wainwright and John Sinclair, who entered a burning building in Farringdon Street, roused two men who were sleeping on the top floor, and then found that their escape by the stairs was cut off by the flames. Eventually a fire-escape was pitched against the third-floor window, and the four men, who were all terribly burned, reached the ground. 1896.

MAY 25

Royal Humane Society's Bronze Medal to W. C. Cartridge, a schoolboy, aged 13, who at great risk to his own life plunged into the harbour at Poole, Dorset, where the water was 14 feet deep, and held up a lad named John Powell, who had fallen in, until they were both picked up by a canoe. **1900.**

Liverpool S. & H. Society's Silver Medal and **Vote of Thanks** to Thomas Murphy for stopping a runaway horse attached to a float at George's Dock Gates. **1906.**

MAY 26

A Durham Farmer sacrifices his Life in trying to save one of his Men. Two farm labourers, named Hetherington and Mitchinson, were engaged in washing sheep in the river Tees at High Coniscliffe, near Darlington, when the former got out of his depth and was in danger of drowning. Mitchinson tried to help him, but failed. Seeing this, Mr. John Winter, their employer, went to the rescue; but although he succeeded in grasping Hetherington, both sank in deep water and were drowned. **1874.**

Liverpool S. & H. Society's Vote of Thanks to P.-C. F. Powell for rescuing six children from a burning house in North Street. **1908.**

MAY 27

A Carmarthenshire Mechanic drowned in saving his Brother. Albert Webb of Llanelly lost his life near Machynys Cliffs through the swamping of an overloaded boat in a squall, whereby several men were drowned. Webb could have got ashore himself, but sacrificed his own life in a noble effort to sustain his brother William. He sank from exhaustion before he could be taken into the boat, which had picked up his brother. **1902.**

East Riding Fisherman drowned in trying to save his Brother. Three brothers named Richard, Arthur, and James Douglas, fishermen of Filey, were returning to shore in their boat in a choppy sea, when Arthur was knocked overboard by a sail he was reefing. Richard, who was at the tiller, jumped in to save him, but the boat drifted away from them, and both were drowned. Arthur Douglas had only been married a week. **1902.**

Liverpool S. & H. Society's Vote of Thanks and £1 to Alfred Woodcock for gallantry in stopping a runaway horse attached to a cart in Brunswick Street. **1908.**

May 28

A gallant Lancashire Blacksmith. At Salford, Philip Bentley, who was unable to swim, heroically jumped into a reservoir to the assistance of a little boy who had fallen into the water. Those ashore took the boy from Bentley's hands, but he, falling back exhausted, was drowned. He left a widow and three children. **1883.**

Fine Devotion to Duty by a Kerry Engine-driver and Fireman. While in charge of an unusually heavy composite train near Glencolt, on one of the steepest gradients in the kingdom, William Renshaw, on applying the brakes at the beginning of the descent, found that they refused to act from lack of power. Renshaw and his driver, Richard Dillon, gallantly stuck to their post in face of certain disaster, they being on a viaduct over a mountain gorge where the line made an acute turn. At this point engine, brake-van, pig-trucks, and carriages plunged headlong into the gorge, nearly 50 feet below. The two were instantly killed, and twelve passengers sustained serious injuries. "Faithful unto death."

1893.

Carnegie Hero Fund. An award of £3 to P.-C. Patrick Burke, who at imminent risk of his life forced open the door of a burning house in Glasgow, and brought out an old man, rendered unconscious by smoke. **1909.**

MAY 29

V.C. Captain C. W. Buckley, **R.N.** (Died 1872.)

V.C. Captain H. T. Burgoyne, **R.N.** Drowned when his vessel, H.M.S. *Captain*, went down off Cape Finisterre, September 6, 1870, with 490 on board, of whom only 18 were saved.

V.C. Chief Gunner Robarts, **R.N.**

V.C. Boatswain Cooper, **R.N.**

The three first named were associated in the audacious feat of firing Russian stores in face of a large force of the enemy. The deed was repeated on June 3, when they were joined by Boatswain Cooper.

Sea of Azoff, Crimea. 1855.

V.C. Captain J. F. Mackay, **Gordon Highlanders.** Gazetted for extreme devotion to the wounded at Crow's Nest Hill, where he carried a man into shelter out of heavy fire. **Boer War. 1900.**

Edward Medal of the First Class to Frederick Watts. Watts, with a man named Isaac Tanner, was at work in Hanham Colliery. After they had prepared four charges for blasting close to each other, the latter set fire to the fuses. Before he could get to a place of safety one of the shots exploded, and a falling stone broke his arm. He found himself unable to move, and called on Watts to help him, whereupon Watts returned to the dangerous spot and dragged him to a place of safety, although aware the other charges might explode at any moment. Tanner died the following April from the effects of his injuries.

1908.

A little Norwich Hero. Walter Holmes, aged 11, with his brother Ernest, aged 9, went to bathe in the river Yare at Thorpe. The younger boy got into difficulties and drifted into the middle of the stream, and Walter, who had left the water, sprang in again to help his brother. Two men went to their assistance, but both boys were drowned. **1901.**

MAY 30

Albert Medal of the Second Class to Mr. Francis Pitts, chief officer of the ss. *Pleiades*, for gallantry in trying to save the life of a seaman who was washed overboard in a heavy gale. Mr. Pitts swam with a line 300 yards, and was himself rescued in an exhausted condition. **1881.**

Lifeboat Service at Porthleven, Cornwall. The brigantine training ship *Polly*, with about fifty people on board, ran ashore on Gunwalloe Reach. The lifeboat *John Francis White* reached the vessel just as she had got clear. One of the lifeboatmen was placed on board, and piloted the *Polly* to Penzance. The weather was moderate but thick at the time, so that on the dangerous Cornish coast the *Polly* ran great risk of disaster but for this timely assistance. **1907.**

Liverpool S. & H. Society's Bronze Medal to P.-C. A. Locke for stopping a runaway horse attached to a lorry in Great Howard Street. **1908.**

MAY 31

Royal Humane Society's Bronze Medal to Joseph S. Smith, second officer of the London steamer *Marie Elsie*, who rescued a man named Louis Durant from drowning in the Seine. Durant had been driving a restive horse which had backed the cart over the bank, throwing the driver into the river. **1901.**

Liverpool S. & H. Society's Silver Medal and Vote of Thanks to P.-C. Robert W. Smith, for stopping a runaway horse attached to a cart in Derby Lane, at great personal risk. **1906.**

JUNE

“ *God of our fathers, known of old—*
Lord of our far-flung battle line,
Beneath whose awful hand we hold
Dominion over palm and pine,
Lord God of Hosts be with us yet,
Lest we forget—lest we forget.

—Rudyard Kipling.

JUNE

JUNE 1

Albert Medal of the Second Class to Captain L. A. De Saumarez, R.N., who jumped from H.M.S. *Myrmidon* at night in the river Congo—infested by sharks—and in a strong current rescued a boy who had fallen overboard and was unable to swim. He guided the lad to the pier, where he supported him until help arrived. **1868.**

Sailor of the R.N. drowned in a fine Attempt to save Life. William Owen, a seaman on H.M.S. *Boomerang*, lost his life off Shortland Bluffs, near Port Philip Heads, Victoria, S. Australia, in a splendid attempt to swim out with a life-line to a wrecked vessel. He had almost accomplished his noble purpose when he sank exhausted. **1853.**

Gallantry of an Oxford Student. John F. Rowlands lost his life in the Thames at Eynsham by going to rescue his friend Mr. Wilks from a sinking canoe. The brave young fellow was an inexpert swimmer, but accomplished his purpose before sinking to his death. **1875.**

JUNE 2

V.C. Sergeant-Major F. H. Kirby, **R.E.** (Born 1871.) Distinguished himself three times, the last occasion being on this date, when he rode back from his troop under hot fire, and brought in a dismounted man on his own horse at Delagoa Bay Railway. **Boer War. 1900.**

Two brave young Ladies of Sussex. Grace Boniface, a dressmaker at Slinfold, near Horsham, hearing screams from the garden of the rectory near by, hurried to the spot, and found a little girl in a pool there. By going into the water up to her waist the fearless girl was able to secure the drowning child. Two little boys then told her their "dear governess" (Miss Margaret Hallett) had jumped into the pond to save their sister. Upon searching the pond this was found to be only too true, but life was extinct when the body was recovered. Miss Hallett was only twenty-three years of age. This was the second occasion upon which Miss Boniface had been instrumental in saving life. **1902.**

JUNE 3

Royal Humane Society's Bronze Medal. When Charles Lloyd fell into the Avon at Bristol—the depth of water being about 20 feet—Walter Latham endeavoured to save him, but also got into difficulties. At great risk, Thomas Biggs, a deaf mute, plunged in and was successful in saving both. **1905.**

Order of St. John of Jerusalem in England. Certificate of Honour to William H. Beadle, a boy messenger, who saved a child which had fallen under a horse attached to a butcher's cart. The driver pulled the horse up on its hind legs, and Beadle jumped under its hoofs and snatched the child from underneath the animal, thus averting what would most probably have proved a fatal accident. **1907.**

JUNE 4

V.C. Sergeant-Major M. Rosamond, **Indian Army.** Cross sold for £54 in 1903. (Two occasions.)

V.C. Sergeant-Major P. Gill, **Loodiana Regiment.** (Three occasions.)

V.C. Private J. Kirk, **10th (N. Lincoln.)** (Two occasions.)

Among other fine deeds, the above three heroes fought their way to an outlying bungalow, and brought Captain Brown and his family safely within the lines. They also saved many other lives from the bloodthirsty assassins, who were butchering every English person they could find at Benares. **Mutiny. 1857.**

Liverpool S. & H. Society's Gold Bramley-Moore Medal to Captain W. Haskell, who by means of a little boat of the schooner *Prepotente*, whose crew, including her gallant commander, numbered only five hands, rescued 42 persons from a sinking steamer in a heavy pampero near the mouth of the Rio de la Plata. Owing to the heavy gale, it was with extreme difficulty and danger that the small boat accomplished so many trips to the wreck. This is the only award of a gold Bramley-Moore Medal, which was founded in 1872 in memory of Mr. John Bramley-Moore. A number of silver and bronze replicas have been given for gallantry in saving life at sea. **1895.**

JUNE 5

V.C. Bombardier T. Wilkinson, **R.M.A.** (Died 1887.) For great courage in repairing advanced batteries under fierce fire at Sevastopol. **Crimea. 1855.**

V.C. Colonel E. B. Hartley, **Cape Mounted Rifles.** (Born 1847.) Showed the greatest devotion to the wounded under heavy fire at Moirosi's Mountain, where, after carrying one man into shelter, he gallantly returned to his humane work. **Basutoland. 1876.**

Norfolk Lifeboat Rescue Work. During a dense fog the ss. *Osprey* collided with another steamer, and was badly damaged. Thirty-six persons were aboard, all of whom were rescued by the Winterton lifeboat, the men making three trips in a heavy sea to the sinking vessel to accomplish this task. **1904.**

JUNE 6

V.C. Sergeant G. Symons, **Royal Artillery.** For splendid heroism in unmasking a battery under tremendous fire, during which plucky performance he was severely wounded, at Sevastopol. **Crimea. 1855.**

V.C. Captain John Mackenzie, **Seaforth Highlanders.** (Born 1869.) "In utrumque paratus." Was severely hit while working two Maxim guns under fierce fire at Dompoassi. Afterwards headed a splendid charge, and cleared the stockade of the enemy, who retreated pell-mell into the bush. **Ashantee. 1900.**

Albert Medal of the Second Class to Quartermaster W. Bridges, R.N., who, after an explosion on H.M.S. *Thunderer*, went down to the shell-room, and by his pluck and presence of mind in wrapping his woollen comforter round some burning fragments of an exploded shell, averted a further catastrophe. **1869.**

A little Devonshire Heroine. Lily Taylor, aged 9, daughter of the Rev. N. Sneyd Taylor, of Farrough Cross, lost her life at Pettitor, S. Mary Church, while trying to save her sister, who had fallen into a pool among the rocks and called to her for help. Their brother tried unsuccessfully to rescue the little girls. **1878.**

JUNE 7

V.C. Captain H. M. Jones, **7th (Royal Fusiliers)** (familiarly known as "Alma" Jones). During the attack on the "Quarries," and while suffering from severe wounds, behaved with cool intrepedity in face of tremendous odds, repelled many fierce attacks of the Russians, and remained at his perilous post throughout the night. He had lost five brothers in action before the Crimean War.

V.C. Gunner T. Arthur, **R.A.** (Died 1902.) Cross sold for £47. For carrying ammunition under fire, and spiking guns at the Redan.

V.C. Corporal M. Hughes, **7th Fusiliers.** For twice carrying ammunition under fire, and saving two lives.

Crimea. 1855.

A Middlesex Boy gives his Life in trying to save his little Brother. While Oliver E. Oldland and his younger brother, Frederick, were bathing in the Grand Junction Canal at Brentford, Frederick got out of his depth and sank. Oliver, who could not swim, gallantly went to help his brother, but both were drowned before assistance reached them. **1875.**

Two Worcestershire Men die in an Attempt to save a Comrade. Charles Lavis, a ganger, and Josiah Jones, a navvy, lost their lives in trying to save that of John Cooper, who had fallen into deep water in the Severn at Folly Point, near Bewdley. The brave fellows sprang to Cooper's assistance, but the strong current of the river drew them under and all three perished. **1901.**

JUNE 8

V.C. Lieutenant-Colonel Alfred S. Jones, **9th Lancers.** "Marte et arte." For the brilliant capture of a gun, which he turned upon a village, driving out the mutineers who held it. Later on, at Agra, Colonel Jones received twenty-two wounds, but recovered from his terrible injuries.

V.C. Sergeant H. Hartigan, **9th Lancers.**
V.C. Sergeant-Major C. Coghlan, **Gordon Highlanders.**

Both gazetted for magnificent courage in saving many lives from the savage Sepoys at Delhi. At Agra, later on, Hartigan was fearfully wounded in a hand-to-hand tussle with four mutineers, from whom he rescued a man they had attacked in a tent. **Mutiny. 1857.**

Edward Medal of the First Class to Miss M. J. Lamb, sister of George H. Lamb, who had gone three times, to rescue five men, into a mine on fire. On ascending a shaft literally ablaze, the poor fellow received fearful injuries, to which he succumbed the next day. The only portion of his clothing not burnt was his leather waist-belt.
Strathcona, Province of Alberta, Canada. 1907.

A Berkshire Lad drowned after rescuing a Companion. While several boys were bathing at Norcot Scours, near Reading, one of them named Wynne got out of his depth. James Rolfe, aged 14, went to the rescue, and succeeded in saving Wynne. Rolfe himself afterwards fell into a ballast hole, into which a sailor dived twice, and brought up the gallant youth, who was, however, dead. 1874.

June 9

V.C. Private T. O'Hea, **Rifle Brigade.** The first man gazetted for an act not performed "in the presence of the enemy," a new clause having been inserted in the Victoria Cross Warrant on his behalf. O'Hea was decorated for fine courage in entering a railway van full of explosive material which was on fire, and extinguishing the flames at imminent peril to his life. This brave man was lost some years later in the Australian bush.

Danville, Canada. 1868.

Fearful Death of a Boy and Engineman near Durham. Jonathan Briggs, aged 12, while attempting to adjust a belt on the machinery of the engine-house at Framwellgate Moor Colliery, caught his sleeve in a cog-wheel and was dragged into the machinery. His screams brought Septimus Turnbull to the spot, but in his haste the gallant fellow stumbled as he reached Briggs, and the fly-wheel—revolving forty times per minute—struck him, and he too was drawn into the machinery, his death being instantaneous. When the lad was at length released it was found he had lost two limbs. A merciful death quickly ended his sufferings. **1868.**

London Fire Brigade Silver Medal to Joseph H. West, who, at a fire in Queen Victoria Street, made his way on to the roof of adjoining premises, and therefrom, by means of an insulated wire, and entering a window on the fourth floor of the burning building, rescued two girls. Later, he pluckily attempted to save another girl, but was rendeied unconscious by the smoke. **1902.**

JUNE

Frank H. Fisher

E B Hartley

Henry M Snead

Alfred S. Jones M.Inst.C.E

J. Caudell

Henry J. Ruby

J Hope

J H Halliday

Charles Ward

Samuel Lake

JUNE 10

V.C. Private J. Lyons, **Yorkshire Regiment.** For picking up a live shell which had fallen in the trenches, and throwing it over the parapet before Sevastopol. **Crimea. 1855.**

Albert Medal of the Second Class to Lieutenant P. Malcolm, 4th Ghurkas, for conspicuous gallantry in attempting to save the life of a friend who had fallen over a precipice near Dalhousie, East India. **1887.**

Albert Medal of the Second Class to Chief Stoker F. Paffett, R.N., who, after an explosion on H.M.S. *Daring* torpedo-boat, made a magnificent attempt amidst scalding steam to reach the valve of the boiler. Although almost overcome by the terrible injuries thus received, he carried a fainting man up to the deck, where he himself fell helpless. His left arm was rendered practically useless for life. **1901.**

Two London Fire Brigade Martyrs to Duty. William J. Abernethy, aged 29, and William B. Smart, aged 21, were crushed beneath a falling ceiling at a fire in Hargrave Park, Upper Holloway. Smart was killed on the spot, and Abernethy succumbed to his terrible injuries a few hours later. **1892.**

Death of two brave Leicester Ladies. Mrs. Elsie Hughes, aged 28, and her cousin, Miss Ethel Cole, aged 20, of Leicester, were drowned at Sheringham, Norfolk, in an attempt to save Mrs. Hughes' little girl, who had been swept off the breakwater. The child was afterwards rescued at great personal risk by a fisherman aged 70. **1902.**

JUNE 11

Albert Medal of the Second Class to Charles Sprankling, chief boatman at Burton Coast Guard Station, Dorset, for a noble and successful effort to save life on the occasion of the capsizing of a Bridport fishing-boat. **1866.**

Albert Medal of the Second Class to Chief Stoker Alfred Stickley, R.N., who, after an accident on a torpedo boat destroyer, forced his way through flames and steam in the stokehold, and made many heroic attempts to open the drencher valve. Finding it impossible to drive back the flames, he ordered the hatch to be opened, and remained below until the four men with him had escaped. The gallant fellow was ill four months from his shocking injuries. **1904.**

JUNE 12

V.C. Colonel T. Cadell, C.B., **Royal Munster Fusiliers.** (Born 1835.) When our troops were forced to retire by overwhelming numbers from the flagstaff on the famous "Ridge" at Delhi, a bugler fell severely wounded, and was rescued by Lieutenant Cadell (as he then was), who later in the day helped to save another wounded man from the inhuman rebels. Both acts were accomplished under terrible cannon and musketry fire. **Mutiny. 1857.**

A Caithness School Teacher sacrifices his Life in trying to save two of his Pupils. While fishing from a boat with two boys near Dunnett, James Ross, of Cross Roads School, was thrown into the water with his companions through the capsizing of their craft in broken water. Ross righted the boat, and managed to get the lads aboard in safety. The boat again capsized, and once more the gallant teacher saved his charges; but a third catastrophe proved too much for his strength, and the trio perished. **1885.**

JUNE 13

V.C. Private S. Shaw, **Rifle Brigade.** Badly wounded by a tulwar cut from a ghazee, whom he despatched after a desperate struggle. **Mutiny. 1858.**

JUNE 14

Liverpool S. & H. Society's Silver Medal, Vote of Thanks, and £2 to John Curtis; also thanks and 30s. each to Edward Wainwright, John Platt, and Thomas Manville, for rescuing at great risk the wounded men on the ss. *Haverford* in Huskisson dock after an explosion. **1906.**

Liverpool S. & H. Society. Fifteen shillings each to William M'Kinley and Thomas Potter for gallantly rescuing a woman who attempted suicide in the canal near Lightbody Street. **1906.**

JUNE 15

V.C. Lieut. J. Rogers, **S. African Constabulary.** By sheer indomitable pluck saved five lives at Thaba Nchu. Took Lieutenant Dickinson (who was dismounted) on to his own horse, carried him into shelter, and then returned and caught riderless horses for four other dismounted men; thus enabling them to escape from the pitiless fire of sixty Boers, who were so close that they called upon the plucky sergeant to surrender, his sole reply to this request being ball cartridge. **Boer War. 1901.**

Liverpool S. & H. Society's Silver Fire Medal for one of the most splendid deeds of heroism ever recorded.

Hearing that a workman was in danger of being burnt to death in a compartment of Stanley Dock railway bridge, Liverpool, which had just been coal-tarred and was on fire, P.-C. Thomas P. Milward tried to go down, but was driven back by the flames and smoke. The compartment was 8 feet deep, 2 feet wide, and 3 feet long, and had been set on fire by the man inside dropping a lighted candle into a bucket of tar. Water was thrown in, and Milward descended again, but failed to get hold of the man, as the man-hole was so narrow. Becoming overpowered by the smoke, the policeman was hauled up into the air. When partially recovered, the hero again plunged into the fearful death-trap, and this time succeeded in placing a rope round the poor fellow before having to be brought to the surface. Yet one more descent—the fourth—was accomplished, and Milward returned this time with his prize—terribly burnt, but still alive. The Committee expressed admiration of the police constable's heroic action, and awarded him £2 and an illuminated Vote of Thanks, as well as the Silver Fire Medal. **1899.**

June 16

V.C. Private G. Rodgers, **Highland Light Infantry.** Single-handed attacked seven mutineers, of whom he killed one, near Gwalior. **Mutiny. 1858.**

Wreck of the *Drummond Castle*. The *Drummond Castle* struck on the Pierres Vertes, off Ushant, at midnight, and 250 lives were lost. Splendid heroism was displayed by those on board at the time of this appalling catastrophe, and to the survivors who helped to save life Silver Medals were awarded by Queen Victoria. **1896.**

Royal National Lifeboat Institution's Gold Medal to Mr. Daniel Rees;

Silver Medal to Mr. Ivor Rees; and
Illuminated Vote of Thanks to Mr. D. Morgan Rees, for great courage and self-sacrifice in saving three men who had been thrown into the sea by the capsizing of a small yacht off Lavernock Point, Gloucestershire. Mr. Daniel Rees went out in a dinghy only six feet long, and succeeded in getting two of the men—one being almost unconscious—into the boat. Their weight, however, so dangerously overloaded the tiny craft that he dared not take in the third man, who was clinging to the bottom of the upturned yacht. Mr. Rees kept near to the derelict, which drifted four miles from the scene of the accident, until his brothers, Mr. Ivor and Mr. Morgan Rees, came to his assistance in a sailing-boat, which Mr. Ivor Rees had fetched by a swim of 200 yards through broken water, he being fully dressed at the time. The whole party reached land in safety.

1907.

June 17

V.C. Major C. Walker-Heneage, **8th Hussars.** (Died 1901.)
V.C. Farrier G. Hollis, **8th Hussars.**
V.C. Sergeant J. Ward, **8th Hussars.**
V.C. Private John Pearson, **8th Hussars.**

Elected under Rule XIII. of the Victoria Cross Warrant in recognition of a desperate charge into the rebel camp at Gwalior, when they dashed into two batteries, captured two guns, and brought them out under terrific fire.

Mutiny. 1858.

Royal Humane Society's Bronze Medal to Maurice Murphy, who at great personal risk rescued John Denneley from drowning at Robert's Cove, County Cork. **1888.**

JUNE 18

FIRST ATTACK ON THE REDAN

V.C. Admiral H. J. Raby, C.B., **R.N.** (Died 1907.)
V.C. Captain of the Forecastle J. Taylor, **R.N.** (Died 1857.)
V.C. Boatswain's Mate H. Curtis, **R.N.** (Died 1896.)

The above gallant trio of naval heroes went out under a deluge of shot and shell and brought in a soldier shot through both legs.

V.C. Major-General Sir Howard C. Elphinstone, K.C.B., **R.E.** Drowned on a voyage to Madeira 1890. "Semper paratus." Hearing the terrible cries of the wounded lying close to the Redan, headed a rescue party and brought in 20 poor fellows himself.

V.C. Lieut.-General Sir Gerald Graham, G.C.B., G.C.M.G., **R.E.** (Died 1899.) "Candide sincere." After having, with splendid pluck, led a party right up to the mouths of the Russian guns, saved the lives of two men under appalling fire.

V.C. Colour-Sergeant P. Leitch, **R.E.** Twice distinguished himself.
V.C. Sapper J. Peirie, **R.E.** Saved a life while himself wounded.
V.C. Colonel W. Hope, **Royal Fusiliers.** "At spes infracta."

Besides on this occasion in broad daylight having helped to carry a wounded officer from under heavy fire from the Russian batteries, on Nov. 15th, by an act of supreme courage, extinguished a fire in a large powder magazine, thus averting a great disaster. Colonel Hope was the inventor of the shrapnel shell.

V.C. Lieut.-Colonel T. Esmonde, **Royal Irish Regiment.** In addition to saving two lives under heavy fire on this date, two days later, by fine promptitude and pluck, extinguished a fire-ball, after ordering his men to take shelter from the perilous missile. Although exposed to fierce fire, the intrepid young soldier was unhurt.

V.C. Lance-Sergeant P. Smith, **17th (Leicester).** Saved several lives under furious fire.

V.C. Sergeant J. Sims, **34th (Border).**

V.C. Private J. Alexander, **Scottish Rifles.**

For repeated acts of gallantry in saving the wounded.

Sevastopol, Crimea. 1855.

Albert Medals of the First Class to Mr. Thomas Worrall and Mr. John Crooks.

Albert Medal of the Second Class to Charles Parkinson, George Higson, Aaron Manley and George Hindley for heroism in saving life after a terrible explosion at Clifton Hall Colliery, Lancashire. **1885.**

JUNE 19

V.C. Private T. Hancock, **9th Lancers.**

V.C. Private J. Purcell, **9th Lancers.**

Associated with a Sowar, Roopur Khan—not gazetted—in the specially gallant rescue of Sir Hope Grant, whose horse was shot under him at Delhi. Hancock gave up his own mount to the officer whom the three heroes had extricated from a perilous plight.

V.C. Private S. Turner, **60th Rifles.** While rescuing Lieutenant Humphreys—mortally wounded—from being mutilated by the inhuman Sepoys by carrying him under cover, was badly cut by a sabre.

Delhi, Mutiny. 1857.

V.C. Captain R. C. Nesbit, **Mashonaland Mounted Police.** A colonial hero who with only thirteen followers fought his way through a large force of Kaffirs, and rescued a number of defenceless women and miners from their hands. **Matabeleland. 1896.**

A Lincolnshire Baby Martyr. Henry Rowbotham, aged 6 years, while playing with his little sister by the river-side at Horncastle, saw her fall into the stream, and pulling off his boots plunged in to the rescue. The depth, however, was too great for the tiny hero, and both children perished. **1874.**

June 20

V.C. Lieutenant W. F. F. Waller, **25th Bombay Light Infantry.** (Died 1885.) "Honor et veritas." With Lieutenant Rose, who was killed, and a few loyal Sepoys, climbed the roof of a house, shot the rebel gunners, stormed the fort of Gwalior, and despatched every mutineer within it. **Mutiny. 1858.**

Albert Medals of the First Class to Mr. Samuel Lake and Mr. W. H. Millett.

During a fearful storm the barque *Diamond*, with 445 souls on board, struck the jagged rocks one and a half miles from Breach Candy, Bombay, where she lay for three days. Heroic efforts to rescue those on board were made by volunteers ashore, conspicuous among whom were the above brave men. Mr. Millett was twice washed by the wild sea out of the boat in which he made fifteen trips, saving 120 lives. Mr. Lake's boat was also twice capsized before he could reach the wreck. When darkness prevented further work, Lake swam ashore, but returned early next morning to the wretched people who had been without food or water for several days. The wreck was now lying, with her back broken, at the mercy of the terrible storm. Mr. Lake worked devotedly; he got those aboard the *Diamond* into boats, and never thought of his own danger until not a man was left on the sinking vessel—409 in all were saved. The above is but one out of many acts of heroism performed by this gallant fellow, who was awarded numerous decorations for saving life. The last was a gold medal from the Swedish Government for splendid self-sacrifice whereby he saved fifteen lives from a wreck on the Corsican coast. This last Medal, however, was received by the widow of the hero, who died suddenly before it arrived in 1887. **1866.**

Albert Medal of the Second Class to Captain Edward Giles, Indian Navy, for conspicuous bravery in saving many lives from the barque *Alicia*, wrecked upon the bar of Kurrachee harbour. **1868.**

Postman's Park Heroine. Tablet 5. Elizabeth Boxall, aged 17, of Bethnal Green, while trying to save a child from being run over, was terribly kicked by a horse. She lingered eleven months in great agony, and died from the effects of the operations, necessitated by her injuries. **1888.**

JUNE 21

V.C. Rear-Admiral C. D. Lucas, **R.N.,** No. 1 on the list of Victoria Cross recipients. The act for which the first award was made was that of picking up a live shell and throwing it into a place of safety. Seven other men during the campaign obtained the Decoration for the same perilous feat, and it was one among the many fine deeds of Sir William Peel, V.C., R.N. (see Oct. 18th).

Bomarsund, Crimea. 1854.

V.C. Lieut.-Colonel F. A. Smith, **43rd.** (Died 1887.) Although suffering from a wound, led a splendid attack on the Maori position at Tauranga, setting his men a fine example of courage by jumping into the rifle-pits and fighting hand to hand with the enemy.

V.C. Sergeant John Murray, **68th (Durham).** A doughty hero, who single-handed attacked a rifle-pit containing ten men, all of whom he either killed or wounded.

Tauranga, New Zealand. 1864.

Royal Humane Society's Bronze Medal to Govind Hiraji, a native policeman at Telnal, India, who jumped into a well 30 feet deep, with 9 feet of water at the bottom, and succeeded in rescuing a girl who had fallen in. **1906.**

JUNE 22

Death of James Braidwood, fireman, who was crushed to death while making heroic efforts to stop the terrible fire in Tooley Street, S.E., which raged for several days. The estimated loss by this fire was £2,000,000. **1861.**

> "Not at the battle front—
> Writ of in story ;
> Not on the blazing wreck,
> Steering to glory.
>
> . . . .
>
> Death found—and touched him with
> Finger in flying :
> So he rose up complete
> Hero undying."
>
> —*Miss Muloch.*

Wreck of H.M.S. *Victoria* off Tripoli. Fine heroism displayed by Admiral Tryon, officers and men. 338 lives lost. **1893.**

"Like the death-plunge of a whale,
Our Leviathan of mail
With its whirring iron flail
Thrashed the waters into blood;
And we heard the peals of thunder,
As the boilers burst asunder,
And the sea-spouts sent from under
Human jetsam of the flood.

Where they foundered let them sleep,
In the sapphire Syrian deep,
Never wind nor tide can sweep
To the breaking of their rest.
There they lie till day of doom,
Hid within the darkened womb
Of their iron girdled tomb—
They, our bravest and our best!"
—"Ballads of Brave Deeds," *Canon Rawnsley*.

A brave Showman (Ireland). Charles Murray, aged 65, seeing a man struggling in the water at Whitehead, near Belfast, swam about 200 yards to his assistance, and tried to clutch a boat near by, but, failing in his purpose, sank from exhaustion. The drowning man whom Murray tried to save was rescued by others. Murray had previously saved five people from drowning. **1899.**

JUNE 23

V.C. Private C. McCorrie, **57th (W. Middlesex).** One of the gallant men who threw a live shell over the parapet at Sevastopol. **Crimea. 1855.**

V.C. Colour-Sergeant S. Garvin, **60th Rifles.** For marked courage throughout the campaign, especially on this date.

V.C. Sergeant J. McGovern, **Bengal Fusiliers.** Carried a wounded comrade out of reach of the enemy's fire. **Delhi, Mutiny. 1857.**

A Jersey Mother's heroic Death. Mrs. Maria Jane Lempriere, aged 37, wife of a clergyman at Jersey, seeing her little child in danger of falling over a precipice near Bonne Nuit, sprang forward and pushed her out of danger. In doing so the brave lady slipped over the rocks, and falling upon her head was instantly killed. Mrs. Lempriere left six little children, the eldest of whom was only seven years of age. **1865.**

Liverpool S. & H. Society's Silver Clasp for his Medal to William H. Prosser, foreman stevedore, for plunging into Wellington Dock to save a drowning man. This was the eleventh rescue for which the brave man had been rewarded by the Committee. **1895.**

JUNE 24

V.C. Major L. S. T. Halliday, **R.M.L.I.** (Born 1870.) "Virtute parta." Although suffering from a smashed shoulder bone and a lung partly torn away, continued to lead a magnificent rush with twenty Marines at the Pekin Legation. When compelled by his shocking injuries to retire—which did not happen before he had killed three of his foes—this fine soldier refused help in getting to hospital, so that the force necessary to oppose the Boxers should not be diminished.

British Legation, Pekin, China. 1900.

Albert Medal of the First Class to P.-C. William Cole, A Division Metropolitan Police, for conspicuous bravery after an explosion in Westminster Hall. **1885.**

A Dumbartonshire Man drowned in trying to save a Boy. While bathing with other boys in the river Leven at Dumbarton, one named M'Cateer sank. James Wilson jumped into the river and tried to save him.

THE BOARD OF TRADE MEDAL.

THE STANHOPE MEDAL.
(Royal Humane Society.)

M'Cateer, however, clutched Wilson so tightly that he could do nothing, and both were drowned before help arrived. **1889.**

JUNE 25

An Oxford Undergraduate's Self-sacrifice. While four students were bathing in Sandford Old Lock pool, Mr. W. Gaisford got into difficulties. Mr. Richard Phillimore, of Christchurch, went to his assistance; but, owing to a great fall of water from the lasher above and from eddies caused by the meeting of two currents, both young men became exhausted and sank. **1843.**

The Gold Medal of the Royal Humane Society awarded to Captain G. B. Milman for saving the lives of five brother-officers, when their boat was upset off Mahebourg, Mauritius. **1848.**

Liverpool S. & H. Society's Silver "In Memoriam" Medallions to the parents of Mr. Ernest E. Taylor and Mr. James W. Gillam, who lost their lives while attempting to save that of a young lady at Blackpool. **1907.**

JUNE 26

Queen Victoria publicly decorated with the Victoria Cross sixty-two heroes of all ranks in Hyde Park. **1857.**

To-day the Queen of all the English land,
She who sits high o'er Kaisers and o'er Kings,
Gives with her royal hand—th' Imperial hand
Whose grasp the earth en-rings—

Her cross of Valour to her worthiest;
No golden toy with milky pearls besprent,
But simple bronze, and for a warrior's breast
A fair, fit ornament.

. . . .

Muscovite metal makes this English Cross,
Won in a rain of blood and wreath of flame;
The guns that thundered for their brave lives' loss
Are worn hence, for their fame!

—*Sir Edwin Arnold.*

V.C. Private Charles Ward, **Yorks Light Infantry.** Volunteered to carry a message asking for reinforcements over 150 yards of ground swept by heavy rifle fire, and was terribly wounded on his return with promise of relief. **Lindley, Boer War. 1900.**

Staffordshire Lad gives his Life in trying to save his Friend. While a youth named Gibbons was bathing in the canal at Darlaston Green, he got out of his depth. T. Dean, aged 17, seeing his friend sink, at once jumped in to save him, but immediately disappeared. Two men leaped into the water and brought up both of the young fellows, but life was extinct in each case. **1878.**

JUNE 27

Two heroic Nottinghamshire Miners. After a fire in the Annesley Colliery, followed by an explosion, Thomas Webster and Joseph Pickard met their death while engaged in rescue work. **1877.**

A gallant little Scotch Laddie: Bruce II. James Bruce, aged 10 years, gave his life in a gallant attempt to save that of his friend, James Smith. The boys were playing on the banks of the Clyde at Glasgow when Smith fell into the river. Bruce stripped and went into the water to rescue his playfellow, but was unhappily drowned. The other boy was saved by some bystanders. **1884.**

JUNE 28

A Sunderland Hero. On the occasion of the terrible calamity at Victoria Hall, whereby 182 children were suffocated, William Robinson, son of an innkeeper, made such tremendous efforts to rescue the poor little victims that he collapsed shortly afterwards from paralysis and died on this day. Young Robinson was a prominent member of the Volunteer Fire Brigade. **1883.**

A brave Boy of Tyrone. Joseph Morrison, aged 13, with his little brother Victor, aged 7, was crossing a ford on the river Blackmore, near Dungannon, when the younger lad slipped into a hole. In trying to rescue him the elder fell in too, and both boys were drowned. **1902.**

A Denbighshire Father drowned in trying to save his Son. Robert Jones, of Santley, near Wrexham, was drowned while endeavouring to save his boy of 18, who was sinking in the Old Mill Pool, where he had gone to bathe. Both perished. **1902.**

JUNE 29

A Sussex Railway Hero. Patrick Shaw, aged 44, was killed at Balcomb station while making a splendid attempt to save a lady who had slipped in crossing the line in front of an incoming train. Both were instantaneously crushed to death. Shaw was in sole charge of the station at the time of the tragic occurrence. **1846.**

Liverpool S. & H. Society's Bronze Medal, &c., to John Noonan, aged 6 years, for pluck in rescuing his four-year-old brother, who had fallen into a pond at Newsham. **1906.**

JUNE 30

V.C. Colonel W. G. Cubitt, D.S.O., **Indian Army.** (Died 1903.) On the retreat from Chinot to Lucknow saved the lives of three men at grave risk of his own from the swarming mass of fanatic Sepoys.

V.C. Corporal W. Oxenham, **32nd (Cornwall).** With great self-sacrifice extricated a man from beneath a ruined verandah under fierce fire from the mutineers.

Chinot and Lucknow, Mutiny. 1857.

V.C. Private S. Hodge, **4th W. India Regiment.** The second of three men of colour who have been awarded the Cross "For Valour." Gazetted for great gallantry at the storming of the stockaded town of Jubabecolong, during which he was fearfully wounded.

W. Africa. 1866.

Five Heroes of the Merchant Service lost while trying to save Life. Out of a volunteer crew of seven men from the Cunard steamer *British Queen*, five lost their lives upon the N.E. Spit, Barbo Bank, Liverpool, in a gale. The boat in which the men put off was the second which was sent to the rescue of a stranded and wrecked schooner. The gallant fellows had succeeded in reaching the wreck, and had brought two of her crew aboard their boat, when a heavy rolling sea broke in upon and swamped her. A passing tug saved two men, but J. Hickey, R. Taggart, T. Ford, J. Miller, and W. Bridge were drowned, with the two men for whom they had given their own lives. **1864.**

Royal National Lifeboat Institution's Silver Medal to Mr. Andrew Noble, coxswain superintendent of the Fraserburgh lifeboat, for rescuing six of the crew of the fishing boat *Henry and Elizabeth*, off Fraserburgh.

1909.

JULY

"Forti non ignavo."

(For the brave, not the coward.)

JULY

July 1

V.C. Colonel J. Travers, **Bengal Native Infantry.** During Holkar's attack on the Indore Residency, Colonel Travers, with only five men, charged the guns and drove away the rebel gunners, thereby saving many English fugitives from their hands. **Mutiny. 1857.**

Four Postman's Park Heroes. Tablet 7. Mr. F. Mills, Robert Durrant, A. Rutter, and F. D. Jones.

A workman named Digby having been overcome by foul gas in a well leading to a sewer at East Ham pumping works, A. Rutter went to his assistance. He also fell in and disappeared down the well. On hearing what had happened, Mr. F. Mills, chief engineer at the works, went down and did not return. Robert Durrant then followed, and met the same fate. Finally, Frederick D. Jones tried to help those in the well, but he also was overpowered. A fifth man named Norman descended, and succeeded in bringing up Jones alive; but the poor fellow expired shortly afterwards, and the others when brought to the surface some hours later were all dead. **1895.**

"When to the horrible pit of mire and clay
To save their fellows, brother men went down,
I saw a glorious angel of the day
Set on each head a crown.

. . . . . .

And still above the pit of dreadful doom,
While the dark flood of sorrow rolls below,
As long as fair forget-me-nots may bloom,
Self-sacrifice shall grow."

—"Ballads of Brave Deeds," *Canon Rawnsley.*

A Canadian's heroic Death by Electricity. Dexter Griffiths was killed by coming in contact with a live wire at the Cataract Power Company's works, near St. Catherine's, while rescuing his companion, Mr. Higgins, who escaped with a severe shock. **1902.**

The Order of St. John of Jerusalem in England. Certificate of Honour to James Newsham, who stopped a bolting horse attached to a fire-engine with firemen on it. Newsham, at great personal risk, caught the reins and succeeded in checking the terrified animal's dangerous career. The engine killed two people.

Kirkham. 1907.

JULY 2

Albert Medal of the Second Class to Tom Lewis (the youngest recipient of the Medal). On the occasion of the collapse of a dock at Newport, where many lives were lost, magnificent heroism was displayed by the rescuers, notably by a boy named Tom Lewis, who went down a narrow chasm 30 feet deep and worked for two hours head downwards trying to release a poor fellow who had been pinned down by a beam for twelve hours. Before, however, the plucky lad could finish his gallant and humane task a terrible sound of cracking timbers and falling sand warned those above of another disaster. Tom Lewis was then drawn up just in time, and fell fainting as he reached the fresh air. It was at first thought that Bardell, the man whom Lewis had been striving to rescue, had perished; but he was the last to be saved, and in hospital was loud in praise of Lewis, whose work had made the later rescue possible. The man recovered. **1909.**

A Wiltshire Gentleman drowned while trying to save the Life of a Guest. Mr. West S. Awdry, son of West Awdry, Esq., lost his life in the river Avon at

Chippenham, while trying to save that of a young lady who was visiting his father's house. Miss Lowther, her younger sister, and Mr. Awdry were in a small boat, which was capsized by colliding with a larger one. The elder girl clung so desperately to Awdry that, although a strong swimmer, he was unable to take her ashore, though he made a desperate effort to do so, and both perished. The Rev. Mr. Clark, who was near, at once plunged into the river, and rescued the younger Miss Lowther just as she was sinking. **1861.**

Gold Medals to Mr. W. Brooks and Mr. A. West;
Silver Medal to F. Mander; and monetary awards to the crew of the British steamer *Star of Australia*, presented by the Canadian Government in recognition of splendid services in rescuing the crew of a sinking barque in the North Atlantic sea. **1904.**

JULY 3

V.C. Seaman J. Trewavas, **R.N.** (Died 1905.) Cut the hawsers of a floating bridge at the Straits of Genitchi under heavy Russian fire. **Crimea. 1855.**

V.C. Colonel Lord W. De la Poer Beresford, K.C.I.E., **9th Lancers.** (Died 1900.) "Nil nisi cruce."
V.C. Sergeant E. O'Toole, **Frontier Light Horse.** Associated in the fine rescue of Sergeant Fitzmaurice, who lay wounded and at the mercy of the Zulus about to assagai him. Lord Beresford caught him up on his own charger, and fought his way through the enemy, while Sergeant O'Toole kept the savage warriors at bay with his revolver.

"Then the bullet-hail hissed, and we answered it back,
Two saddles are emptied, a third man is down,
And his horse, at a gallop, has followed our track—
Shall Beresford leave him, a prey to the pack,
Or dare for Old England a deed of renown?

No moment to ponder! but back at full speed,
With his hand at his holster, and rowels red-rose,
He has dashed to his comrade-in-arms at his need,
Has lifted the man, wounded sore, to his steed,
Has mounted behind him in face of the foes."

—"Ballads of Brave Deeds," *Canon Rawnsley.*

V.C. Captain C. D'Arcy, **Frontier Light Horse.** For a splendid attempt to save a wounded trooper from the Zulus. **Ulundi, Zululand. 1879.**

V.C. Lieutenant W. J. English, **2nd Scottish Horse.** After a fine defence of a desperate position at Vlakfontein, fetched cartridges under heavy fire at less than 30 yards range. **Boer War. 1901.**

Lifeboat Rescue Work. The schooner *Broughty Castle*, of Ramsey, laden with salt, stranded on the Causeway Rock in a strong N.W. breeze. The lifeboat *Christopher Brown* went to her assistance, and attempted to heave her off, but the hawser parted. The lifeboat returned ashore with the vessel's crew of three men. **1906.**

JULY 4

V.C. Private H. G. Crandon, **18th Hussars.** While scouting with Private Berry at Springbok Laagte, the latter was wounded, his horse also being shot. Crandon rode back, placed his comrade on his own mount, and himself made his way on foot to shelter, for over 1000 yards under fire at 100 yards range. **Boer War. 1901.**

A Cumberland Miner drowned in trying to save his Friend. Edward M'Kenna, aged 20, and James Grant were bathing at Cleator Moor, near Whitehaven, when the latter, who could not swim, got out of his depth. M'Kenna, who was also unable to swim, went to his assistance, and both were struggling for life in deep water, when a man who was passing made a splendid attempt to save the poor fellows. The attempt nearly proved fatal to their would-be rescuer, who was after all unable to save the young men. **1869.**

Plucky London Policeman. P.-C. Joseph Taylor, B Division, seeing a boy drowning in the Thames at Chelsea, plunged fully dressed into the river, in which there was a very strong current. The constable, after swimming about 200 yards, seized the boy, whom he supported until assistance arrived. He was awarded £10 on August 24, 1909. **1909.**

July 5

V.C. Sergeant A. H. L. Richardson, **Lord Strathcona's Corps,** under heavy fire at 300 yards' range picked up a wounded and dismounted trooper, and carried him on his own horse, which was so injured that the party could only proceed very slowly into a place of safety.

Wolve Spruit, Boer War. 1900.

Gallant Attempt to save Life by Lanarkshire Miners. James Graham and Hugh McGlanahan with sixteen others went down the shaft of a disused coal-pit at Gartsherrie Colliery, Coatbridge, near Glasgow, in search of two men who had become overpowered by a sudden outburst of deadly gas. The shaft, which was full of water to within 25 fathoms of the top, had been utilised as a water supply for some adjoining ammonia works, and the workmen had descended to repair the machinery, when the gas surprised and stifled them. The entire rescue party suffered more or less injury, but the above-named men, and those they gave their lives in trying to save, perished. **1883.**

JULY 6

V.C. Captain J. D. Grant, **8th Ghurka Rifles.** "Stand Sure." (522. Last name gazetted.) Together with Havildar Karbir Pun (native sergeant), crawled on hands and knees up the steep rocky height of Gyantse Yong, under heavy concentrated fire and an avalanche of rocks and stones hurled from above. The passage was not wide enough for two to walk abreast. Both men were wounded, and the Havildar fell 30 feet. Despite their injuries, however, the doughty pair returned to the attack, and the position was captured, this success being greatly due to Captain Grant (then lieutenant) and his colleague. The latter received the Indian Order of Merit.

Thibet. 1904.

The Order of St. John of Jerusalem in England. Certificate of Honour to P.-C. Albert Linnell of Northampton, who was seriously injured while stopping a runaway horse attached to a trolley, the driver of which had been thrown off. The gallant policeman was dragged a considerable distance, but succeeded in effecting his purpose despite his injuries. **1905.**

JULY 7

V.C. Gunner W. Connolly, **Bengal Artillery.** For magnificent pluck in sticking to his gun although twice fearfully wounded. Later in the day he was again badly hit, but kept on loading his gun until he fainted from loss of blood and was carried off the field.

Jhelum, Mutiny. 1857.

Albert Medals of the Second Class to Ambrose Clarke and Robert Drubble, for gallantry displayed on the occasion of an accident which occurred in a sinking shaft near Rotherham, Yorkshire. **1891.**

Two Hampshire Heroes. James Shopland, clerk of the works, and Walter Mussell, labourer, were suffocated at Southampton Corporation Wharf while trying to save two men overpowered by carbonic acid gas which had escaped from a sludge well into an ejector chamber. Six others, who gallantly risked their lives to save them, received monetary rewards and certificates of bravery.

1900.

JULY 8

Heroic Death of two Lanarkshire Platelayers. While repairing the line on the Glasgow and Paisley Railway near a lofty viaduct, two men named Alexander Jamieson (uncle and nephew) saw a half-drawn out sleeper, which would probably have caused a frightful accident to an approaching passenger train. They nobly attempted to pull the sleeper entirely out, and had just succeeded in doing so, when the train dashed up and killed both the gallant fellows instantaneously. **1874.**

" Stand back ! the fire-devourer comes !
The signal dips ! the line is clear !
He scatters dust upon the way,
Too proud to ask if mortal clay
Be cast therewith, while darkened homes
Are fruitage of his mad career.

Stand back ! but men, their brothers, saw
That Jamieson's eyes were filled with light,
That Jamieson leapt upon the rail,
There in the six-foot drove the nail,
To mend the 'sleeper's' deadly flaw,
And bade the younger clinch it tight.

Then, safe on its triumphant way
The fiery-footed monster fared,
High o'er the ringing arch of stone,
And left a mother's heart to moan,
And left a widow, well-a-day !
To weep for those who died, but dared."

—" Ballads of Brave Deeds," *Canon Rawnsley.*

A Kentish Father's splendid Heroism. Richard Kenknight, a labourer, lost his life under the following circumstances at Cliffe-at-Hoo, near Rochester. A lamp having exploded, setting the room ablaze, Kenknight carried his wife, whose clothes had become ignited, outside. He then returned to the cottage, and groped through the flames to the room where his little girls, aged seven and four respectively, had been left. He was afterwards found clasping the dead children in his arms in the cellar, the floor of the room having fallen through with the three victims. **1901.**

JULY 9

V.C. Lieutenant W. A. Kerr, **Bombay Native Infantry.** With a handful of men, stormed the rebel stronghold of Kolapore, killing, wounding, or capturing the whole of the large garrison. By this officer's splendid promptitude and pluck the mutiny on the Malabar Coast was at one stroke practically crushed. **Kolapore, Mutiny. 1857.**

V.C. Major-General Sir Henry Tombs, K.C.B. (Died 1874.)
V.C. Lieut.-General Sir James Hills-Johnes, G.C.B. (Born 1833.)

An instance—of which there are several—of one Victoria Cross hero saving the life of another. Lieutenant Hills (as he then was) was engaged on a magnificent defence of two guns menaced by rebel cavalry, whom he charged single-handed. The young soldier was thrown and disarmed, and his heavy riding-cloak becoming twisted round his neck nearly choked him. As he lay at the mercy of a sowar, who was about to despatch him, Colonel Tombs rode up and shot the mutineer. Lieutenant Hills was, later on, again in mortal peril, and received a fearful sword cut on the head, when his life was saved a second time by his superior officer.

V.C. Private James Thompson (**60th King's Royal Rifles**). Elected under Rule 13 of the Victoria Cross Warrant for repeated acts of gallantry during the siege of Delhi, where he saved his captain (Wilmot) from being murdered by a party of Ghazees. **Delhi, Mutiny. 1857.**

Stanhope Medal to Gunner G. B. Chainer, R.N., who was one of a bathing party from H.M.S. *Dryad* off Retina, Crete. Their boat capsized, and Chainer swam ashore with a drowning man a distance of 200 yards. He swam out again three times, and each time took a man ashore, saving in all four lives. **1897.**

July 10

Albert Medal of the Second Class to James Carney, who jumped on to the four-foot way at Dinapore (India) and saved a native who had fallen before an oncoming train, holding down the struggling man until the train had passed over them both. The rescuer narrowly escaped being struck by the axletree of one pair of wheels. **1881.**

A Glasgow Child drowned in trying to save his Friend. Patrick Collins, aged 11, lost his life by jumping into the river Kelvin to the assistance of Thomas Murray, aged 14, who had sunk in mid-stream. The gallant little lad did his utmost, but the task was beyond his strength, and he shared his chum's fate. **1884.**

Liverpool S. & H. Society's Gold Clasp to Medal (won in 1889) to Captain Henry W. Hayes for gallantly rescuing a young lady who was in great danger of being drowned at Seascale, Cumberland. Also Vote of Thanks to Dr. Garstang, of Gloucester, for assisting. **1899.**

JULY

W. J. English

Henry George Crandon V.C.

A. H. L. Richardson V.C

J. D. Grant

[illegible]

Israel Harding

W. E. Gordon

Basil J. D. Guy.

[illegible]

Patrick Mullane.

A noble Death and a gallant Rescue: Somersetshire. While a number of boys were bathing at Lady's Bay, near Clevedon, one of them got out of his depth. Harry Knowles, aged 16, swam to his assistance, but was seized by the drowning boy, and they both sank. Harold Brownsey then swam to the spot, and found the boy whom Knowles had tried to save, face downwards and insensible. He got beneath the youth's body, brought him to the surface, and with great difficulty got him ashore. The tide was going out, and the gallant lad with his burden sank three times. On reaching land Brownsey and several other lads restored the boy to consciousness, but he remained in a critical condition in hospital for some time before eventually recovering. Poor young Knowles was drowned. **1901.**

JULY 11

V.C. Chief Gunner J. Harding, **R.N.** Picked up a live shell and threw it overboard H.M.S. *Alexandria* during the bombardment of Alexandria. **Egypt. 1882.**

V.C. Captain D. R. Younger, **Gordon Highlanders.** Mortally wounded while trying to save a gun at Leehoehoek, after having taken out a volunteer party who dragged in a R.A. waggon under furious fire at 850 yards range.

V.C. Lieut.-Colonel W. E. Gordon, **Gordon Highlanders.** When Captain Younger had been mortally hurt, led the desperate effort to save the gun. Afterwards remained in the awful hurricane of lead until all the wounded had been removed. **Boer War. 1900.**

London Fire Brigade Silver Medal to Thomas Lynch, who at a fire in Goodge Street, Tottenham Court Road, saved two people, one after another, from the third floor of the house, while the whole of the lower part, including the staircase, was on fire. **1881.**

A Sunderland Baby Hero and Martyr. Robert Shields, aged 6 years, was playing with two other children by the river, when one of them fell in and shrieked for "Robbie." Little Robert sprang after his friend, whom, however, he was unable to save. The boys were found clasped in each other's arms. **1902.**

JULY 12

V.C. Private P. Mylott, **84th (Yorkshire and Lancashire).** For distinguished pluck on many occasions from July 12 to November. **Mutiny. 1857.**

Postman's Park Baby Hero and Martyr. Tablet 35. William Fisher, a gallant little lad of 9, was killed in Walworth while trying to save his younger brother from being run over. **1886.**

Three Westmorland Men killed in a Limekiln in trying to save a Comrade. Miles Wright, Miles Thompson, and George Dixon, lost their lives at some lime works at Plumgarths, near Kendal, while making a splendid attempt to save a fellow-workman. After tipping a load of limestone into one of the kilns, a man entered to level the stones, and was at once overcome by the gas. The above noble trio went to the rescue in turn, but perished in their attempt, with the man they tried to save. **1889.**

Three Postman's Park Heroes and Martyrs. Tablet 41. Many years later, on this same day, Godfrey W.

Nicholson, George F. Elliot, and Robert Underhill successively went down a well at a Stratford distillery to rescue a comrade, and were all poisoned by foul gas.

1901.

JULY 13

V.C. Lieut.-Colonel G. D. Dowell, **R.M.A.** With three others saved the crew of a disabled rocket boat, keeping her afloat, under heavy Russian grape and musketry fire, until she was towed into safety.

V.C. Captain of the Mast George Ingoueville, **R.N.** While suffering from a wound and under furious fire, caught the painter of a cutter and saved her from drifting under a Russian battery. **Baltic, Crimea. 1855.**

V.C. Lieutenant B. J. D. Guy, **R.N.** Over ground literally ploughed by bullets tried to carry a mortally wounded seaman. Failing to do so alone, he gallantly sought and found willing helpers in his errand of mercy, and conveyed the dying man into shelter.

Tientsin, China. 1900.

London Fire Brigade Silver Medals to David Wall and James J. Jago, the former of whom saved one and the latter four lives at a fire in Hackney Road. **1878.**

A brave little Cheshire Lad. While John McHugh, aged 11, and Samuel Cartwright, aged 10, were bathing in the clay pits at Saltney, the latter got into difficulties. Neither could swim, but McHugh sprang to help his friend, exclaiming, "Here's my life or nothing." Cartwright, however, seized him by the legs and pulled him under, and neither came up again. **1901.**

N

July 14

London Schoolboy Hero and Martyr. Thomas Yellowly, aged 15, plunged into the Thames at ebb tide near the Embankment to the assistance of his little friend who was drowning, but both lads sank in the mud.

1901.

London Fire Brigade Silver Medal to A. Oates, who, by means of a fire-escape, succeeded in rescuing a woman from a room on the second floor at Great St. Andrew Street, Seven Dials. The gallant fireman was severely burned on the face and hands while entering the room.

1904.

Fourteen-year-old Hero. William Grierson, a lad of 14, was bathing with Arthur Saunders in the Leeds and Liverpool Canal, near Aintree racecourse, and the latter got into difficulties. Grierson went to his aid, but the drowning boy gripped him round the neck, and after a struggle they sank together. **1909.**

July 15

V.C. Boatswain J. Sheppard, **R.N.** Decorated for two heroic attempts to blow up a Russian battleship in Sevastopol harbour. **Crimea. 1855.**

Albert Medal of the Second Class to William H. Burt, of Devizes, for conspicuous bravery at a fire, which broke out on the premises of an Italian warehouseman in the market-place of that town. The gallant man entered the shop and succeeded in bringing out a box containing eleven pounds of gunpowder, thus preventing a disastrous explosion. **1881.**

A Morayshire Railway Porter's Heroism. While three ladies were bathing in the river Lossie they got beyond their depth, whereupon Peter Grant at once sprang into the water to their assistance, when two of the drowning women clutched their rescuer and dragged him under. Grant perished, but the three ladies were eventually saved. **1881.**

JULY 16

V.C. General Sir H. M. Havelock (afterwards Havelock-Allan and son of the famous Sir Henry Havelock), Bart., K.C.B., **10th (N. Lincoln).** For two brilliant charges at the rebels' guns at Cawnpore and Lucknow. General Havelock was killed in the Khyber Pass on December 30, 1897. **Mutiny. 1857.**

Postman's Park Hero and Martyr. Tablet 28. William Donald, a Bayswater railway clerk, aged 19, was drowned in the river Lea while trying to save a lad from a dangerous entanglement of weeds. **1876.**

JULY 17

Liverpool S. & H. Society's Gold Medal to Mr. Eyton P. Owen, B.A., schoolmaster at Waterloo High School. While bathing near Crosby, three of his pupils were swept away by the heavy sea and two were drowned. Mr. Owen gallantly plunged into the broken water, and with great difficulty managed to bring the third lad, who was unconscious, ashore. It was some hours before the attempts to restore animation proved successful. **1893.**

Liverpool S. & H. Society's Vote of Thanks to Samuel Henderson for rescuing a child from being run over by a tramcar in Park Road. **1907.**

JULY 18

V.C. Colonel R. Wadeson, **Gordon Highlanders.** For saving the lives of two wounded English soldiers by killing a couple of mutineers who had attacked them.

Delhi Mutiny. 1857.

Two noble Lancashire Doctors. During an epidemic of typhus fever at Bolton, Dr. Richard Robinson and Dr. William Hatton devoted themselves so entirely to the poor patients that both contracted the disease and died of it. The mother, brother, and two servants of Dr. Hatton helped him in his noble work of nursing the victims, cleansing their horribly insanitary houses, burning rubbish, and doing everything possible to stem the "plague" (as it was called). Dr. Robinson died on July 18, and Dr. Hatton on August 31. **1847.**

Postman's Park ten-year-old Hero and Martyr. Tablet 20. John Clinton, a cabman's son, slipped back into the Thames near London Bridge and was drowned, after saving the life of another boy. Shortly before, this tiny hero had saved his baby brother's life by tearing off the child's clothes, which had been set on fire. **1894.**

"We live in deeds, not years."—*P. J. Bailey.*

Postman's Park Railway Heroes and Martyrs. Tablet 2. Walter Peart, driver, and Harry Dean, fireman of the Windsor express, while forcing their way through flames and steam to stop their engine, were both so fearfully scalded and burned that they died the next day. "Never mind," said Peart, while being carried to the hospital, "I stopped the train."

This heroic deed averted a terrible catastrophe, as the train was travelling at a great speed when the engine became unreliable. **1898.**

JULY 19

A Lancashire Baby Hero and Martyr. Richard Spencer, aged 6 years, made a gallant attempt to save the life of his brother, aged 4, in the river Ribble at Preston. James got out of his depth while bathing, and in trying to save him Richard lost his life also.

1877.

A gallant Scotch Laddie. A youth named Gordon, aged 14, seeing a little boy fall from a ledge of rock into the river near Tay Bridge at Dundee, sprang to his assistance. The drowning child clutched his would-be rescuer so tightly by the throat that both boys were drowned. **1897.**

A humble Hero of the R.N. James Ellis, a rope-maker on the gunnery ship *Cambridge*, lost his life in trying to save two lads in Torpoint harbour, Devonshire. Ellis was fully dressed, and one of the drowning lads seized him round the neck, dragging him under water. Both perished. The other boy was saved by the crew of a yacht. **1897.**

JULY 20

Liverpool Lifeboat Tragedy. Three Men lost. Emanuel Roderique, William Ruffler, and Daniel Morgan lost their lives in going to the assistance of the *Maxwell* in a terrific sea at midnight. When close to the vessel their boat was completely turned over. Some of the crew managed to cling to the boat and re-enter it when she righted; but as oars and everything else had been washed away, the craft drifted in pitch darkness over Burbo Bank into the Rock Channel, and was cast ashore about 6.30 the next morning at Leasowe. Two men were found to be missing, and D. Morgan died afterwards in Hoylake Hospital from his injuries. **1892.**

A Boy Hero of Northumberland. Joseph Gardiner, aged 13, was drowned in the river Tyne while trying to save his friend, Joseph Allen. The gallant boy jumped into the water to his friend's assistance with all his clothes on, and these weighed him down. Allen also perished. Both were sons of widows. **1901.**

The Order of St. John of Jerusalem in England. Silver Medals to Archibald M. M. Bomphrey, George Williamson, and William Foley for extreme bravery on the occasion of a boiler explosion on a launch at Southampton. All three men rushed through the flames, in order to rescue a boy who was imprisoned in the boiler-room. **1907.**

JULY 21

V.C. Sergeant J. Ross, **R.E.** Displayed extreme courage on three occasions, upon one of which he placed and filled twenty-five gabions under fearful fire from the Russian batteries before Sevastopol. **Crimea. 1855.**

A Bristol Boy's Self-sacrifice. Stephen St. George Showers, aged 14, son of Major Showers, while boating on the Severn near Tewkesbury with two companions named Roberts and Dixon, lost his life in a gallant effort to save the latter. Dixon had fallen overboard, and, in trying to haul him into the boat, Showers was dragged into the river, both being drowned. **1869.**

Heroism of a West Riding Mill Foreman. Near the South Pier at Bridlington, while racing the waves of the tide, two boys were caught and swept out to sea. Mr. Edward Peel, who could not swim and was in feeble health, ran into the sea to help the lads, who were afterwards rescued by the coxswain of the local lifeboat. The heroic man who first went to their aid, however, met the fate from which he tried to save them. **1902.**

A noble Record. Albert Labrum, an attendant at Northampton Corporation Baths, fetched a man out of eight feet of water, in which he was drowning. The man clung so tenaciously to Labrum's shoulder that both narrowly escaped death. This was the gallant fellow's sixty-third rescue. **1909.**

JULY 22

Albert Medal of the First Class to T. A. Shuttleworth, Esq., Deputy-Conservator of Forests at Alibagh, for distinguished courage on three occasions, on each of which he saved the life of a shipwrecked mariner at great risk of his own. **1866.**

A Warwickshire Child loses her Life in trying to save her Friend. Two children named Minnie Hornsley and Alice Deane were playing on the bank of the Leam at Leamington, when the latter fell into the water. Minnie went to her assistance, but she was dragged in by the drowning girl, and both were lost. **1886.**

A little Cheshire Hero. William Rumsey, aged 13, of Victor Street, Chester, and Edward Middleton, aged 10, were bathing in the river Dee, when the latter got out of his depth. He was struggling for his life when Rumsey, with great bravery, went to his assistance, but both perished. **1887.**

The Order of St. John of Jerusalem in England. Certificates of Honour to James Simmons, Thomas Simmons, and Joseph Dawber for a gallant attempt to rescue their foreman, who had been overcome by gas in the Douglas Bank Colliery, Wigan. Dawber and James Simmons each in turn tried to reach the victim of the deadly fumes, and, being themselves overpowered, were rescued by Thomas Simmons. **1905.**

July 23

London Fire Brigade Silver Medal to Edward Epps, who saved four lives at a fire in Aldersgate Street. **1879.**

A Warwickshire Lad drowned in trying to save Life. Three boys were playing on a barge at East Dock, Cardiff, when one of them fell into the canal. Henry Reed, a street musician from Birmingham, jumped in after him, but was unable to save the drowning boy, and lost his own life in the attempt. **1892.**

Royal Humane Society's Bronze Medal to William Tull, a schoolboy aged 13, who jumped from Horseferry Stairs, Rotherhithe, into 18 feet of water, and rescued T. Malham, who had fallen into the river and was unable to swim. **1904.**

July 24

V.C. Major N. R. Howse, **New South Wales Medical Staff.** Decorated for carrying a wounded man into shelter under severe cross-fire at Vredefort. **Boer War. 1900.**

Bristol Doctor loses his Life in trying to save a Patient. While attending an operation for tracheotomy on a patient in the Infirmary, Mr. William C. Lysaght, seeing that the tube had become choked, sucked out the moisture with his lips as the only chance of saving the patient's life. The doctor's heroic act was in vain, as the man (who was suffering from malignant scarlatina) died, and the doctor, having caught the deadly complaint, followed him to the grave shortly afterwards. **1887.**

JULY 25

Heroism of a Norfolk Gentleman. James Bradshaw, of Thorpe Hamlet, Norwich, while bathing with Mr. G. Clarke at Lowestoft, noticed that the latter was in difficulties and swam to his assistance in a heavy sea, but in a few moments both disappeared. Those on shore endeavoured to launch a boat, which capsized, and it eventually reached the spot too late to save them. **1870.**

JULY 26

V.C. Major A. Scott, **Bengal Staff Corps.** For great gallantry in saving an officer's life from three murderous Pathans at Quetta. **Beloochistan. 1877.**

V.C. Captain E. W. Costello, **Indian Staff Corps.** Under heavy fire, with the help of two Sepoys, rescued a Lance-Havildar who was lying wounded 60 yards away on a field swarming with the enemy's swordsmen. Was twice wounded during the Malakand campaign.
Punjab Frontier. 1897.

Albert Medal of the Second Class to Mr. William Yaldwyn, in recognition of conspicuous gallantry in rescuing six persons from a flood at Charlesville Colony of Queensland. **1886.**

Postman's Park. London Fire Brigade Martyr. Tablet 14. George Lee, aged 26, on entering a burning building in Smithfield for the third time, found a girl whom he carried some distance to the window, falling many times, but refusing to abandon her. On reaching the escape he threw her in first and followed himself, but both succumbed to their terrible injuries. **1876.**

Heroic Death of Six Men at a Durham Chemical Manufactory. James M'Cuskin, W. Parkinson, G. Robertson, J. M'Tiernan, H. Storey, and R. Johnson sacrificed their lives while trying to save that of William Heslop, who had fallen with a condenser which had caught fire and collapsed. The six men rushed to rescue their comrade, when three more condensers suddenly fell, burying all seven men beneath their ruins. Six out of the seven victims were killed outright, but M'Cuskin could be seen, through a chink between the mass of girders, beams, and huge stones, still alive and suffering intense agony from his injuries and also from the fumes of the acid. The deadly atmosphere greatly impeded the heroic efforts made all through the night to release the unfortunate victim, and an air-pump was procured; but at eight o'clock in the morning the man died after having borne his dreadful injuries with heroic patience throughout. **1891.**

Liverpool S. & H. Society's Silver Medal and Vote of Thanks, and a suit of clothes to Edward Rudd, aged 13, for most gallantly and at great personal risk rescuing a boy from a "live" electric rail on the Lancashire and Yorkshire Railway, near Freshfield. Attracted to the spot by hearing a girl crying, Rudd found a boy named Partington with his feet fast on the live rail and his head on the running rail. Covering his hand with his cap, which was unfortunately wet with the rain, he attempted to pull the boy off, but received a shock which flung him back some yards. He then took off his coat and placed it over the boy, and, with the assistance of a boy named James Hasitt, succeeded in clearing Partington from the rail. Another boy, named James Smith, also went to Rudd's assistance, but fell on the live rail and received a severe shock. Hasitt and Smith were each awarded 15s. and a Vote of Thanks. **1906.**

July 27

V.C. Sergeant-Major P. Mullane, **R.H.A.**
V.C. Gunner J. Collis, **R.H.A.**

A pair of heroes, who after the awful disaster at Maiwand proved their mettle in deeds which will never be forgotten. Collis, when the pursuing Afghan cavalry were firing upon the limber of his gun, upon which the wounded had been placed, in a narrow passage, deliberately went to the side of the road and drew the enemy's fire upon himself to give his disabled comrades a chance of life. This is but one of the gallant gunner's fine acts. Mullane, when the enemy were but a few yards behind, seeing the driver of a gun carriage fall wounded, ran back and lifted him to the limber of his own gun, where, however, he succumbed to his hurts.

Afghanistan. 1880.

Albert Medal of the Second Class to Private Anthony Gerrighty, Royal Marines, for saving a lunatic who jumped from a transport ship. The man fought desperately with his rescuer, striking at him with a knife before the brave soldier was able to effect his humane purpose. **1878.**

A Memorial bearing the following Inscription is to be found at North Berwick. "Erected by public subscription in memory of Catherine Watson, aged 19, who was drowned in the East Bay, 27th of July 1889, while rescuing a drowning boy. The child was saved; the brave girl was taken." **1889.**

JULY 28

Postman's Park Heroine and Martyr. Tablet 16. Ellen Donovan lost her life while trying to save some children supposed to be in the top floor of a burning house in Lincoln Court, Great Wild Street. No one was there; but when the brave woman turned to descend, her escape was cut off and she perished in the flames. **1873.**

A Deed worthy of the highest Recognition. During the night attack on Malakand, Lieutenant Ford was badly hit. When Surgeon-Lieutenant V. Hugo came to him and struck a match amid a splutter of bullets, he saw that the femoral artery was severed and that the patient had fainted from loss of blood. Knowing it was impossible to move the unconscious man, the doctor promptly seized the artery to arrest the flow of blood, and knelt, passive amid the fearful tumult of war and exposed to incessant fire, holding a man's life between his finger and thumb through the long night. When morning broke, the doctor, cramped and weary but still holding the artery, had his charge carried into quarters to receive medical care. This fine act, lasting not merely for a few breathless moments of excitement, but for long, perilous hours which would try the toughest nerves, was acknowledged by the Golden Badge of the D.S.O. Many have thought that a simple Maltese Cross of bronze would have been a more fitting recognition of one of the most noble deeds in British warfare.

N.-W. Frontier of India. 1896.

Stanhope Medal to Mr. John H. Collier for the rescue of a lascar in a sea too heavy for any boat to be launched. At great personal risk Mr. Collier, second officer of the ss. *Sultan*, went overboard with a line and eventually both men were hauled aboard. **1896.**

JULY 29

V.C. Major A. C. Bogle, **Seaforth Highlanders.** (Died 1900.) At Oonao was fearfully wounded while forcing his way with a few followers into a loop-holed house full of armed mutineers, all of whom he captured.

Mutiny. 1857.

Heroic Death of a Monmouthshire Labourer. As William Dowling was seeing a relative off by train from Newport, a Mrs. Bower, who accompanied him, slipped between the platform and carriage as the train started. Dowling made a desperate effort to save the woman; but he also missed his footing and fell, and two of the coaches passed over him, killing him instantly. The woman had a miraculous escape, being quite uninjured. **1901.**

July 30

Two out of Four Civilian Wearers of the Victoria Cross, on whose behalf a new clause was added to the Royal Warrant, July 8, 1859.

V.C. W. F. McDonnell, Esq., **Bengal Civil Service.** (Died 1894.)

V.C. R. L. Mangles, Esq., **Bengal Civil Service.** (Died 1905.)

During the pathetic attempt to relieve the doomed garrison of Arrah, with its 15 English and 50 Sikhs hemmed in by 4000 mutineers, some of the finest deeds in the history of the Great Mutiny were performed by the above two civilians. Out of the 450 who made the attempt and were trapped by the rebel troops, 300 perished. Mr. Mangles, among many splendid deeds of mercy during the awful retreat, carried a heavy man six miles through incessant fire across a rough swamp under the tropical heat of the Indian sun, having had no food for twenty-four or sleep for forty-eight hours. Mr. McDonnell, while dangerously wounded, released a boat laden with refugees from her moorings under a hurricane of lead. His action saved thirty-five of our soldiers from certain death. These are but samples of the deeds of these silent heroes, in which they were associated with Private Dempsey, V.C. (see March 14).

Mutiny. 1857.

Two heroic Solicitors. Mr. E. W. Field, aged 67, and Mr. H. Ettwood, aged 58, gave their lives to save that of a gentleman unable to swim at Moulsford, Upper Thames. The two supported their friend for some time until their strength failed and they sank. Their friend was rescued by those on shore. **1871**

A Hero of the Royal Navy. On the occasion of an explosion on the cruiser *Forth*, in which Engine-room Artificer R. Moses sustained fatal injuries, Engineer-Lieutenant Henry Wolfe attempted to enter the stokehold, but was so overcome that the crew had to play the hose on him to bring him round. Steam was still issuing in clouds from the stokehold, but the gallant Lieutenant again went down, only to find Moses dead. **1909.**

JULY 31

Albert Medal of the Second Class to Mr. William Buyers for gallantry in saving life from a wreck near Shanghai in a heavy sea. **1878.**

Postman's Park Hero and Martyr. Tablet 27. Edmund Emery, aged 21, leapt from a steamboat on the Thames at Chelsea, and perished in trying to save a drowning child. **1874.**

AUGUST

" There limned in lightning on the scroll of fame,
The record of earth's bravest ye may read."

—James Rhodes.

AUGUST

August 1

An Oxford Girl of 8 dies in trying to save her little Brother. Seeing her little brother James fall into the river at Deep Martin, Annie Fox took off her shoes and got hold of him from the steps of a landing-stage, but was pulled into the water herself, and both were drowned. **1869.**

Two Men sacrifice their Lives attempting to save others. While acting as guides to a holiday party boating at Barmouth, Mr. William Paton and Mr. Percival Gray lost their lives in attempting to save those under their care. In the twilight a sudden squall lashed the great tidal wave running up the estuary and engulfed the boat. One of the two brave men, after doing all he could to save a lady, struck his head against a rock in the gathering darkness, and sank in deep water. The other, who could easily have saved himself, also perished in trying to rescue a lady. **1894.**

> " Now Sorrow on from cape to headland wails ;
> And childless mothers weep along the shore
> For those dear dead so silent on the sands ;
> But two bright stars have risen to set no more,
> And Christ, the Saviour, cries with wounded hands—
> ' Love that will lose its life alone avails.' "
>
> —" Ballads of Brave Deeds," *Canon Rawnsley.*

AUGUST 2

V.C. Lance-Corporal W. House, **Royal Berkshire Regiment.** Was badly hit by a Boer marksman while making a splendid attempt to save a wounded comrade at Mosilikatse Nek. **Boer War. 1900.**

A gallant little Yorkshire Lad. Two boys, aged 9, named John G. Armstrong and Daniel Keller, were bathing in the Ouse, near York, at a part where the bed of the river suddenly shelves and the water deepens from 4 to 6 feet. Keller got out of his depth, and Armstrong pluckily went to the rescue, but both lads were drowned. **1858.**

Death of a Worcestershire Mother while trying to save her Children. Kezia Bishop, wife of a lock-keeper at Stoke Prior, near Bromsgrove, lost her life in trying to rescue her two little boys, aged 4 and 6 years. The children fell into the canal, and the mother at once plunged in to the rescue, but, being unable to swim, her heroic attempt was unavailing, and all three were drowned. **1882.**

Postman's Park Child Hero and Martyr. Tablet 40. Edward Morris, aged 10, seeing his companion sink while bathing in the Grand Junction Canal, went to his assistance. Unhappily he was powerless to save the other lad, and lost his own life in the attempt. **1899.**

AUGUST 3

Albert Medal of the Second Class to John S. Summers, for great courage and exertion in saving six lives from a wrecked boat near Buchaness in a dangerous cross sea. **1876.**

Albert Medal of the Second Class to Mr. Henry Wesley, for rescuing the crew of a vessel wrecked on the bar of the river Volta. **1879.**

Albert Medal of the Second Class to Richard W. Toman, R.N., engineer, who, after a terrible explosion on H.M.S. *Foam*, shut off steam from the main-stop valves of boilers in the stokehold. After twice falling, he then forced his way through the scalding steam, and turned the fire extinguishers on to the boilers. After this, a third journey was made to the engineers' room to see if any one had been left behind. Toman was severely scalded in the execution of these intrepid deeds. **1898.**

A Derbyshire Youth of 18 drowned in trying to save his Brother. Harry Hyde, aged 18, and his brother, three years younger, were bathing in a reservoir at Mellor, near New Mills, when the latter called out that he was sinking. Harry at once went to his assistance, but both got into deep water and were drowned before help could reach them. Their mother was a widow. **1888.**

August 4

V.C. Colonel F. C. Elton, **55th (Border Regiment).** Displayed magnificent pluck in the advanced trenches before Sevastopol, where, under terrific cross-fire, he worked with a pick and shovel, and by his fine example encouraged his men to persevere in their perilous work.

Crimea. 1855.

"When such things happen on any of the battlefields of life—believe not that the deeds begin upon battlefields, that they are the first heroism of their doers. Only souls wonted to sweetness and self-forgetting brim over at such hours. The little thing that makes a moment great is never all done *at* the moment."—*William C. Gannett.*

A West Riding Miner loses his Life in trying to save his Sons. Richard Swallow was drowned on the occasion of the flooding of a mine at Raventhorpe, near Dewsbury. When the water burst into the pit, Swallow had ample time to escape, but went to warn his lads of their danger, and in so doing sacrificed his own chance of life. **1892.**

Wreck of the *Maori*. When the liner *Maori* was wrecked in a terrible sea at Slangkop Point, 20 miles south of Table Bay, George Stewart, the boatswain, showed splendid gallantry in rescuing survivors. Twice he swam out 80 yards through the boiling surf, and each time saved a life. Yet a third time he plunged into the surf to rescue a drowning comrade, but the latter sank just as Stewart clutched him, and it was with the greatest difficulty that the heroic man himself regained the shore. **1909.**

August 5

V.C. Private F. Corbett, **60th.** Gazetted for great self-sacrifice in remaining with and succouring a mortally wounded officer, being himself all the time a target for the enemy's fire. **Kafr Dowar, Egypt. 1882.**

Sussex Chemist suffocated in an Attempt to save Workmen. Hearing that two men had succumbed to foul air in a tank at the Sewage Company's works at Hastings, Mr. John T. Porter, aged 22, with a man named Harris, went down taking a lighted candle. This speedily went out, and Harris, losing sight of his companion and feeling very ill, returned to the fresh air. When somewhat recovered, he made three more gallant attempts to rescue the victims, in which noble task he was assisted by other employés of the company. At length the two workmen were brought out of the tank, but both were dead. Mr. Porter could not be found, and his body was not recovered till three days later, when it was discovered in a sewage pipe a quarter of a mile from the scene of the tragedy. **1870.**

Heroic Death of an Irish Gentleman. Mr. Cormac Rooney, a merchant of Manor Hamilton, County Leitrim, during his wife's absence from home awoke to find his house on fire. He rushed through suffocating smoke towards the nursery, where his three children and their nurse were sleeping. This he was, however, unable to reach, falling back on his way thither and perishing in the flames. Efforts at rescue were unavailing, and the remains of the five victims were afterwards found charred almost beyond recognition. **1901.**

Royal Humane Society's Silver Medal to Jeremiah Smith for a splendid attempt to rescue John Hallam from a large flue full of gas at Brybo Steel Works, near Wrexham. Smith succeeded in dragging the man to one of the openings, when he also succumbed to the poisonous fumes. Both were got out in an unconscious state; but, while Smith recovered shortly, Hallam died six hours later, despite all efforts to restore him. **1908.**

August 6

Albert Medal of the Second Class to Major T. Cropper, West Kent Militia, for great gallantry in trying to save a suicide, who jumped from the ss. *Idaho* in San Francisco Bay in a high sea. Major Cropper was rescued after being twenty-five minutes in the water. **1878.**

A gallant Police Sergeant of Kent. George Coomber, who had served through the Crimea and possessed a Medal for that campaign and also a Turkish Medal, died in a cess-pit at Gravesend, from which he was endeavouring to rescue some men who had succumbed to the noxious vapours. **1864.**

Two noble "Stagemen" of Cheshire. Samuel Dear and William Nicholls, seeing four men from a capsized punt trying to reach the landing-stage at New Brighton, put off in a boat to their rescue. Shortly after starting, their own boat also capsized; and, despite their being expert swimmers, they were carried out to sea by the ebbing tide, while the men they tried to succour were saved. Their bodies were never recovered. **1894.**

A Leicester Solicitor drowned in trying to save his Friend. Four gentlemen were bathing at Poldhu Beach, Cornwall, when two, named Webb and Wykes, got into difficulties. Mr. Albert Dexter, of Leicester—a strong swimmer—succeeded in saving Mr. Webb; and then, in a heavy ground swell, he swam out to the rescue of Mr. Wykes. The additional strain, however, was too great for his strength, and both he and his friend were drowned. **1900.**

AUGUST 7

V.C. Lieutenant T. Lawrence, **17th Lancers.** While on patrol duty with Private Hayman, the two were attacked by fourteen Boers, Hayman being hit and his horse shot. Lawrence placed his comrade on his own mount, and on foot kept the enemy at bay until the other was out of range. He then retired, followed by the Boers for two miles, until help came.

Essenbosch Farm, Boer War. 1900.

Albert Medal of the Second Class to Mr. Alfred Hunt, of Longport, for gallantly endeavouring to save the life of his brother Robert at Tunstall. The two brothers were employed at Messrs. Johnson Brothers' Pottery in cleaning out a tank containing hot water and oil, under the engine-house floor, when Robert Hunt, who was bending over the opening of the tank, fell in. Alfred Hunt was working close by at the time, and, hearing his brother's cry, immediately jumped in after him—although he knew the water must be very hot—and succeeded in pulling him out. Robert succumbed to his injuries. **1908.**

Captain C. S. S. Stanhope, R.N. (after whom the Royal Humane Society's premier decoration is named) was awarded the **Silver Medal** of the Society for an extremely gallant rescue at sea, off the west coast of South America, while serving on H.M.S. *Asia*. **1850.**

Some gallant Redcoats at Malta. Private William Thirkill, King's Own Light Infantry, was drowned near Malta in attempting to save a comrade, who was, however, dashed against a rock and killed before help could reach him. Several men of the Derbyshire Regiment and a Lance-Corporal also displayed much bravery on this occasion. Thirkill had previously saved two lives. **1901.**

August 8

Albert Medal of the First Class to Seedie Farabini for one of the most splendid deeds throughout the Albert Medal records. A fugitive slave-boy having jumped overboard from H.M.S. *Wild Swan*, this gallant hero plunged after him, although an enormous shark had already attacked the boy when Farabini caught him and brought him ashore. Three other sharks were close by, and it is marvellous that either man or boy escaped with life. **1880.**

Billposter's heroic Death in Co. Down. On being told that a little boy was in the cellar of a house which had partly collapsed in North Street, Newry, Laurence Kearns, despite the warning of a Fire Brigade man that the rest of the building was about to fall, persisted in going to the rescue, because he could hear the child's voice. As the noble fellow disappeared down the cellar steps the rest of the house crashed in, completely burying Kearns, who was afterwards found dead. The child was unhurt, having been protected by some rafters, which, falling against the wall so as to form a shelter, had prevented the debris touching him. **1898.**

Postman's Park Hero and Martyr. Tablet 18. John C. Cambridge, aged 23, a clerk in the London County Council offices, was drowned off the beach at Ostend, after saving the life of a lady who was unable to swim. **1901.**

"In the service of others he found his happiness. Probably the manner of his death would most impress those who did not know him; his friends feel that it would be easier to die as he died than to live as he lived."—*Extract from the pamphlet to be obtained from the Park Keeper, St. Botolph Churchyard, E.C.*

August 9

Albert Medals of the First Class to Mr. A. R. Margary and Mr. John Dodd for noble self-sacrifice in taking out, first, a boat, which was capsized, and, later, a rope, by which four lives were saved from a wrecked barque near Ke-lung harbour. They were only just able to reach the wreck through the boiling surf; it broke up as the last man was brought off. Mr. Dodd was seriously injured by the boisterous waves, which dashed him against the wreck. **1871.**

Albert Medal of the Second Class to Edward Scullion for conspicuous gallantry in attempting to rescue two men and a boy. These had been overcome by fumes in the air-shaft of an unused sulphuretted hydrogen sewer connected with the Newcastle and Gateshead Chemical Company. **1886.**

Two gallant Durham Boys. William Watkins, aged 13, and John Hall, aged 12, lost their lives in trying to rescue a companion bathing in a pond at Stockton. The lad was in difficulties when the two others went to his aid. All three perished. **1882.**

More Durham Heroes. Thomas Quin and Thomas Swinburne, hearing that a child was overcome by poisonous gas down an air-shaft in a chemical sewer into which he had ventured, went to his assistance. Gallant efforts were made to rescue the unfortunate trio, the two men having also been overcome by the fumes; but Quin and the boy were already dead when brought up, and Swinburne was in a comatose state. He was restored after two hours' exertion on the part of the doctors, and lingered a couple of days, when he too expired. **1886.**

August 10

Heroism of a Lancashire Labourer. John Strode, aged 48, lost his life at Hooley Hill, Ashton-under-Lyme, in trying to save his mate, who had succumbed to foul gas at the bottom of a sewer shaft 64 feet deep. Another man afterwards descended, strapped to a "hop-pit," and succeeded in bringing Strode to the surface, who, however, was dead. **1901.**

Royal Humane Society's Bronze Medal to Jeremiah Sweeney, aged 14. Two lads, while bathing in the Taff

AUGUST

T. Lawrence
Lieut & Riding Master
18th Q.M.O. Hussars

[illegible]

H. Gough

Thomas Ashford
V.C

Dunmore.

R.K. Adams

Hector Maclean

at Cardiff, got into danger in 10 feet of water, the tide being very strong at the time. Sweeney plunged in and succeeded in saving one of them, also making a gallant but unsuccessful attempt to rescue the other. **1904.**

Royal Humane Society's Bronze Medal to Herbert Bathie, aged 13, who at great risk plunged into the Thames at the Adelphi steps, fully clothed, and rescued a boy who had fallen in. **1905.**

AUGUST 11

V.C. Private J. Prosser, **1st (Royal Scots).** Had previously caught and brought back a soldier deserting to the enemy, and on this date carried a wounded man out of the trenches, both acts being performed under severe fire before Sevastopol. **Crimea. 1855.**

Magnificent Heroism at a Suffolk Gun Cotton Factory. After a terrific explosion of a magazine containing twelve tons of gun cotton at Stowmarket, there was imminent danger of other large stores of explosives becoming ignited. A box of cartridges was lying in a shed adjoining the flaming building, and with intrepid valour, worthy of the Victoria Cross itself, Inspector Edward Prentice and his son William determined to remove the dangerous box. Unhappily, as they were trying to effect their heroic purpose, the cartridges caught fire, a second awful explosion occurred, and father and son were literally blown to pieces. A third shock followed, and so finished the terrible destruction. Seventeen were killed and seventy-two wounded in this fearful catastrophe. **1871.**

Liverpool S. & H. Society's Medal and Vote of Thanks, and £1 to Frances Polding, aged 15, of St.

Helen's, who went to the assistance of a police constable lying unconscious on the ground and being kicked by three drunken men. The girl flung herself across the constable's shoulders, and so protected his head, in all probability saving his life. She also blew his whistle, and brought others to the rescue. **1906.**

AUGUST 12

V.C. Rear-Admiral J. Bythesea, C.B., C.I.E., **R.N.** (Died 1906.) Second name on the Victoria Cross list. "Mutare vel timere sperno."

V.C. Stoker W. Johnstone, **R.N.**

Disguised as Russians, these naval heroes were associated in a most ingenious and perilous enterprise, which took three days to accomplish, whereby the enemy's despatches and three prisoners were captured at Wardo Island. **Baltic, Crimea. 1854.**

V.C. Lieutenant-Colonel J. P. H. Crowe, **Seaforth Highlanders.** (Died 1876.) "Skagh McEnchroe." For great gallantry in being the first to enter a redoubt at Busherutgunge. **Mutiny. 1857.**

A Glamorganshire Railway Ganger killed while saving Passengers from a wrecked Train. On the occasion of a train being thrown down an embankment near Trefort station, William Jones, of Blaennart Yorysybwl, clambered under the overturned coaches and extricated several people. A rope was afterwards fixed to a coach, which was then pulled by helpers into position; but Jones somehow failed to run back in time, and was knocked under by the moving mass. He was extricated alive, but received terrible injuries, which proved fatal shortly after. **1893.**

Young Scotch Lady drowned in trying to save her Brother. While Mary Duncan, aged 22, and her brother James, aged 14, were bathing near Kingsbarns, 8 miles east of St. Andrews, the latter got into difficulties. His sister tried to save him, but both perished before further aid arrived. **1902.**

Crippled Man's Bravery. George Stevens, a labourer, incapacitated from work on account of paralysis of the nerves, rushed into a room in White Cross Street, St. Luke's, and found a child named Elizabeth North in flames. Despite his affliction, he tore her burning clothing off, receiving terrible injuries to his arms and hands. The child, however, despite his heroic efforts, died in St. Bartholomew's Hospital. **1909.**

AUGUST 13

V.C. Sergeant-Major A. Young, **Cape Police.** Charged alone, ahead of a few followers, at Commandant Erasmus, who fired three times at point-blank range at his assailant. The Boer General was eventually compelled to surrender to the dashing young Colonial.

Ruiter's Kraal, Boer War. 1901.

Warwickshire Youth gives his Life in trying to save his Friend. George Gregory, aged 16, and a boy named Wright were bathing in the river Anker at the Ashlands, near Tamworth, when the latter got out of his depth. Gregory went to his assistance, but the drowning boy seized him and dragged him under water. Two young men dived into the river soon afterwards and brought the boys out, both dead. **1871.**

Heroism in Ireland. Miss Eileen Nicolls, M.A., daughter of Mr. Nicolls, secretary to the Loan Fund Board of

Ireland, went to bathe with Miss Kate Crohan and Miss Marie Kehane. Seeing Miss Crohan in difficulties, Miss Nicolls swam to her assistance, but became exhausted and sank. Miss Kehane, who was on the shore, dashed into the sea, but was powerless to help, and her life was only saved by Miss Crohan's brother, Donough Crohan, aged 18, who, having brought her ashore, swam out fully clothed to the others. Before he could reach them, he too sank. When Miss Crohan was eventually picked up by a boat, she was unconscious, but recovered later. **1909.**

August 14

A gallant Gloucester Lad. William Llewellyn, aged 12, with his brother James, aged 10, and two other boys, was bathing in the river Severn, when the younger lad got out of his depth. William, who could not swim, tried to pull him ashore, but his strength failed, and both were carried away by the tide and drowned. **1842.**

Death of a Durham Lad in trying to save his Brother. Three youths, named Gibson, were bathing in the sea at South Shields, when, in consequence of a strong off-set of the tide, the eldest brother was carried out of his depth. Leonard, the youngest of the trio, who swam to his assistance, was drowned; but the brother he went to help clung to the rocks and was saved. **1880.**

August 15

V.C. General Sir Charles J. S. Gough, G.C.B., **Bengal European Cavalry.** "Faugh-a-ballagh." Distinguished himself on four separate occasions, saving two lives, one of which was that of his brother, Sir Hugh Gough, V.C. Sir Charles Gough is the brother of one and the father of another V.C. hero, his son, Colonel

Gough, having won the decoration in 1903 (see April 22). This is the only instance of three Victoria Crosses in the same family. **Mutiny. 1857.**

A plucky Yorkshire Laddie. Although unable to swim, John Goulden, aged 8, of Hull, saved his playmate, a lad named Phillips, aged 7, from drowning. The younger lad got out of his depth and was being carried out to sea. **1909.**

A very young Hero. Jack Benson, aged 4, very pluckily saved the life of his little brother, aged 2, who had somehow got out on to the window-sill, and was falling over when Jack grasped his clothing and held on to him. He managed to support the baby, who was very heavy, until older hands lifted the child into safety. **1909.**

"Art little? Do thy little well, and for thy comfort know,
Great men can do their greatest work no better than just so."
—*Goethe.*

AUGUST 16

V.C. Lieut.-Colonel W. St. Lucien Chase, C.B., **Bombay Staff Corps.** (Died 1908.)
V.C. Sergeant T. Ashford, **Royal Fusiliers.**

Between them carried a wounded man over 200 yards under terrible fire into safety at Deh Khoja. **Kandahar, Afghanistan. 1880.**

Stanhope Medal to George W. Bennett. Three persons in trying to cross the South Esk river, near Avoca, Tasmania, were swept away, the river being in flood and 15 feet deep. Bennett plunged in, and after a hard struggle managed to save them all. **1875.**

Heroic Death of a Staffordshire Schoolmaster. John T. Savage, aged 23, a schoolmaster, lost his life in an attempt to rescue a workman, who was overcome by foul gas in a well at Hanley Hayes farm. Mr. Savage was also immediately overpowered, and, falling into 4 feet of water, was drowned. **1882.**

London Fire Brigade Silver Medals to J. Coombes and T. Williams, who after saving three people from a burning house in Baltic Street, St. Luke's, by means of a fire-escape, again entered the building in search of any one left behind, but owing to the fierceness of the fire were compelled to retreat, narrowly escaping with their lives. **1896.**

Boy of 12 who has saved Five Lives. Roland Mitchell, a half-time mill operative at Preston, dived half-dressed into 10 feet of water, and brought out a four-year-old lad who had fallen in, but was dead. This brave little half-timer had already saved five lives. On his return home after his gallant attempt, his reward from an appreciative mother was a thrashing for getting his clothes wet. **1909.**

August 17

V.C. Major The Earl of Dunmore, M.V.O., **16th Lancers.** (Born 1871.) "Furth fortune and fill the fetters."

V.C. Major-General R. B. Adams, C.B., **Indian Staff Corps.** (Born 1856.) "In cruce salus."

V.C. Lieutenant H. L. S. MacLean, **Indian Staff Corps.** "Virtue (*i.e.* Valour) mine honour."

Gazetted for a fine attempt to save the life of Lieutenant Greaves, who was shot and surrounded by tribesmen at Nawa Kili, Upper Swat. The gallant trio had succeeded in driving off the enemy, and were placing the wounded officer on a horse, when he was again shot and killed. His sad fate was shared by one of his would-be rescuers, Lieutenant MacLean, who received mortal injuries. **Punjab Frontier. 1897.**

Denbighshire Clerk drowned while trying to save his Companion. Mr. John Pritchard, of Wrexham, and Mr. Campbell, of Liverpool, were bathing at Douglas, Isle of Man, when the latter shouted for help. Although the water was shallow, Mr. Pritchard also got into difficulties, and both were drowned before help reached them. **1875.**

An Edinburgh Lad drowned while trying to rescue his Friend. Two lads, named Connelly and Macnab, were bathing at Portobello, when the ebb tide carried them beyond their depth. Macnab was rescued, but James Munroe, a young compositor, who tried to save Connelly, was dragged under by him and both were drowned. **1882.**

Brave London Girl. Rose Thompson, aged 17, seeing a man assaulting P.-C. Humphrey in Mill Lane, West Hampstead, went to his assistance, and blew his whistle for help. A second man also struck the constable a heavy blow on the ear, knocking his helmet off. Miss Thompson, having assisted the policeman to secure his first assailant, then ran for the ambulance, on which the struggling man was taken to the station. At the Police Court the magistrate complimented Miss Thompson on having behaved with great courage and with the greatest possible credit to herself. **1909.**

August 18

A gallant Cadet. Mr. Percy Saunders, a young military officer, seeing an old gentleman in danger of drowning at Saltburn-on-Sea, North Riding, swam to his assistance.

He had almost effected the rescue, when he became exhausted, and was carried away by the tide and drowned. Mr. Saunders had served in the Afghan and Egyptian campaigns. **1883.**

Gorleston Policeman Martyr to Duty. While trying to arrest a man who had been violently ill-treating his wife, P.-C. Allgar was shot by Thomas Allen, who fired point blank at the poor fellow. After wounding several other people, the miscreant was arrested. Allgar left a widow and several children. **1909.**

AUGUST 19

London Fire Brigade Silver Medals to George W. Ralph and Alfred Smeeth. At a fire in Linton Street, New North Road, Ralph, hearing that some one was alive on the second floor, effected an entrance through the window. He found one man lying on the floor and another trying to help him, and carried the injured man to the window, passing him out to Smeeth. Meanwhile the flames had burst out from the first floor, setting the fire-escape alight, and Smeeth was badly burned while descending with his burden. **1894.**

A little Hero of Devon. Bertie Matters, aged 10, and his brother Freddie, aged 13, were playing on a floating raft in an estuary of the river Tamar, when the elder boy fell into deep water. Bertie jumped in to help his brother, but the impetus of the leap carried him under another raft. Two gentlemen went to the rescue of the boys, and brought Freddie out safely, but the gallant little Bertie was drowned. **1899.**

AUGUST 20

A gallant Devonian Shoemaker. Edward Stephens, a shoemaker of Ilfracombe, jumped into 19 feet of water at high tide to the assistance of Miss Bailey, a

AUGUST

H G Grace-Browne

J W Chaplin

Color Sergeant Instructor of Musketry
Harry Hampton V.C.
The Kings (Liverpool) Regt

L Sgt William. E. Heaton. V.C
1st Batt Kings Lpool Regt

E Durrant
2nd Batt
Rifle Brigade

Peterborough visitor, who was drowning. Stephens succeeded in supporting her until a rope was thrown from the quay, by means of which the lady was hauled up safely; but her intrepid deliverer was struck by a wave and carried out to sea. The lady undertook to provide for Stephens' wife and children. **1845.**

A Welsh Undergraduate's Self-sacrifice. Mr. Reginald Griffith, aged 22, of Jesus College, Oxford, brother of Captain Griffith, of Llanfair Hall, Carnarvon, was drowned in Menai Straits while endeavouring to rescue Mr. J. Blanchard, who had been seized with cramp. The drowning man threw his arms round the other's neck, and both perished. **1875.**

AUGUST 21

V.C. Colonel H. G. Gore-Browne, **32nd (Cornwall's Light Infantry).** (Born 1830.) "Loyal en tout." For extreme gallantry in leading a sortie, spiking two guns, and attacking the rebel gunners, of whom 100 were slain.

Lucknow, Mutiny. 1857.

STORMING OF TAKU FORTS

V.C. Colonel J. W. Chaplin, C.B., **Hampshire Regiment.** (Born 1840.) Was seriously wounded after planting the Queen's Colours on the fort, also on the *cavalier* of the fort, which he was the first man to mount.

"Fortune gives her hand to the bold man."—*Virgil.*

V.C. Captain N. Burslem, **67th (Hampshire).**
V.C. Private Thomas Lane, **67th (Hampshire).**

Associated in a deed of exceptional pluck. Before any of our men had gained an entrance, the doughty pair swam a ditch, enlarged a breach in the walls, and entered the fort, both being severely wounded.

V.C. Major-General R. M. Rogers, C.B., **44th (Essex Regiment).**

V.C. Private J. McDougall, **44th (Essex Regiment).**

V.C. Major E. H. Lenon, **67th.**

During the assault on the North Taku Forts these three brave men swam a water-course and entered by an embrasure, in the order given.

V.C. Hospital Apprentice A. F. Fitzgibbon, **Indian Medical Establishment.** While ministering to those stricken down was severely wounded under a torrent of bullets. **China. 1860.**

V.C. Colour-Sergeant H. Hampton, **8th (Liverpool Regiment).** (Born 1870.) When ordered to retire after holding a position against a large number of Boers, saw all his men under cover, and then went out to the aid of a wounded man, with whom he stayed until another shot killed the poor fellow. Hampton was himself twice badly hit.

V.C. Sergeant H. J. Knight, **8th (Liverpool Regiment).** With four men held a position against fifty Boers until two of his four were killed and the others rendered *hors-de-combat*. This gallant soldier then found shelter for one of the wounded men, and carried the other two miles into camp under severe fire all the way.

Van Wyks Vlei, Boer War. 1900.

A Brother's Heroism. Mr. Booley and his two sons were bathing in the river Dee at Holywell, when the younger boy got into difficulties. Peter E. Booley pluckily went to his brother's assistance and succeeded in saving him, but lost his own life. **1890.**

A Suffolk Man who saved 77 Lives. William Adams, swimming instructor and bathing-machine proprietor of Gorleston, who during a period of thirty years has saved 77 lives (thus earning the soubriquet, "The hero of Gorleston Pier"), possesses many decorations for his numerous rescues. One of his most remarkable feats was that of saving the son of a lifeboatman, for whom he dived 30 feet, fully dressed, from the pier. Among his sixty trophies he has already received the **Bronze Medal** of the **Royal Humane Society,** two clasps, and several diplomas. **1909.**

Two gallant Yorkshire Boys. William Gannon, aged 12, and Edward Lawn, aged 13, seeing two of their schoolmates in difficulties in a swimming bath at Huddersfield, went to their assistance and brought one of the two to the side of the bath, but unhappily the child was dead. There are plenty of life-saving appliances in the baths, but the boys were either too small or too excited to reach them. **1909.**

August 22

A Wiltshire Labourer's devotion to his Mate. James Draper, in attempting to rescue a bricklayer overcome by carbonic acid gas in a well near Devizes, fell a distance of 45 feet, and when help arrived both men were dead. **1857.**

A similar Case in Essex. Twenty-four years later, John Walker perished in a like manner through his devotion to a fellow-workman, who had succumbed to foul air in a well at Primrose Hill, Chelmsford, and the man he gallantly tried to save also died. **1881.**

AUGUST 23

V.C. Corporal W. Heaton, **Liverpool Regiment.** At terrible risk under fearful fire took a message asking for relief for his Company, which was in danger of being wiped out. By his heroic act help was obtained, and they were thus saved from the humiliation of surrender.

Geluk, Boer War. 1900.

Royal Humane Society's Bronze Medal to Samuel Smith. While Mr. E. Walker and his daughter were bathing in Red Wharf Bay, Anglesey, the latter got into danger, and her father swam out 300 yards to her assistance, when he also got into difficulties. Samuel Smith then went out, and made a splendid attempt to rescue them; but both father and daughter perished. **1904.**

AUGUST 24

A Waterford Man drowned in trying to save his Friend. While Thomas Burke was bathing with a friend at Stradbally, the latter got out of his depth, and Burke, seeing him in great peril, went to his assistance, but both perished. **1882.**

A Banffshire Clergyman's Self-sacrifice. The Rev. Matthew Moggridge, Rector of St. Michael's, Dufftown, Banffshire, who had gone with his choir and Sunday School excursion to Lossiemouth, seeing two boys in difficulties in the sea, went to their assistance. He succeeded in saving them, but died from exhaustion himself before he could be taken out of the water. **1891.**

Royal Humane Society's Bronze Medal to Herbert O. Turner, aged 13, who plunged into the river Dart at

Dartmouth, the depth of water being 10 feet, with a 3 or 4 knot tide running, and rescued a boy named W. Kellond, who had fallen into the water while at play. **1905.**

Rescue by a London Carman. George Smith, of Sabberton Street, Poplar, seeing William Kitts, aged 61, stumble on the towing-path of the Lea Cut into the water, dived in fully clothed and brought him to the bank. He then applied artificial respiration with success, but the man died from the effects of the immersion. The jury highly commended Smith, who said he had saved other lives, and the coroner told him he deserved a Medal from the Royal Humane Society. **1909.**

AUGUST 25

Albert Medal of the Second Class to Lieutenant Lecky, R.N., of H.M.S. *Widgeon*. While in Kosi Bay, 50 miles south of Delagoa Bay, Lieut. Lecky saved Lieut. Gray and Trooper Trethowen from a heavy sea infested with sharks; afterwards, with his servant, he did all in his power to restore animation, and after two and a half hours Lieut. Gray regained consciousness. **1900.**

Postman's Park Hero and Martyr. Tablet 33. Ernest Benning, aged 22, who with others was upset from a boat on a dark night off Pimlico pier, grasped an oar with one hand, while supporting a woman with the other. She was rescued, but he sank. **1883.**

Postman's Park two Heroes and Martyrs. Tablet 46. Arthur Strange, carman, and Mark Tomlinson, while making a desperate attempt to save two girls from a quicksand in Lincolnshire, in which they were struggling for life, were themselves drawn in and perished. **1902.**

"Men still own that life to be the highest which is a conscious voluntary sacrifice."—*George Eliot.*

AUGUST 26

Albert Medal of the Second Class to Dr. Henry Grier, who at imminent risk to his own life applied his lips to the wound after an operation for diphtheria (tracheotomy) had been performed on Lieut. Graham of the 10th Regiment, thus restoring power of breathing for a time. This gallant attempt to save the patient's life was unhappily of no avail. **1880.**

A Glamorganshire Mining Contractor's heroic Death. On the occasion of an explosion at Park Slip Colliery, Aberkenfig, James Bowen lost his life in an endeavour to find a way of safety for his gang of 19 men. Some of them wished to accompany him on this perilous quest, but Bowen insisted on going alone from a position of comparative safety into the gas-choked galleries, from which he never emerged alive. His men were afterwards rescued by other means. **1892.**

A Fifeshire Colliery Tragedy. On this date at 1.40 P.M. soft peat or moss began to flow into a heading of one of the pits at the Donibristle Colliery, and engulfed a number of men. Thomas Rattray, oversman; William Hynd, Andrew Paterson, and James B. M'Donald, miners, descended the pit, endeavouring to save their comrades, and were never seen alive again. Four months later (Dec. 14th) the noble quartette were found starved to death, their retreat having been cut off by over 12,000 tons of moss. In M'Donald's pocket the time-book was found, in which the doomed miners had kept a pathetic diary. The following are a few extracts:—

"I am thinking about Wee Donil. God bless him!"

"William Hynd says for his wife to go back to America with the bairns."

PRESENTED
BY THE
GLASGOW HUMANE SOCIETY
TO

FOR
INTREPIDITY OF CONDUCT
AND SUCCESS IN RESCUING
FROM DROWNING

The Glasgow Humane Society's Medal.

The Order of St. John of Jerusalem.

"Andrew leaves his love to Annie, and the bairns; Good-bye! God bless you all."

"The Boss (Rattray) leaves his love to his wife and family. God help them all!"

"The moss is creeping on us. We have no hope of getting 'but.'"

"All prepared to die. . . . Failing now. We are very. . . . No food, but plenty of moss to . . . and drink. . . . Farewell all! . . . Oh, Bella, dear, good-bye. Failing now." &c.

1901.

AUGUST 27

V.C. Lance-Corporal E. Durrant, **Rifle Brigade.** When a man, delirious from a wound in the head, was running towards the enemy at Bergendal, this plucky soldier went after the poor fellow, slung him across his shoulder, and carried him 200 yards under fearful fire into safety. He then returned to his own position in the firing-line.

Boer War. 1900.

Albert Medal of the Second Class to Giovanni Bilocca and Guiseppe Zammit for great bravery in saving the lives of fellow labourers from poisonous fumes in a shaft at H.M. dockyard, Malta. **1901.**

The Order of St. John of Jerusalem in England. Bronze Medal to Private Arthur W. Laing, Ambulance Brigade, for great courage in jumping on the rails in front of an express train at Queen Street Station, Exeter, and saving a boy who had fallen on to the line. Laing escaped death by only a few inches.

On the same day a **Certificate of Honour** was earned by a porter named Frederick A. Gibson at Ashford Station, Kent, for a similar heroic deed. **1907.**

Fine Heroism of a Cardiff Miner. Owing to the snapping of one of the rods of the reversing gear of the winding engine, an empty ascending cage at Ely Pit, Penycraig, crashed into the sheaves at the pit-top and was precipitated upon a double-deck cage. The men on both decks of the cage were hurled on each other, those on the lower deck being imprisoned by the walls of the sump in such a manner that the only means of rescuing them was by digging into the sump and getting them out through a narrow passage. Seven men were killed and twenty-one injured by this terrible mishap.

In connection with the rescue work, a fine deed of heroism was performed by a hitcher named James Vaughan, who cut away the timbering, dug a hole in the sump, crawled down and released the imprisoned men from the lower deck, handing them out severally to two comrades. In doing this Vaughan was in imminent danger of being killed by falling timbers from the destroyed shaft.

Mr. Leonard Llewellyn, general manager of the colliery, will apply to the proper quarters for the Edward Medal for Vaughan. **1909.**

August 28

Albert Medal of the Second Class to Ernest W. Owens for jumping, fully and heavily clothed, from a vessel off Cape Horn and holding up a boy who had fallen overboard. When picked up both were almost dead, having been in ice-cold water nearly twenty minutes. **1875.**

Manchester Workman killed while trying to save a Comrade. John Spencer and James Howcroft, employed at Mr. Bealey's chemical works, Radcliffe Close, near Manchester, lost their lives when trying to help a comrade who had fallen into a tank full of poisonous vapour. The three were soon brought out, and the man who first fell in recovered, but Howcroft was dead, and Spencer died the same night. **1858.**

AUGUST 29

V.C. Colonel R. H. M. Aitkin, **Bengal Native Infantry.** (Died 1887.) Earned the decoration over and over again for various acts of gallantry, of which the following are examples. Once under fierce fire prevented stores of explosives being set alight by the mutineers; twice went into the garden of the besieged residency and brought in cattle for the garrison; and on this date, with only four followers, captured a rebel gun in a sortie.

Lucknow, Mutiny. 1857.

His Life for his Brother's. Two brothers named Thomas were bathing in a pond at Merthyr Tydvil, when the younger child got into deep water, and James, the elder, in trying to save him was drowned. The younger boy was saved. **1886.**

Staffordshire Father's heroic Deed. Mr. Jonathan Brammer, a Biddulph colliery owner, lost his life in trying to rescue his boy, who had gone into a "foothill," or narrow decline, towards a mine, and had been overcome by foul gas. A search-party found and brought them out alive, but both died a few minutes after reaching fresh air. **1902.**

Royal Humane Society's Bronze Medal to J. H. Meikle, aged 15. When Edward Carter accidentally fell overboard from the training ship *Wellesley*, in the Tyne off Jarrow, the water being 34 feet deep with a strong ebb tide, young Meikle immediately plunged in and supported him until they were picked up by a boat. **1905.**

Gallant Tyneside Fisherman's Exploits. Robert Drane, of Newcastle, who achieved his first rescue at the early age of thirteen, has, by bringing three children safely to land, made up his total of lives saved to eighty-two. As far back as 1889 Drane was awarded the **Silver Medal** of the **Royal Humane Society**, and since then three bars have been placed thereon. Another of his trophies—the Tyneside Trust Medal—was handed to him when his record of rescues reached fifty. In all he has twelve Medals, but these only represent a portion of the public presentations made to him. **1909.**

August 30

V.C. Sergeant J. Coleman, **97th (Royal West Kent).** After exhibiting distinguished courage under fire so furious that nearly all around him were either killed or wounded, carried a disabled officer into a place of safety. **Sevastopol, Crimea. 1855.**

Albert Medal of the Second Class to Mr. Arthur Hardiment. While the Cromer express, on its way from Norwich to London, was approaching the level crossing at Tivetshall at the rate of 50 miles an hour, Hardiment and Horace Bloomfield, the crossing-keeper, were standing near one of the gates, about 29 feet from the track, when Bloomfield's little child, aged 18 months, was seen to be making for the line from the opposite side to join his father. He continued on his way despite the cries of the men, and Hardiment thereupon dashed across the line towards the child, knowing that the father, who had lost a leg and an arm, was incapacitated from attempting rescue. Before he was clear of the track the footplate of the engine had struck his left forearm, fracturing both the bones and hurling him into a hedge 9 feet away. He had the satisfaction, however, of seeing that the child had turned away from the approaching train and had escaped unhurt. **1907.**

A Surrey Man suffocated while trying to save his Brother. While William and Spencer Lucas were engaged in deepening a well at Boothland Farm, Spencer went down first and was overpowered by foul air. William went to help him, but unfortunately he too succumbed. **1876.**

An Aberdeen Fisherman gives his Life in a gallant Effort to save his Brother. Joseph Stewart, aged 24, lost his life in Aberdeen Bay while endeavouring to save his brother George, aged 17, who had fallen from their boat in a heavy sea. **1892.**

AUGUST 31

V.C. General Sir Samuel J. Browne, G.C.B., K.C.S.I., **Bengal Native Infantry.** (Died 1901.) "Fortitur et fidelitur." Inventor of the well-known "Sam Browne" belt. While capturing a gun at Seerporah had a terrible struggle with the rebel gunners, during which he was severely wounded in one knee and received a fearful sword cut, which slashed his left arm off at the shoulder. **Mutiny. 1858.**

A little Derbyshire Hero. While several children were sailing a toy boat on a reservoir near Glossop, Charles Thompson, aged 9, fell into the water. His brother Joseph, aged 11, at once jumped in and did all that he could to rescue the younger boy, but both were drowned. **1878.**

Board of Trade Silver Clasp to Jacob Don, pilot's apprentice, to be worn with the Silver Medal already awarded to him; and a Silver Medal to Emanuel

Frederik Vogelaar, seaman, of the Dutch pilot cutter, No. 11, of Rotterdam, in recognition of their services in assisting to rescue the shipwrecked crew of the British steamship *Sydney*, of London, which foundered off Dungeness. **1908.**

SEPTEMBER

"*Hero-worship* IS *nevertheless, as it was, always and everywhere, and cannot cease till man himself ceases.*"—THOMAS CARLYLE.

SEPTEMBER

SEPTEMBER 1

V.C. Captain G. G. E. Wylly, **Tasmanian Imperial Bushmen.** (Born 1883.)

V.C. Lieutenant J. H. Bisdee, **Tasmanian Imperial Bushmen.**

Each saved the life of a wounded man, at imminent risk of capture, under furious fire.

Warm Bad, Boer War. 1900.

Heroic Limekiln Workers. During a press of business at some works near Bury St. Edmunds, coke instead of coal had been used in one of the kilns. Robert Catton, who was unaware of this, was increasing the draught when he was overcome by the stifling fumes. William Wells, aged 17, went to his aid, but was also overcome. A man named Henry Crooks then ventured into this veritable death-trap to assist his fellow-workmen, but he too shared their sad fate. **1843.**

A Herne Bay Hero. Robert Collingwood, a bathing-machine assistant at Herne Bay, seeing two ladies in the sea struggling for life, swam to their assistance. He was bringing them both ashore, when he was heard to call out, "Don't cling to me so tightly or you will drown me." A boat put off and the ladies were rescued, but Collingwood sank from exhaustion. **1882.**

SEPTEMBER 2

V.C. Private A. Ablett, **Grenadier Guards.** (Died 1897.) Cross sold after his death for £62. Gazetted for picking up a live shell and throwing it over the trenches. In this case the deadly missile had alighted in the midst of ammunition barrels. **Sevastopol, Crimea. 1855.**

V.C. Colonel P. A. Kenna, **21st Lancers.** (Born 1862.)

V.C. Captain the Hon. R. H. L. J. de Montmorency, **21st Lancers.** "Dieu ayde." Killed in the Boer War, 1900.

V.C. Private T. Byrne, **21st Lancers.**

V.C. Lieut.-Colonel N. M. Smyth, **2nd Dragoon Guards.**

Each of the above quartette won the decoration for fine gallantry in saving lives of wounded soldiers during the famous cavalry charge at **Khartoum. 1898.**

Royal Humane Society's Bronze Medal to Abani M. Das, Inspector of Police at Dumka, India, who plunged into a tank 10 feet deep to the rescue of a woman who had thrown herself in, and after three attempts succeeded in bringing her out. **1906.**

SEPTEMBER 3

Wreck of the *Princess Alice*: a Merchant Service Hero and Martyr. Captain William R. H. Grinstead, commanding officer of the ss. *Princess Alice*, lost his life off Woolwich in the wreck of that vessel, in which nearly 700 perished. The captain was last seen in the water by a young girl, whom he implored to seize a floating plank which lay between them—thereby giving up his one chance of life—and immediately after sank. Three members of Captain Grinstead's family also perished in this disaster. **1878.**

Heroic Scotch Lassie. Helen Currie, a servant, was killed at Barassie station, near Kilmarnock. She had crossed the line in safety; but, seeing her master, aged 92, coming in front of the Stranraer express, sprang forward and tried to drag him out of danger. Both were killed. **1879.**

SEPTEMBER 4

A Hero of the Hopfields. A man named Sheleen while going to the hopfields made a splendid effort to save a woman who had fallen before a train at Paddock Wood Junction. He leaped on to the metals and dragged her away, but both were shockingly injured. Sheleen died in Maidstone Hospital, but the woman recovered. **1895.**

A Renfrew Man drowned while trying to save a Boy. William Groves, seeing a little boy fall off a pier at Greenock, jumped after him, but the tide carried them both away. **1901.**

SEPTEMBER 5

V.C. Sergeant-Major J. Champion, **8th Hussars.** For fortitude in remaining on duty while severely hit through the body, and for other acts of bravery.

Mutiny. 1858.

R.H.A. Hero and Martyr. Bombardier F. Scattergood, aged 25, T Battery, 2nd Brigade, lost his life in trying to rescue victims from the gallery of Exeter Theatre, where 120 people were burnt to death. Unfortunately the brave fellow's efforts were fruitless, and his remains were found beneath the débris the following day. He was buried with full military honours at Higher Cemetery, Exeter. **1887.**

SEPTEMBER 6

V.C. Ensign J. Craig, **Scots Fusilier Guards.** Was severely wounded while, under heavy grape fire, carrying Captain Buckley to shelter. Captain Buckley died on the way.

V.C. Private G. Strong, **Coldstream Guards.** Another hero of the trenches, who picked up a live shell and threw it over the parapet.

Sevastopol, Crimea. 1855.

V.C. Midshipman D. G. Boyes, **R.N.** (Died 1869.)
V.C. Captain of the After-Guard T. Pride, **R.N.** (Died 1893.)

During the desperate attack on Simonisaki, Mr. Boyes carried the Colour ahead of his party, and two sergeants, of whom Pride was one, followed him. The Colour was riddled by bullets, Pride was seriously wounded, and the other sergeant killed.

V.C. Seaman W. Seeley, **R.N.** For gallantry in carrying out scouting operations alone, and for leading a charge while badly hit. **Japan. 1864.**

V.C. Surgeon W. J. Maillard, M.D., **R.N.** Through a deluge of bullets, which perforated his clothing but failed to hit him, made a desperate attempt to carry a dying man into shelter at Candia. **Crete. 1898.**

Postman's Park Boy Hero and Martyr. Tablet 32. George Blencowe, aged 16, pluckily went to the assistance of a friend who was drowning in the river Lea, but both lads perished. **1880.**

Postman's Park Little East End Hero and Martyr. Tablet 42. Solomon Galaman, aged 11, saved his younger brother from being run over in the crowded traffic of Commercial Street, but fell himself beneath the wheels. "Mother," he said, as he lay dying, "I saved him, but I could not save myself." **1901.**

SEPTEMBER 7

V.C. Ensign E. Mackenna, **65th (York and Lanc.).** After his superior officers were rendered *hors de combat*, displayed the utmost coolness and courage in opposing a large number of Maori rebels in a dangerous rocky country.

V.C. Lance-Corporal John Ryan, **65th (York and Lanc.).** Cross sold for £58 after his death, which was caused by trying to save a drunken comrade from drowning.

Together with Privates Bulford and Talbot of his regiment (both of whom received the Medal for distinguished conduct), stayed all night guarding a dying officer from the Maoris in the bush.

Cameron Town, New Zealand. 1863.

Grace Darling, daughter of the lighthouse-keeper at the Farne Islands, together with her father, William Darling, launched a coble and rowed to the help of several persons who had taken refuge on a ledge of rock, after their steamer had been wrecked. By these gallant exertions five lives were saved. The Royal Humane Society and the Glasgow Humane Society awarded Gold Medals for this fine service, and a large sum of money was collected for the benefit of the brave father and daughter. Grace Darling died of consumption in 1842. The rescue was accomplished on this day. **1838.**

"Together they put forth, Father and Child!
Each grasps an oar, and struggling on they go—
Rivals in effort; and, alike intent
Here to elude, and there surmount, they watch
The billows lengthening, mutually crossed
And shattered, and re-gathering their might;
As, if the tumult, by the Almighty's will,
Were in the conscious sea roused and prolonged

That woman's fortitude—so tried, so proved—
May brighten more and more!
. . . .
Though young, so wise, though meek, so resolute
Might carry to the clouds and to the stars,
Yea, to celestial Choirs Grace Darling's name!"
—*Wordsworth.*

Loss of H.M.S. *Captain*. H.M.S. *Captain*, during her first ocean trip with the Channel Squadron, foundered off Cape Finisterre soon after midnight and went down in three minutes, having on board 483 officers and men, including Captain H. T. Burgoyne, V.C., her commander, Captain Cowper Coles, her designer, and Midshipman Childers, son of the then First Lord of the Admiralty. Of the entire ship's company only eighteen were saved. On a beautiful brass tablet, close to the Wellington mausoleum in St. Paul's Cathedral, are engraved the names of all who were lost. Within eight months of the disaster a sum of nearly £60,000 was raised for the benefit of the widows and orphans. **1870.**

Saved 400 Lives. Mr. Frank Shooter has saved no fewer than 400 lives during the thirty-six years he has acted as superintendent of the Exeter bathing ground. He possesses all the chief awards of the Royal Humane Society.

Lancashire Carter's Heroism. Evan Rutter, aged 21, of Chorley, with George Sumner and George H. Gerrard, were working in a sandhole belonging to the Gorse Hall Sand and Gravel Company. On looking up to the top of the hole, 50 feet above, the two last-named saw the sand beginning to run down. Sumner seized Rutter by the shoulders, and, despite his own danger, tried desperately to drag him to safety; but in vain, for he was buried, face downward, under forty tons of sand.

1909.

SEPTEMBER 8

FINAL ATTACK ON THE REDAN

Out of a total of nine Victoria Crosses bestowed on this occasion, the following seven recipients were decorated for deeds of mercy to the wounded under appalling fire from the Russian batteries.

V.C. Major-General Gronow Davis, **R.A.** (Died 1891.) "Solem fero." Went out twice and helped to bring in Lieutenant Sanders and several other wounded men.

V.C. Surgeon-Major T. E. Hale, M.D., C.B., **7th (City of London).** "Vera sequor." Assisted by Sergeant Fisher of his regiment (not gazetted), carried many wounded and dying men into shelter.

V.C. Sergeant D. Cambridge, **R.A.** Was severely hit while carrying in a stricken man, after having helped to spike a gun, during which he was also wounded.

V.C. Surgeon W. H. T. Sylvester, M.D., **23rd (Royal Welsh Fusiliers).** Brought in Lieutenant Dyneley, who was dying, and attended numerous other stricken men.

V.C. Corporal R. Shields, **23rd (Royal Welsh Fusiliers).** Associated with Dr. Sylvester, V.C., in above gallant act.

V.C. Private John Connors, **3rd (The Buffs).** Rescued an officer who was surrounded by Russians, of whom he despatched a couple.

V.C. Ensign A. Moynihan, **90th (2nd Scottish Rifles).** Saved an officer who was lying helplessly stricken.

V.C. General Sir Frederick F. Maude, G.C.B., **3rd (Buffs, East Kent).** (Died 1897.) "Virtute securus." With a handful of men dashed for a traverse, which he gallantly held until all hope of relief was at an end, and each member of the party was badly wounded.

V.C. Major C. H. Lumley, **97th (Royal West Kent).** During an obstinate fight with three Russians, of whom he overcame two, was horribly wounded by a bullet in the mouth. **Crimea. 1855.**

Gallant Lifeboat Service in Kent. During a WSW. gale about 3 P.M. a vessel off Dungeness was seen to be making signals of distress. No. 1 lifeboat was promptly launched, and found a French fishing lugger, leaking badly, with 5 feet of water in her hold. The master could not speak English, but by signs the coxswain of the lifeboat made him understand that the lugger should be beached to prevent her sinking. The crew of eight hands were taken ashore in safety. Tugs subsequently towed the vessel to Folkestone for repair. **1906.**

September 9

A gallant Doctor. William Campbell, M.D., F.R.C.S., of 18 Westbourne Place, Eaton Square, was drowned at Coatham, Redcar, after saving a lad's life. It was thought that cramp must have attacked the doctor, who was a fine swimmer. **1880.**

Stanhope Medal to Thomas M'Dermott. While the sailing cutter of H.M.S. *Swallow* was anchored off Uzi Island,

Zanzibar, the two men left in charge began to bathe, when a large shark was seen within a few feet of them. Thomas M'Dermott, boatswain, at once sprang in right over the shark, and the sudden splash frightened it away long enough for the men to regain the boat. **1892.**

> "No time had he to doff his coat,
> Who scarce had time for dread;
> The Bo'sun sprang from out the boat
> Full at the monster's head.
>
> . . . .
>
> He chanced the stroke of furious fin,
> He met the mouth of greed;
> That so his men their boat might win,
> M'Dermott did this deed."
>
> —"Ballads of Brave Deeds," *Canon Rawnsley.*

Board of Trade Silver Medal to Albert Warman, commissioned boatman, coastguard, and **Bronze Medals** to Arthur Laccohee, boatman, coastguard, and to Patrick J. Connor and James M. Kennedy, civilians, for their services in descending a cliff and rescuing the master of the Russian barquantine *Orient*, which foundered off Ballydavid Head. **1908.**

September 10

V.C. Private J. Divane, **60th Rifles.** Dangerously wounded while leading a charge against the rebels at the Delhi trenches. **Mutiny. 1857.**

Stanhope Medal to Lieutenant J. de Hoghton, 10th Foot, who jumped from the yacht *Dart* in Lowestoft harbour on a dark, stormy night, and kept a drowning man afloat in the rushing tideway until both were hauled aboard. **1874.**

Postman's Park Youthful Hero and Martyr. Tablet 9. Daniel Selves, aged 12, gave his life in a fine attempt

SEPTEMBER

John Hilton Bisdee

R. H. de Montmorency.

Paul A. Kenna

N. M. Smyth.
Major.

Thos Egerton Hale.

Henry T. Sylvester.

A. Moynihan Lieut
2nd Battn. 8th Regiment

Henry Evans.

to save a companion from drowning in the Thames at Tripcock Point. Both lads were found clasped in each other's arms in fifteen feet of water. **1886.**

SEPTEMBER 11

V.C. Colour-Sergeant P. Green, **Gordon Highlanders.** For a specially fine rescue of a comrade, who had fallen wounded when the picquet was hotly pressed by a large force of mutineers at Delhi. **Mutiny. 1857.**

Albert Medals of the First Class to Henry Davies and John Harris.

Albert Medals of the Second Class to William Simons, Charles Morgan, Thomas Herbert, Miles Moseley, Lewis Harris, Charles Preen, and William Walters.

For splendid heroism in going down a pit at Abercorn Colliery, after a terrible explosion whereby 260 lives were lost, in a gallant attempt to rescue any who might perchance have escaped. **1878.**

A Derbyshire Boy's heroic Death. Charles Darwin, aged 12, lost his life in Little Eaton Canal in a gallant attempt to save his younger brother, who had fallen into the water. Charles, in trying to catch hold of him, slipped in also, and both boys perished. **1873.**

Glasgow Twins die together. Andrew Goldie, a young lad, was drowned in the High Tetherton Pond at Glasgow Iron and Steel Works, while making a gallant effort to save his twin brother George, who was struggling in the water. **1891.**

SEPTEMBER 12

Edward Medal of the First Class to Henry Everson for his gallant action in saving the life of a fellow-workman at the Penallta Colliery. The barrel, by means of which water was being raised from a depth of 345 feet, came into contact with the scaffold suspended in the shaft and broke it from its chains, precipitating it with two men 30 feet into 12 feet of water. Everson, who was at the top of the shaft, at once descended the pit by means of a 4-inch pipe, a distance of 270 feet. He then got into the barrel, and was lowered till he came upon one of the men hanging on a thin wire, up to his neck in water, almost exhausted, who but for this timely aid must have perished. The two were brought safely to the surface. The second man was drowned. **1907.**

Two gallant Gentlemen. William Wilson, seeing his two daughters out of their depth in the sea at Dunbar, went with his son James, aged 18, to their assistance. Unfortunately the receding tide was too strong for them, and all four were carried out to sea and drowned before help could reach them. **1857.**

Boy Hero of Caithness. Kenneth Sutherland, aged 13, and six other boys were fishing in a small boat at Wick, when their craft capsized and all were thrown into the sea. Sutherland brought ashore those boys who were unable to swim, with one exception. While on his way back to rescue this last lad, the gallant little chap, exhausted by his previous efforts, sank. The other boy was saved. **1871.**

September 13

V.C. Bugler W. Sutton, **60th Rifles.** Elected under Rule XIII. for great bravery in making a reconnaissance, and other gallant deeds. **Delhi, Mutiny. 1857.**

V.C. Major W. M. M. Edwards, **Gentleman-at-Arms, 74th (Highland Light Infantry).** (Born 1854.)

"Quid leges sine moribus." For great pluck in rushing alone into an Egyptian battery, where he was knocked down and, but for the timely arrival of aid, would have been slain. **Tel-el-Kebir. 1882.**

Albert Medal of the Second Class to W. Simpson, R.N., for great gallantry in saving the crew of the ship *Avonmore*, wrecked on the coast of Cornwall. **1869.**

Stanhope Medal to Walter Cleverley. When a lascar fell overboard from the ss. *Rewa* in the Gulf of Aden, which abounds with sharks, Cleverley jumped from the poop, a height of 30 feet, and supported the man for forty minutes till they were picked up. **1883.**

Stanhope Medal to William H. Parr. The ss. *Illovo* was at anchor in the Inhambane river, on the East African coast, when a boat with some thirty natives and one white seaman on board was capsized in trying to reach the ship. Instantly the natives clutched the sailor and dragged him under. Parr saw this from the ship, and plunging overboard he liberated the man from the frantic natives and swam away with him. They were picked up about twenty minutes after. **1907.**

September 14

THE BLOWING UP OF THE CASHMERE GATE AT DELHI

V.C. Lieutenant D. C. Home, **Bengal Engineers.** Killed by an accidental explosion the following month.

V.C. Lieutenant P. Salkeld, **Bengal Engineers.** Received shocking injuries to legs and arms, to which he succumbed in a few days.

V.C. Bugler R. Hawthorne, **52nd.** Cross sold for £108 at Glendenning's in 1909.

V.C. Sergeant John Smith, **Bengal Sappers and Miners.** Also Sergeants Carmichael and Burgess, who were killed, and a few others whose names have not come down. Equal in pure heroism to the magnificent feat of blowing up the magazine on May 11th was the above fine deed, which was accomplished just before the great assault on the stronghold of the mutineers.

> "Gashed with honourable scars,
> Low in Glory's lap they lie;
> Though they fell, they fell like stars,
> Streaming splendour through the sky."
> —*James Montgomery.*

V.C. Lance-Corporal Henry Smith, **52nd.** Cross realised £70 after his death. Carried a wounded comrade through fearful fire from the Chandin Chouk.

V.C. Lieutenant A. S. Heathcote, **King's Royal Rifle Corps.** For distinguished gallantry throughout the whole siege from June to September. Elected under Rule XIII.

V.C. Colour-Sergeant G. Waller, **King's Royal Rifle Corps.** For capturing one of the enemy's guns, and successfully defending our own.

V.C. Surgeon-General H. T. Reade, **61st (S. Gloucester).** (Died 1897.) "Cedant arma togæ." With ten men charged a body of mutineers, who were firing down from the housetops on his patients. He wounded and dislodged them. Later on helped to spike a gun.

V.C. Sergeant J. McGuire, **European Bengal Fusiliers.**
V.C. Drummer M. Ryan, **European Bengal Fusiliers.**
Three out of five boxes of ammunition having caught fire and exploded, this fearless pair seized the other two boxes and threw them over the parapet into the water.

V.C. Captain R. H. Shebbeare, **Bengal Native Infantry.** (Killed in China three years later.) Fearfully wounded in the face and head while making an heroic attempt to capture a serai.

Great Attack on Delhi, Mutiny. 1857.

Board of Trade Bronze Medals to sixteen gallant fishermen of Knightstown, Valentia, for services in rescuing the crews of two fishing-boats which were swamped.

1908.

SEPTEMBER 15

V.C. Boatswain J. Kellaway, **R.N.** (Died 1880.) After escaping from an ambush, went back to help a fallen friend, when both were captured despite fierce resistance.

Sea of Azoff, Crimea. 1855.

Gave his Life to save his Sister. Arthur B. Holbertson, aged 18, his sister, and another lady, were in a boat on the Thames, which capsized in deep water near West Middlesex Waterworks. Young Holbertson succeeded in supporting his sister until help arrived, but he then sank from exhaustion. The other lady was also drowned.

1881.

SEPTEMBER 16

V.C. Major-General G. A. Renny, **Bengal Horse Artillery.** (Died 1887.) With magnificent courage mounted the wall of the magazine, in face of almost certain death from furious fire, and threw a number of shells with lighted fuses among the rebels who were trying to recapture the building.

V.C. Colonel E. T. Thackeray, K.C.B., **R.E. (Bengal).** Gazetted for fine heroism in going into an ammunition shed which was alight, under fire from the enemy. By this young officer's bravery in stamping out the fire a terrible explosion was averted. **Delhi, Mutiny. 1857.**

V.C. Major T. C. Watson, **R.E.** Led two splendid charges against a large number of tribesmen at Bilot, during which he was badly wounded.

V.C. Major J. M. C. Colvin, **R.E.**
V.C. Sergeant James Smith, **The Buffs (East Kent).**
When Major Watson was disabled at Bilot, the above pair of heroes continued the attack, and afterwards helped to convey the wounded from the village, which was on and under fire. **Punjab Frontier. 1897.**

Albert Medal of the Second Class to John Barber, R.N., for gallantry, in being the means of saving a crew wrecked off Amour Point, Forteau Bay, coast of Labrador. **1889.**

A gallant Stewardess. When a fire occurred on the outward bound ss. *Iona* off Clacton, Edith M. Leadingham, of Gateshead, the young stewardess, rushed into the flames to fetch a little child who had been forgotten. Her heroism was unavailing, and the two bodies were found charred to ashes when the fire was extinguished. **1895.**

"She has taken the little one safe in her hand,
Angel of help, she has turned for the door—
This eloquent heap of ash on the floor
Is seal of her will, and is sign of her doom ;
But her feet so swift for the purpose planned
Are set, God knows, in a larger room.

. . . . . .

SEPTEMBER

Mordaunt Edwards.

P. Salkeld

W. [illegible]

L. G.

Edward Talbot Thackeray

T. C. Watson

Jas C. Colvin.

Llewelyn Price-Davies

[illegible]

Think of her gratefully, girls of the Tyne
Whose blood is salt with the Northern sea!
The salt that shall keep our England free
From the savour of Death is a salt of flame,
Salt of self-sacrifice, salt divine,
That is sprinkled on all, as we name her name."
—"Ballads of Brave Deeds," *Canon Rawnsley.*

SEPTEMBER 17

V.C. Captain L. A. E. Price-Davies, D.S.O., **King's Royal Rifles.** (Born 1878.) "Mentioned" repeatedly throughout the campaign for gallant conduct. Was fearfully wounded while making a desperate effort to save the guns at Blood River Poort. **Boer War. 1901.**

Albert Medal of the Second Class to Captain N. B. Forbes, R.N., who jumped to the rescue of a boy who had fallen from H.M.S. *Rapal* on a dark night off Gibraltar. When picked up by the ship's boat both were nearly dead. **1870.**

Scotch Boy's Self-sacrifice. James Allison, aged 14, having fallen into a quarry hole full of water on a farm near Glasgow, his brother Frederick, aged 12, bravely attempted to rescue him, but both were drowned. **1886.**

A Lancashire Miner dies to save his Son and a Comrade. While working at Lindal Moor Mines, Ulverstone, John Wilkinson saw that a fall of the roof was imminent. His son and a comrade were with him, and, making a tremendous effort, the splendid fellow pushed them both from the dangerous spot. He was, however, unable to escape himself, and was buried in the falling débris. **1901.**

SEPTEMBER 18

V.C. Ensign E. A. L. Phillipps, **Bengal Native Infantry.** "Ducit amor patriæ." Was wounded three times during the terrible fighting in the streets of Delhi, and, after capturing with a few followers the Water Bastion, was killed on this day. **Mutiny. 1857.**

Albert Medal of the Second Class, also **Stanhope Medal** to Commander A. C. Lowry, R.N. When the ss. *Charkich*, of London, was wrecked in the Doro Channel, Isle of Andros, three men climbed the foremast as she sank. A boat from H.M.S. *Empress of India* was at once put off to save them in a very heavy sea. Lieutenant (afterwards Commander) A. C. Lowry swam to the mast with a line, and ultimately managed to rescue them all. **1900.**

Some gallant Herefordshire Children. Elizabeth Marsh, aged 13, with a companion named Hill, was walking through a dark tunnel beside the Ledbury and Hereford Canal near Widemarsh, when the latter fell into the water, and in trying to save her Marsh shared the same fate. A little boy of 8, who tried to help them, was dragged in too, but was saved by a school-fellow. Both the girls were drowned before help arrived. **1874.**

SEPTEMBER 19

Two Warwickshire Heroes. Mr. Sidney Hasluck and Thomas Jenkinson, gardener, lost their lives—the former in trying to save his little sister who had fallen from a boat into a pond at Handsworth, Birmingham, and the latter in going to help the young gentleman. All three were drowned. **1868.**

Lanarkshire Collier dies in trying to save a Comrade. On the occasion of an explosion at Addington, near Glasgow, Robert Wyper, with four other men, went to the rescue of a comrade. All five were overpowered by the deadly fire-damp, but with the exception of Wyper they were brought out of the pit alive, although unconscious on reaching the fresh air. **1876.**

SEPTEMBER 20

ALMA

Victoria Crosses awarded as under :—

V.C. Major-General Luke O'Connor, C.B., **23rd (R. Welsh Fusiliers).** When Lieutenant Anstruther, who was carrying the Queen's "Colour," fell drenched with his life-blood, this brave soldier snatched the Colour from the dead man's grasp, and, although himself badly wounded, carried it throughout the day. At the end of the action there were twenty-six holes in it. He also displayed great gallantry at the Redan, where he was shot through both thighs.

V.C. Lieut.-Colonel R. J. Lindsay (afterwards The Right Honourable Lord Wantage, K.C.B.), **Scots Fusilier Guards.** (Died 1901.) "Loyauté m'oblige."

V.C. Major J. S. Knox, **Scots Fusilier Guards.**

V.C. Sergeant J. McKechnie, **Scots Fusilier Guards.**

V.C. Private W. Reynolds, **Scots Fusilier Guards.**

Made a magnificent defence of the "Colours," which were in great danger of capture, the line of formation having become disordered.

V.C. Major-General E. W. D. Bell, C.B., **23rd (R. Welsh Fusiliers).** Captured a Russian gun single-handed;

and, finding all his senior officers — he was then a Captain—killed or disabled, took command and brought his regiment successfully out of action.

Crimea. 1854.

"And our sons unborn shall nerve them for some great deed to be done,
By that twentieth of September, when the Alma's heights were won.
. . . .
O thou river! dear for ever to the gallant, to the free,
Alma, roll thy waters proudly, proudly roll them to the sea."

—*Richard Chevenix Trench.*

Royal Humane Society's Silver Medal to Miss D. Milman, and **Resuscitation Certificate** to Miss R. Milman, who, with a friend, Miss D. F. Richmond, went out in a boat some distance on Lake Windermere with the intention of bathing. Miss Richmond, who was a poor swimmer, got into difficulties, and Miss D. Milman, on going to her assistance, was dragged under water. An oar was thrown to them from the boat, which had then drifted away, but this was insufficient to support them both. Meantime Miss R. Milman paddled ashore, secured another boat, and rowed out again, and the sisters by their united efforts then succeeded in getting Miss Richmond out of the water. Artificial respiration was practised for half-an-hour, before they were noticed and assisted back to land. The treatment was there continued, ultimately proving successful. **1904.**

September 21

V.C. Captain G. F. Day, C.B., **R.N.** (Died 1876.) Displayed the coolest audacity in making a reconnaissance, venturing alone for two days waist-deep in a dangerous swamp to within 200 yards of the Russian vessels. A

French officer who had previously essayed the same perilous feat lost his life.

Genitchi, Sea of Azoff, Crimea. 1854.

V.C. Lieutenant-Colonel W. Rennie, **90th (Scottish Rifles).** (Died 1896.) On this date, and also on September 25, charged ahead of his regiment, on each occasion rescuing imperilled guns from the rebels at Lucknow.

V.C. Sergeant P. Mahoney, **1st Madras Fusiliers.** While doing duty with volunteer cavalry at Mungulwar, captured a Colour from the rebels. **Mutiny. 1857.**

Gallant little Aldershot Boy. H. J. Langwith, aged 11, pluckily saved S. Morris from the canal at Aldershot.

1907.

September 22

V.C. Captain The Hon. A. G. A. Hore-Ruthven, **Highland Light Infantry.** (Born 1872.) "Deed shaw." Carried a wounded Egyptian officer from within 50 yards of the advancing Dervishes under fearful fire, having several times to lay down his burden in order to fight off the enemy. The two eventually reached cover in safety.

Nile. 1898.

A Gloucestershire Woman burnt to Death in trying to save her Friend. While Minnie Frost, aged 35, was trimming a paraffin lamp at Bristol it exploded, setting fire to the dress of another woman in the room. Minnie Frost endeavoured to extinguish the flames, but her own dress caught, and she rushed into the garden enveloped in fire. Both women were so fearfully burned that they expired shortly after. **1887.**

Stanhope Medal to Captain T. C. Mackenzie, R.A.M.C., who, while a passenger on board the Messageries Maritimes ss. *Saghalien* in the Ionian Sea, plunged after an apprentice who had fallen overboard, and kept him afloat until they were picked up by a boat forty minutes later. The *Saghalien* was steaming at 12½ knots an hour at the time through a choppy sea. **1904.**

SEPTEMBER 23

Liverpool S. & H. Society's Silver Medal and Vote of Thanks to Richard Courtney who, with great presence of mind, rescued a diver whose dress and air-tube had become entangled by a parted hawser at Portland. Courtney pluckily lowered himself over the side of the boat, unscrewed the diver's mouthpiece, cut the hawser adrift, and so saved the man's life. **1907.**

Carnegie Hero Fund: First Case on the List. An allowance of £2, 10s. per month to the widow of Thomas Wright, who died in attempting to save a fellow-workman in the Baxter Chemical Works, St. Helens, Lancs. A workman, when attending to some machinery, fell into a vat 6 feet deep and was overcome by the fumes of a chemical substance. While rescue apparatus was being fetched, Wright, fearing the man would die before it arrived, went down into the vat to render assistance, and was himself overcome. The first man was afterwards taken out and recovered, but Wright succumbed, leaving a widow and family of seven. **1908.**

Liverpool S. & H. Society's Silver Medal, Vote of Thanks, and £2 to Peter Littler and John Maguire for rescuing two men asphyxiated by sulphur fumes from a well at a chemical works at St. Helens. Unfortunately one of the men, named Thomas Wright, was found to be beyond aid. **1908.**

SEPTEMBER

Luke O'Connor V.C. C.B.

C. Hore-Ruthven.

Francis C. Maude

Anthony D. Home
Dy Surgeon Genl Army Med Staff

Chas C. Fraser

W. Blair

C. J. Melliss Colonel
Comdg 53rd Sikhs F.F.

Corporal William Bees.
V. C.

SEPTEMBER 24

V.C. Sergeant R. Grant, **5th (Northumberland).** For saving the life of a private, whose leg had been shot away, by carrying him into camp from under severe fire. **Lucknow, Mutiny. 1857.**

Albert Medal of the Second Class to Mr. Frederick M. Timme for saving life during a cyclone at Darjeeling, Northern India. **1899.**

Postman's Park Hero and Martyr. Tablet 31. James Hewers, while trying to save the life of a man at Richmond, was run down by a train and killed. **1878.**

SEPTEMBER 25

FIRST RELIEF OF LUCKNOW

V.C. General Sir William Olpherts, G.C.B., **Bengal Artillery.** (Died 1902.) Known as "Hell-fire Jack" for his dashing courage and absolute scorn of danger. Among many deeds of intrepid valour was that of capturing two of the rebel guns in the face of awful fire, after which he again faced the inferno of lead, and brought up horses and limbers to carry off his prize.

V.C. Major-General Sir H. T. Macpherson, K.C.B., **Seaforth Highlanders.** (Died 1886.) "Touch not the cat but a glove." Led a splendid charge on this historic occasion, and captured two guns.

V.C. Surgeon V. M. McMaster, **Seaforth Highlanders.** Remained all night in devoted ministration to the wounded under continuous fire.

V.C. Inspector-General J. Jee, C.B., **Seaforth Highlanders.** (Died 1899.) Was all night in great peril from a force of rebels, who surrounded him and his wounded charges in the Mote-Mehal Hall. Carried many disabled men out of the rebels' power earlier in the day.

V.C. Private Henry Ward, **Seaforth Highlanders.** Guarded all night Captain Havelock, V.C., who had been wounded and was placed in a dhoolie. In the morning another wounded man was added. Ward then guided the bearers through terrific musketry and ordnance fire, and by his splendid pluck and coolness eventually conducted his party into safety.

V.C. Hon. Lieutenant-Colonel A. Boulger, **84th (York and Lancaster).** For great pluck in twelve separate actions. On this date he stormed a bridge, and was the first man inside a masked battery.

V.C. Colonel F. Cornwallis Maude, C.B., **R.A.** (Died 1900.)
V.C. Private J. Holmes, **84th (York and Lancaster).**
Colonel Maude was noted for cool heroism under the most terrific fire, and the first relief was in a great measure owing to the magnificent dash of this officer, who forced his battery through fearful cannon and musketry fire. Private Holmes, V.C., was decorated for fine behaviour in conjunction with Colonel Maude.

V.C. Sergeant-Major George Lambert, **84th (York and Lancaster).** For distinguished conduct on three occasions, of which this was the last. **Mutiny. 1857.**

A humble Hero of Peace. Joseph Guest, aged 44, a well-sinker, lost his life by going down a well at Hemsworth Hall, near Barnsley, to the rescue of his comrade overcome by foul gas. Assistance was at hand, but the air was so poisonous that no one else ventured down. The men were recovered, but both were dead. **1875.**

SEPTEMBER 26

THE HEROES OF DHOOLIE SQUARE

V.C. Surgeon-General Sir Anthony Home, K.C.B., **90th (2nd Scottish Rifles).** (Born 1823.) "Tuebor."

V.C. Surgeon W. Bradshaw, **90th (2nd Scottish Rifles).**

V.C. Private P. McManus, **5th Northumberland.**

V.C. Private J. Hollowell, **Seaforth Highlanders.**

V.C. Private J. Ryan, **Madras Fusiliers.**

Also Private Ward, V.C. (See September 25th.)

When Havelock entered Lucknow, Dr. Home was in charge of the wounded, who were carried in dhoolies. His small escort was almost wiped out, and, being in the rear, Dr. Home and his little party were cut off from the main column. Hotly pursued by the savage mutineers, the fugitives sought shelter in a house, which their relentless foes set on fire. They then escaped to a shed, which they defended for twenty-two hours against fearful odds; and when relieved from their terrible plight only six men besides the brave doctor were able to fire. The valour of the above party was almost superhuman, and the safety of all concerned was due to their magnificent courage.

V.C. Lieutenant S. H. Lawrence, **32nd (Cornwalls).** "In cruce salus." Two occasions on which he performed acts of unusual courage. On this date he charged in advance of a party with only two men and captured a gun.

V.C. Private T. Duffy, **Madras Fusiliers.** Cross sold in 1902 for £53. Saved a gun from being captured by the mutineers.

S

V.C. Colour-Sergeant S. McPherson, **Seaforth Highlanders.** Under a storm of bullets, went from the Residency and carried in a badly wounded comrade.

All at First Relief of Lucknow, Mutiny. 1857.

V.C. Driver F. G. Bradley, **R.F.A.** One of five men who volunteered to fetch ammunition under fearful cross-fire at Itala, Zululand. Bradley also helped to carry one of the men, who was wounded, into safety. The others concerned received the Medal for Distinguished Conduct. **Boer War. 1901.**

Two Scotch Medical Heroes of Alma. The names of Dr. Richard J. Mackenzie, M.D., of Edinburgh (a volunteer doctor), aged 33, and his friend Dr. Scott, of the 79th Regiment, are foremost on the splendid roll-call of noble doctors whose names are absent from the list of the V.C. Both spent many hours during and after the "Alma" tending the wounded, while exposed to the fire of the batteries. Dr. Mackenzie, in addition to extracting numerous bullets and dressing a multitude of wounds, performed twenty-seven capital operations. He accompanied the army on its march, and was thought to be in good health; but the strain had been too heavy, and he succumbed to an attack of cholera, passing away after two days' illness. The kind doctor was idolised by the soldiers, and it was said that his loss was more sincerely lamented than that of any man who fell at Alma. **1854.**

"The beloved physician."

Carnegie Hero Fund. An award of £20 to George Davis, of Poplar (London), for rescuing a boy from drowning in the Thames at Limehouse. This gallant fellow had previously saved many lives, and held a Medal and eight Certificates from the Royal Humane Society.

1908.

THE CARNEGIE MEDAL.

SEPTEMBER 27

V.C. Bombardier J. Thomas, **Bengal Artillery.** Gazetted for saving a wounded man from the Sepoys, who would otherwise have tortured him to death. This fine deed was performed under heavy fire.

V.C. Private W. Dowling, **32nd (Cornwall).** Decorated for spiking the mutineers' guns on three separate occasions. **Mutiny. 1857.**

V.C. Colonel P. Roddy, **Bengal Army** (unattached). (Died 1895.) An officer who rose from the ranks. He was decorated for a specially courageous encounter with a rebel at Kuthirga.

V.C. Major-General Charles G. Baker, **Bengal Police Batt.** (Died 1906.) "Finis coronat opus." Charged, with only 60 horsemen, a force of 1000 rebel infantry at Suhejnee, near Peroo, and utterly routed them.

V.C. George B. Chicken, **Naval Brigade (late Indian).** For a gallant attack on a number of rebels, by whom he was badly wounded. **Mutiny. 1858.**

Liverpool S. & H. Society's Silver Medals and Votes of Thanks to Captain D. A. Wood and Mr. W. Barrow (third officer); and £1 each to ten men of the crew of the lifeboat of the ss. *Wayfarer*, for the rescue of the crew—seven in number—of the American schooner *Elmer E. Randall*, 25 miles south of the southern entrance to the Mississippi. When sighted, the schooner was dismasted and had lost her rudder. Owing to the gale and heavy sea, the *Wayfarer's* lifeboat was unable to get alongside the schooner, neither could a line from the schooner reach the boat. After repeated attempts, the lifeboat's crew was so exhausted that they had to return to their vessel, and it was with the greatest difficulty that they were got on board, the boat breaking adrift and being abandoned. The *Wayfarer* stood by the schooner during the night, and next day after much trouble successfully achieved the rescue. **1906.**

SEPTEMBER 28

V.C. Lieutenant Robert Blair, **2nd Dragoon Guards.** "Amo probo." Received a fearful sword cut—which nearly severed one arm at the shoulder—while, with a handful of followers, fighting his way through sixty mutineers.

V.C. Private P. Donohoe, **9th Lancers.** Supported Lieutenant Blair after his terrible injury, assisting him into camp. He also showed great courage during the fierce encounter.

V.C. Sergeant B. Diamond, **Bengal Artillery.**
V.C. Gunner R. Fitzgerald, **Bengal Artillery.**

After every other man belonging to their gun had been shot, these brave men continued to work it, and by their devotion to duty succeeded in clearing the road of every mutineer.

V.C. Captain the Hon. A. H. Anson, **84th Regiment (York and Lancaster).** "Nil desperandum." Distinguished for "the greatest gallantry on every occasion." In an encounter with the rebels on this date he was unable—in consequence of a wounded hand—to stop his horse, which carried him right into the middle of a number of the enemy. His escape was one of the many miracles of warfare.

V.C. Private J. R. Roberts, **9th Lancers.** Decorated for carrying a wounded comrade into safety from murderous fire.

V.C. Lance-Corporal R. Kells, **9th Lancers.** Seeing Captain Drysdale wounded and disabled, dashed to his aid, and kept the Sepoys at bay until help arrived.

Boolundshuhur, Mutiny. 1857.

Some gallant Kentish Gipsies. Ambrose Lee, a gipsy, with his brother John, hearing the cries of two lads who had fallen into a clay-pit near Folkestone, went to help them. Both dived into deep water, and John, after remaining for some time below the water, came to the surface in a dying state, expiring as he was taken out. One of the lads he died to save also perished. **1897.**

Heroic Death of a Carnarvonshire Widow. During a fire at Port Dinorwic, near Carnarvon, Margaret Evans, aged 57, went up a ladder and entered a room in which an old lady was sleeping. She came to the window and told those below that the woman was dead; but instead of descending the ladder, Mrs. Evans turned back into the room and was never again seen alive. **1902.**

SEPTEMBER 29

V.C. Major-General Sir C. C. Teesdale, K.C.M.G., **R.A.** (Died 1893.) Cleared a redoubt of the enemy during a night attack, rallied the Turkish artillerymen under terrific fire, and, later on, saved many wounded Russians from being butchered by the Turks. This latter magnificent act was seen by the Russian General in command, who thanked the intrepid Englishman for his noble conduct.

Kars, Asia Minor, Crimea 1855.

Albert Medal of the First Class to Stoker Edward Lynch, R.N., who sustained terrible injuries from a bad explosion on board H.M.S. *Thrasher*. Despite intense agony from scalds, the gallant fellow refused medical aid until his comrade had received attention. It afterwards transpired that Lynch had nobly sacrificed his own chance of quitting the stokehold in order to help the other sufferer to escape. **1897.**

Stanhope Medal to Francis O'Neill. An explosion occurred at noon in the Annagher pit, Coalisland, Tyrone, four men being at work at the time. Two of these got out alive, but the other two were struck down by the deadly after-damp. Francis O'Neill, miner, made three attempts to descend the shaft, being driven back each time. At the fourth attempt he reached the bottom, and, finding a man named Hughes, got him into the cage, he himself falling unconscious, and both were drawn up. On recovering, O'Neill again went down and brought out the fourth man, only to find him dead. **1889.**

SEPTEMBER 30

V.C. Colonel C. J. Melliss, **Indian Staff Corps.** (Born 1862.) Distinguished himself upon four occasions, on one of which (the present date) his foot was shot and became paralysed while he was leading a small party against a large force of the enemy. These, after a desperate hand-to-hand encounter, he dispersed.
Obassa, Ashantee. 1900.

V.C. Private W. Bees, **Notts and Derbyshire Regiment.** In order to relieve the terrible thirst of six wounded comrades, fetched water from a spruit within 100 yards of furious Boer rifle fire and in full range of their guns. Although the bullets rattled like hail on the kettle holding the precious liquid, the man who carried it was preserved as by a miracle. **Moedwil, Boer War. 1901.**

London Fire Brigade Silver Medal to Henry Girault, who rescued three women from a second-floor room of a burning house in Finsbury Road, W. Brompton. He again entered the room in search of five children said to be there, but owing to the intense heat and dense smoke could get no further. It was afterwards discovered that the children were not in the house. **1887.**

Kentish Lifeboatmen's Heroism: Death of Five Men of the *Walmer* Crew. Frederick Jordan, John Jordan, George Beecham, John Cross, and Albert Arnold lost their lives by the capsizing of a galley punt—not a lifeboat—in which they had gone to the assistance of the barque *Carmorney* in the Downs off Deal. The mast of the galley punt fouled some of the *Carmorney's* projecting gear, and the men became entangled in the sails as she capsized. All were lost. **1899.**

OCTOBER

"*It is an everlasting duty—the duty of being brave.* VALOUR *is still value. The first duty for a man is still that of subduing* FEAR. *A man shall and must be valiant; he must march forward, and quit himself like a man—trusting imperturbably in the appointment and* CHOICE *of the upper powers, and on the whole not fear at all.*"—THOMAS CARLYLE.

OCTOBER

October 1

An Oxfordshire Man's heroic Deed. While Samuel Coleman was engaged with other men in carrying wood across the Great Western line near Banbury, a plank was dropped thwart the track of an on-coming train. Although the engine was within three yards of him, Coleman dashed forward to remove the obstruction, and was struck on the shoulder and hurled on to the four-foot way, the train of thirty waggons passing over him. The poor fellow died of his terrible injuries in Horton Infirmary. **1880.**

A devoted Mother. Eliza Smart, a widow, aged 35, of Lime Grove, Hackney, was earning 4s. per week as an upholstress, of which she paid 2s. for rent. In order that her ten-year-old boy might have sufficient to eat, she literally starved herself to death, the doctor certifying that want of proper nourishment was the direct cause of her death. **1884.**

"God's love, O mother, is greater than thine,
And He calls thee away to a peace divine."
—*Bishop Walsham How.*

Royal Humane Society's Silver Medal to Ernest W. Nealier, stoker, R.N., and **Bronze Medal** to John D. Bradley, A.B., for great gallantry in jumping into the Solent on a dark night to rescue a man who had fallen from a cutter of H.M.S. *Eclipse.* They supported him until another boat picked them up, 200 yards astern of the ship. **1907.**

OCTOBER 2

V.C. Lieutenant-Colonel J. C. C. Daunt, **Bengal Native Infantry.**

V.C. Sergeant D. Dynon, **53rd (Shropshire).**

Associated in the brilliant capture of two guns from the mutineers at Chota Behar. Colonel Daunt also distinguished himself a month later, when he was dangerously wounded.

V.C. Private P. McHale, **5th Northumberland.** (Died 1866.) Celebrated for his prowess in attacking the mutineers at Lucknow. Twice, under galling fire, he was foremost in capturing their guns. **Mutiny. 1857.**

V.C. Ensign J. T. Down, **57th (W. Middlesex).** (Died during the war.)

V.C. Drummer D. Stagpool, **57th (W. Middlesex).**

Between them, and under fierce fire, carried a wounded man out of the bush swarming with Maoris, into shelter. **Pontoko, New Zealand. 1863.**

Albert Medal of the Second Class to Arthur Eccleshall, porter at Bushbury railway station. Some children were making their way over a level crossing at the end of the platform, when a light engine approached. Eccleshall shouted to them, and two of them got clear, but the third, a little boy, instead of getting off the line, ran along the ballast between the rail and the platform. The engine had almost reached him, when Eccleshall sprang from the platform and pulled him out of danger, in performing which act he was himself knocked down and rendered unconscious. Fortunately he fell clear of the wheels. **1908.**

Carnegie Hero Fund. Award of £10 to Arthur Eccleshall (mentioned above), to recoup him for loss sustained. **1908.**

Heroic Death of a Northumberland Police Constable. Seeing a man fall from the quay into the river, at 1 A.M., P.-C. John Robinson, aged 22, lowered himself by a rope to the drowning man. The rope being too short, he also fell in and sank. George Craig, one of a family well known for life-saving, plunged in and brought him out, but life was extinct. **1894.**

Fine Heroism of two Devonian Boatmen. Richard Souch and his son, seeing a ketch flying signals of distress on Briton's Rock, Ilfracombe, went to the rescue in their boat and brought off four people. The boat was, however, wrecked on Hillborough Rocks on her return journey, and all her occupants perished. The elder Souch, who had previously saved four lives at the same perilous spot, left a widow and a large family. **1895.**

October 3

Heroism of an Antrim Workman. A small tank of varnish over a gas stove at a blind manufactory at Belfast having become ignited, set fire to the clothes of a workwoman. Messrs. James and Frederick Anderson, proprietors of the business, and a workman named George Green rushed to the rescue; but their own clothing caught fire, and all sustained serious injuries. Green died shortly after his admission to the hospital, but the others recovered. **1881.**

Board of Trade Awards. Silver Medals and Diplomas sent by the Greek Government to Mr. Henry Forbes, master, Mr. James W. Harriss, Mr. John Fanning, and Mr. Richard H. Buck, officers of the British ship *Augustine*, for gallantry in saving eight lives from a Greek steamer. **1904.**

OCTOBER 4

A Yorkshire Martyr. Fred Landley, aged 26, seeing his brother attacked by a rabid dog at Hepworth, near Holmfirth, West Riding, went to his assistance, and the dog, turning upon the brave fellow, bit him in the wrist. The attack of hydrophobia which supervened proved fatal. **1887.**

Carnegie Hero Fund. Captain James T. Belton, of the ss. *City of Dundee*, lost his life in St. George's Channel, when his ship was struck by another steamer during a dense fog and sank within fourteen minutes. All the passengers, with one exception—a lady—were quickly transferred to the other vessel, and by his plucky efforts Captain Belton succeeded in saving this last passenger, but at the cost of his own life. He left a widow and two children.

The Trustees of the Carnegie Hero Fund have granted Mrs. Belton an allowance of £2, 5s. per calendar month for each of her two children towards their support and education, for such length of time as the Trustees may consider suitable. She has also received a memorial Medallion. **1908.**

OCTOBER 5

Two forgotten Heroes of the Alma. After the battle on the banks of the Alma, whereon "the grey acre" of 750 wounded Russians lay for upwards of sixty hours, Dr. James Thomson, M.D., of the **44th Regiment,** with but a flag of truce to protect him from the vindictive fury of the Cossacks hovering near, spent days and nights in relieving the agony of the sufferers. His servant, whose name cannot be ascertained, was his faithful companion in this magnificent and long-drawn-out deed of mercy. Afterwards, at great personal risk (having incurred the danger of being left behind alone with the enemy), the doctor rejoined his regiment at Balaclava, only to perish of cholera on this day. **1854.**

"Worship of a Hero is transcendental admiration of a Great Man. No nobler feeling than this of admiration for one higher than himself dwells in the heart of man. It is—the vivifying influence in man's life."—*Carlyle.*

Stanhope Medal to Captain H. N. McRae, who at great risk rescued a trumpeter of the R.A., who had fallen down a well in the compound at Rawal Pindi, India. The well was 88 feet deep, with 12 feet of water in it. **1886.**

OCTOBER 6

V.C. Corporal J. Sinnott, **84th (York and Lancaster).** (Died 1896.) For assisting several other men—by whom he was chosen to receive the Decoration—to rescue Lieutenant Gibaut from heavy fire at Lucknow, after that officer had been mortally wounded. **Mutiny. 1857.**

V.C. General C. A. Goodfellow **(late Bombay R.E.).** The last Cross awarded for fine deeds during the Mutiny. Went through severe fire to a soldier lying under the walls of Beyet Fort, only to discover, after having with great difficulty carried the poor fellow into cover, that he was dead. **Mutiny. 1859.**

V.C. Field-Marshal Sir George S. White, G.C.V.O., G.C.I.E., G.C.B., G.C.S.I., **Gordon Highlanders.** (Born 1835.) "Vigilans et audax." Served through numerous campaigns, from the Indian Mutiny to the great Boer War, 1899–1902, where he defended Ladysmith from November 1899 to March 1900 with a small but heroic garrison, decimated by disease and privation, against a huge besieging army of Boers. The two deeds for which Sir George White was gazetted were—the capturing a gun, and (on this date) the leading of a small party against a large force of Afghans up a precipitous mountain, where he rode alone in advance of his men, shot the Afghan leader, and by his brilliant dash so disorganised the enemy that they fled and the position was carried.

Charasiah and Kandahar, Afghan War. 1879.

V.C. Lieut.-Colonel A. S. Cobbe, D.S.O., **Indian Army.** (Born 1870.) "In sanguine vita: Moriens cano." Some of the companies having retired, and he being left alone in front of the line with a Maxim gun, worked it and afterwards brought it in during the action at Erego. Also carried in a wounded man, within twenty yards of the enemy, under galling fire. **Somaliland. 1902.**

Board of Trade Bronze Medals to William Tyson, chief officer; Edward Hobbs, chief boatman; Edward Hayman, commissioned boatman; James Cole, commissioned boatman; William C. Cock, coastguard boatman; George Cluett, coastguard boatman; John Lander, coastguard boatman, and Mr. W. H. Mitchell, farmer. All these were received by the King and had their Medals from his hand for the following deed. The British brigantine *Try Again* stranded at Dodman Point, Cornwall, and two of her crew managed to climb the cliffs, leaving the master and two hands on the rocks. Search-parties under Mr. Tyson and Mr. Mitchell went up and down the cliffs in a dense fog searching for them, and brought the three men at great risk to the top of the cliffs. **1908.**

Nurse's fine Devotion to Duty. Nurse Murray, of the South-Eastern Hospital (London), who had undergone five operations, and had been warned against lifting any weight, was in charge of the receiving room when an urgent case of diphtheria, necessitating an immediate operation, was brought in. Risking the double danger of infection and injury, Miss Murray, knowing that the least delay might prove fatal, did not wait for the porter, but carried the patient—a little girl of five—some distance to the operating theatre. The operation was successful and the child recovered, but the humane nurse was afterwards incapacitated for duty, and on January 16, 1909, the Local Government Board awarded her a gratuity of £50. Nurse Murray rendered fine service during the small-pox epidemic, 1901–2. **1908.**

October 7

Postman's Park Fireman Hero and Martyr. Tablet 25. Joseph A. Ford, aged 30, of the Metropolitan Fire Brigade, saved six people from a burning house in Gray's Inn Road. The flames caught the canvas shoot of the escape as Ford brought out the last person—a woman—and he had to let her drop. She, however, escaped without serious injury, but the heroic fireman became entangled in the wire net-work of the machine, and was literally burned alive. Life was not extinct when he was released, but he expired after fearful agony in the Royal Free Hospital at eight o'clock the same night. **1871.**

FORD, THE FIREMAN

Why glints the autumn sun on glittering helms?
  Why the Dead March, with its funereal beat?
Why this vast crowd, whose silence overwhelms
  The roaring of the street?

The marching column has a martial air;
  Its tramp is timed like tread of well-trained troop.
Is it some famous Captain that they bear
  To where the dark yews droop?

A common man !—a fireman !—what, no more?
  Why tears? Why sobs? Why grief on every face,
As though it were some hero that ye bore
  To his last resting-place?

Not always, true, are purest laurels won
  Amid red carnage in fierce battle's strife,
But earned by humble duty, bravely done,
  In saving human life!

This was a hero! yet he never strove
  To win distinction for his simple name.
His way through flame, and stifling smoke he clove
  For duty—not for fame!

With single purpose acted he his part,
  Conscious of living in his Maker's ken;
And well the lesson had he learnt by heart
  Of Him who died for men.

'Twas so he died! from out a fiery grave
  He snatched the helpless, weak with wild despairs.
Then in his wonted work's performance gave
  Freely—his life for theirs.

Before that plain deal coffin bow the head!
  That land's secure which may such heroes boast.
Write Joseph Ford among the honoured dead
  Whom England prizes most!

—*Written by* THOMAS HOOD, the younger,
for "Fun," No. 837, 1871.

OCTOBER 8

V.C. Corporal C. Anderson, **2nd Dragoon Guards.**
V.C. Trumpeter T. Monaghan, **2nd Dragoon Guards.**

Anderson's Victoria Cross is now in the United Service Institute, Whitehall, London. Monaghan's was sold in 1903 for £43. After a desperate struggle in a jungle with a body of fierce Sepoys, the above pair protected Colonel Seymour (who had received two sword-cuts) and kept between thirty and forty of the miscreants at bay, thus saving their officer's life.

Sundeela, Oude, Mutiny. 1858.

Northamptonshire Bricklayer's heroic Death. Two men had descended the well at a new pumping station at Kettering Waterworks, but found on reaching the bottom that the foul gas was overpowering them. On their making signals of distress, Samuel Bryant pluckily volunteered to go to their rescue. When he had descended about half-way, the noxious air overcame him and he fell to the bottom of the well, perishing with those he had tried to save. **1887.**

Postman's Park Medical Hero and Martyr. Tablet 38. Dr. William Lucas contracted diphtheria while ministering to a child in Middlesex Hospital, and died there shortly afterwards, at the early age of 23. **1893.**

October 9

V.C. Able-Seaman G. Hinckley, **R.N.** Decorated for saving two lives under circumstances of great peril. Hinckley carried one wounded man 150 yards under heavy fire, and afterwards, while still under fire, brought in another sufferer. **Fung-wha, China. 1862.**

A Daughter's unavailing Heroism. On descending a large disused water-tank, in which a quantity of brewers' grains had been compressed, an old man, named Charles Gregory, fell senseless, overcome by the poisonous gas generated by the compressed grains. His daughter Charlotte, aged 31, seeing this at once followed to help him, but also fell. On an alarm being raised, Joseph Tacy and Charles Freeman went down, but they also collapsed, and when the four victims were brought quickly to the air life was extinct in each case. **1863.**

OCTOBER

Mr Stagpool. V.C

[illegible]

[illegible]

[illegible]

[illegible]

E. D. Brown-Synge-Hutchinson
Colonel 14th Hussars

Calichson
Mil. Attaché

Eccles Wood

OCTOBER 10

V.C. General the Right Hon. Sir Dighton M. Probyn, G.C.V.O., K.C.B., K.C.S.I., P.C., **2nd Punjab Cavalry.** (Born 1833.) Decorated for numerous acts of distinguished gallantry in personal encounters with the mutineers at Agra; also for capturing one of the enemy's standards.

V.C. Private J. Freeman, **9th Lancers.** Freeman's Cross is in the United Service Institute, Whitehall, London. He killed the leader of some rebel cavalry, and kept them at bay while protecting his officer, Lieutenant Jones, who was badly wounded and in great peril, and ultimately saved his life. **Agra, Mutiny. 1857.**

Brave Deed of a Warwickshire Mill Manager. A railway porter named Barnwell, and two men named Francott and Roberts, went with a horse and cart through flooded fields at Clifton, near Rugby, to try and rescue some cattle. Being near the river, where the current was very strong, the enterprise was attended by considerable danger. The water nearly reached the horse's neck. Francott, who was driving, said he knew every inch of the ground, but as he spoke the horse and cart disappeared into a deep cavity. Two of the men sank and were not seen again, but Barnwell jumped out; and Mr. Alfred Barnett, manager of Clifton Mill, who was on horseback and who went to his assistance, also perished. Finally, with the aid of ropes, Barnwell was dragged to a place of safety. **1875.**

OCTOBER 11

V.C. Admiral of the Fleet Sir John E. Commerell, G.C.B., **R.N.** (Died 1901.)

V.C. Chief Officer of the Coastguard W. J. Rickard, **R.N.** (Died 1905.) Cross sold in 1906 for £80.

Associated with Seaman G. Milestone (not gazetted) in the daring feat of firing a huge store of Russian forage. The gallant trio walked 2½ miles in the darkness, after rowing in a little boat across the Spit of Arabat. The Cossacks, who were close by, aroused by the flames, pursued the brave English sailors for some distance with heavy rifle fire. On the way back, Milestone, becoming exhausted, sank in the mud, but was extricated and brought into safety by his companions.

(*N.B.*—In most accounts it is asserted that Rickard only helped Milestone, but this is not the case. The truth was communicated to the compiler by one in possession of all the facts.)

Isthmus of Arabat, Crimea. 1855.

London Fire Brigade Silver Medal to Walter Hogwood, who saved two lives at a fire in Mansell Street, Aldgate. **1879.**

The Order of St. John of Jerusalem in England. Certificate of Honour to Thomas H. Jones, driver, and George B. Helliar, guard, of a motor 'bus near Crawley. Seeing a miller's van with two runaway horses coming towards the " Vanguard " 'bus, of which they were in charge, these two men got their passengers out, drew the vehicle to the side of the road, and then, at imminent risk, sprang forward and stopped the big, spirited animals. **1905.**

Carnegie Hero Fund. Award of £10 and a **Bronze Medal** to Thomas Watson, of Bristol, who rescued a companion from drowning in a deep pool of stagnant water in a disused clay-pit. Without waiting to divest himself of any of his clothing, Watson plunged into the water, and, after a severe struggle, succeeded in getting his companion sufficiently near the bank for others to assist in completing the rescue. This was the sixth occasion on which he had been the means of saving life. **1908.**

OCTOBER 12

Heroism of a Carnarvonshire Coastguard Officer. Mr. John K. Richards lost his life while warning the men of a schooner off the promenade at Carnarvon in a violent gale. As he was shouting through the storm, the brave man ventured too near the edge of the wall, in which the sea had made a breach, and fell into the water. Although several attempts were made, the men on the schooner were unable to rescue him from the furious sea, and he was drowned. **1870.**

The Order of St. John of Jerusalem in England. Bronze Medals to Frank Paice, Frederick Wiseman, and David Phillips for a splendid attempt to save the life of a man suffocated by foul gas in a sewer at Hackney Wick. Phillips was ill for some time afterwards and narrowly escaped with his life. He is a corporal in the St. John's Ambulance Brigade. **1906.**

Carnegie Hero Fund. Thirty shillings per month for one year awarded to Edwin Colcomb, gateman, aged 50, who saved two boys from being run over at Grovehill level crossing, Beverley. The children were crossing the line contrary to the gateman's warning, and, becoming confused, walked right in front of an engine. Colcomb, shouting to them, rushed forward to save them, and they stepped back just in time, but the coupling-rod of the engine caught the brave man, knocking him down and breaking his thigh. **1908.**

OCTOBER 13

V.C. Colonel E. D. Browne-Synge-Hutchinson, **14th Hussars.** (Born 1861.) "Non sibi sed toti." For great gallantry in saving three lives on one day. Under furious fire he assisted two dismounted men to regain their horses, and, later in the day, carried Trumpeter Leigh out of action. **Geluk, Boer War. 1900.**

Albert Medal of the Second Class to George Hoar, R.N., who made two gallant attempts—the second of which was successful—to rescue an unconscious man left aboard a wrecked and deserted schooner in a terrific gale off Tynemouth. **1891.**

London Fire Brigade Silver Medal to William Wells, who saved a life at a fire in King Street, Tower Hill. **1878.**

OCTOBER 14

V.C. Colonel H. C. T. Jarrett, **26th Bengal Native Infantry.** "Consilio et armis." Gazetted for a fine attempt to enter a house in a narrow lane at Baroun strongly held by Sepoys. Having, however, but four followers, the project had to be abandoned, and the gallant quintette were forced to retire under a tornado of bullets. **Mutiny. 1858.**

Albert Medal of the Second Class awarded to a Lady. During a violent gale the stone belfry of the Sutton National Schools was blown down, and crashed through the roof of the infants' schoolroom. Nearly 200 children were assembled there at the time, of whom one was killed outright and many others injured. Miss Hannah Rosbotham, who was teaching in another part of the school at the time, deliberately entered amid the wreckage, although well aware of the great danger to which she was exposed, and remained there until every child had been removed to a place of safety. At imminent risk to her own life, Miss Rosbotham rescued four infants who were partially covered with the débris and a little girl who was completely buried. The latter must inevitably have perished had not such gallantry been displayed by this heroic teacher. **1881.**

Albert Medal of the Second Class to Frederick Jaggers for courageously going out with a rope in a bad storm to the aid of a stranded vessel. A tremendous sea was dashing over rugged rocks at the time, and Jaggers was washed off his feet and rendered insensible, in which condition he was hauled ashore. He had previously done fine and successful rescue work. **1881.**

Postman's Park Hero and Martyr. Tablet 43. John Bannister, aged 30, of Bow, lost his life in a fine attempt to rescue another from a burning shop. **1901.**

"A hero is a hero at all points; in the soul and thought of him—first of all—a wise, noble-hearted man."—*Carlyle.*

October 15

Schoolmaster and Pupil drowned in an Endeavour to save others. Robert Speciall, tutor, aged 22, and Robert Baird, aged 17 (son of Sir David Baird, Bart.), while bathing with a large number of boys and masters from Grange Academy, Sunderland, lost their lives in a gallant endeavour to save the younger brother of Baird and another lad, both of whom had been swept out of their depth by a strong sea. Mr. Wilson and Mr. Downes, two other masters, rescued several lads who would otherwise have shared the fate of the above-named heroic pair. **1845.**

"It is a thing for ever changing, this of Hero-worship; different in each age, difficult to do well in any age."

—*Carlyle.*

Liverpool S. & H. Society's Silver Medals and Votes of Thanks to Captain Thomas Potter and First Officer Lieutenant S. G. M'Neil, R.N.R.; also 10s. each to the crew of the lifeboat of the steamer *Etruria*, for rescuing the crew of the Swedish barque *Orion* in the North Atlantic. The barque had sprung a leak and was rapidly settling down, when a boat was lowered from the *Etruria* and took off the captain and nine men. **1905.**

October 16

Northumberland Lifeboatman's Death. Mark A. Fairhurst lost his life through the capsizing of the North Blyth lifeboat on its way to a wrecked sloop outside the harbour. When the boat righted, all her crew save Fairhurst managed to get on board. The coxswain made a splendid attempt to rescue the drowning man, and succeeded in bringing him ashore, but all attempts to restore animation failed. **1898.**

The Order of St. John of Jerusalem in England. Certificate of Honour to P.-C. Frederick Harding, metropolitan police, for great courage and presence of mind at Holborn Bars on the occasion of the opening of the new Post Office buildings by His Majesty. The horses in Sheriff Bowater's state carriage bolted, and Harding at once rode towards the runaways to stop them. He was thrown to the ground, sustaining serious injuries; but his prompt action stopped the horses, and what might have proved a catastrophe among the dense crowd in the street was thus averted. **1905.**

OCTOBER 17

V.C. General Sir Collingwood Dickson, G.C.B., **R.A.** (Died 1904.) "Fortes fortuna juvat." Under a hurricane of Russian shell-fire went many times to fetch barrels of powder from the magazine. This fearless soldier also stood for hours, exposed the whole time to fearful fire, directing the unloading and storing of ammunition. He was said to be to the gunners what Captain Peel, V.C., R.N., was to the Navy.

Siege of Sevastopol, Crimea. 1854.

Postman's Park Doctor Hero and Martyr. Tablet 12. Dr. Stewart Brown, of Holly Bank, Brockley Road, London, while suffering from severe injury to the spine from an accident, jumped into the sea at Boulogne and rescued a drowning man, afterwards spending two hours in his drenched clothes trying to restore animation. This noble act of self-sacrifice hastened the doctor's death, which took place on this date. **1900.**

Master of a Monmouthshire Vessel drowned in trying to save one of his Crew. Charles Dixon, of Chepstow, seeing one of his crew fall into the river Usk, near Newport, tried to rescue him, and in doing so fell overboard himself. Both perished. **1901.**

OCTOBER 18

V.C. Captain Sir William Peel, Bart., K.C.B., **R.N.** "Industria." (Died 1858.) One of the most gallant heroes on the roll of honour. His exploits included the flinging of a lighted shell over a parapet, a magnificent defence of the "Colours," and a share in the capture of Lucknow.

Inkermann, Redan, &c., Crimea. 1854.

"Kind to man and kind to beast,
Loving greatest in the least;
Iron-willed, but tender-sweet,
Gentle-hearted to the core;
Peel, the darling of the Fleet!
Peel, the hero of the shore!"
—"Ballads of Brave Deeds," *Canon Rawnsley.*

A Surrey Heroine: the Oldest in the Book. Harriet Kenward, aged 82, of Limpsfield, upon an outbreak of cholera in that village, was the only person who volunteered to nurse the stricken people. Her devotion cost her her life; she caught the disease, and entered into rest on this date. **1866.**

Postman's Park Heroine and Martyr. Tablet 26. Amelia Kennedy, aged 19, was fatally burned while trying to save her sister from their burning house in Edward's Lane, Stoke-Newington. **1871.**

Stanhope Medal to Hedley Hill, who plunged into the Avon at Bristol on a dark night, and with great difficulty and peril to himself rescued a girl who had walked into the water by mistake. **1887.**

October 19

V.C. Field-Marshal Sir H. Evelyn Wood, G.C.B., G.C.M.G., D.L., **17th Lancers.** (Born 1838.) "Defend."

Sir Evelyn Wood, who began his distinguished career in the Navy, was, as a youth of 16, recommended for the Victoria Cross by Captain Lushington during the Crimean War. It was, however, not until 1858 that it was awarded for two gallant acts at Sindwaho and Sindhora, by which time the young officer had exchanged into the Junior Service. Sir Evelyn Wood possesses numerous decorations, has served in eight campaigns, was mentioned in despatches twenty-five times, and has been thanked for his services in Parliament.

Mutiny. 1858.

Carnegie Hero Fund. A grant of £4 per month to the widow and children of James Williams, who lost his life at Bedlinog, Glamorgan. On the occasion of a flood in the street on a dark night, Williams, hearing that some children were in a house in the direction in which the torrent was flowing with great force, went to their assistance, but fell into the water and was carried a mile down the valley, where his lifeless body was found the next day. **1908.**

October 20

V.C. Captain H. S. Pennell, **Sherwood Foresters.** Killed while tobogganing at St. Moritz-Dorf, January 1907. Gazetted for two fine attempts to carry Captain Smith of the Derbyshire Regiment, who was badly hit, out of a fearful hurricane of bullets. He only desisted from his labours when he found that the wounded man had expired.

V.C. Private E. Lawson, **Gordon Highlanders.**
V.C. Lance-Corporal S. Vickery, **39th Dorsetshire.**

Decorated for saving lives of wounded comrades during the famous storming of the heights. Lawson carried two men into safety, and was severely hit himself in the accomplishment of his gallant work.

V.C. Piper G. Findlater, **Gordon Highlanders.** While shot through both feet, sat up under fearful fire and played the regimental march to encourage his comrades in the assault. Findlater was decorated by Her late Majesty Queen Victoria at Netley Hospital.

Punjab Frontier. 1897.

"Historians say when at the 'Trott'
The natives then a thrashin' got,
They threw their weapons on the spot,
And ran awa' frae 'Turra.'

But Findlater, a native loon,
When shot in battle, jist sat doon
And blew his pipes and played a tune,
As if he'd been in 'Turra.'

And when the Queen, as jist she can,
Gied him the 'Cross' wi' gracious han',
And said, 'Far come ye frae, my man?'
He proodly answered, 'Turra.'

May heaven frae a' bad things defend it,
And wi' a watchfu' ee attend it.
Prosperity may He aye send it—
Oor birthplace, 'Turra.'"

V.C. Lieutenant A. C. Doxat, **3rd Battalion Imperial Yeomanry.** Gazetted for rescuing a dismounted man under furious fire at 300 yards range at Zeerust.

Boer War. 1900.

"An' you, good yeoman,
Whose limbs were made in England, show us here
The mettle of your pasture. Let us swear
That you are worth your breeding; which
I doubt not."

—*King Henry V.*

OCTOBER

George Findlater V.C

E Lawson.

Corporal Sam Vickery

M F M Meiklejohn
Captain

W Robertson

E H Sartorius

W. Hewett

Albert Medals of the Second Class to William Rolleston, Arthur McKee, and John Adams. After one disastrous attempt to save the crew of a wrecked barquantine off Newfoundland, this brave trio set out on a second effort, and in a tiny boat made two journeys through an awful sea and brought off the crew of the sinking vessel. **1882.**

Postman's Park Medical Hero and Martyr. Tablet 8. Dr. Samuel Rabbath, knowing well the grave risk he ran, sucked an obstruction through a tube in the throat of a child, upon whom tracheotomy had been performed in the Royal Free Hospital. He caught the disease, and died on this day. **1884.**

"Had the child lived, for whom thy life was spent,
We think we had not grudged the bitter cost;
But both have died, and, some will say, in vain
Thy calm, heroic spirit has been lost.

And yet, perchance, beyond the veil of sense,
At our poor folly angels may have smiled,
Seeing a young man enter perfect life,
And in his arms a little loving child."

—*C. C. L. in the* "*Spectator.*"

OCTOBER 21

V.C. Captain M. F. M. Meiklejohn, **Gordon Highlanders.** (Born 1870.) While making a splendid rally of the Highlanders, who were beginning to waver under fearful Boer fire, had, in addition to other terrible injuries, his right arm so badly hurt that amputation was necessary. "Hæc manus ob patriam" (This hand for my country).

V.C. Hon. Lieutenant W. Robertson, **Gordon Highlanders.** (Born 1865.) Was dangerously wounded in the body, and had one arm badly fractured, while defending a position he had previously taken under murderous Boer fire.

V.C. Major C. H. Mullins, C.M.G., **Imperial Light Horse.**

V.C. Captain R. Johnstone, **Imperial Light Horse.**

This brilliant pair of Colonials, by a splendid rush at a most critical moment, enabled an important flanking movement to be carried out which decided the issue of the day. Captain Johnstone was wounded while accomplishing this fine act. **Elandslaagte, Boer War. 1899.**

Albert Medal of the Second Class to Mr. John W. Thomson. While on duty at Stirling railway station he was told that a man was lying on the metals of the down main line. An engine was rapidly approaching, and Thomson, without hesitation, sprang to render assistance. He managed to drag the man (of very heavy build and quite unable to help himself) on to the six-foot way. With the exception of a few cuts which Thomson received about the face, both escaped without injury. **1905.**

October 22

Albert Medals of the First Class to William Smith, mate, and Arthur Rea, second engineer, of the steam trawler *Crane*, of Hull.

Albert Medals of the Second Class to Charles Beer, mate, Harry Smirk, chief engineer, and Edwin Costello, boatswain, of the steam trawler *Gull*, of Hull.

While passing through the North Sea at night, the Russian Baltic Fleet came upon the Hull fleet of steam trawlers fishing on the Dogger Bank, and (by mistake) at once opened fire. The captain and third hand of the *Crane* were killed outright; all the other hands, with one exception, were wounded; and the vessel was so badly damaged that she began to sink. W. Smith, the mate, was severely wounded, but finding the captain was dead, he took charge of the sinking boat and signalled for assistance. The chief engineer being wounded and unconscious, another man named Rea took charge of the engines, and by his prompt action in drawing the fires averted an explosion. Charles Beer, H. Smirk, and E. Costello put off from the *Gull* in a boat in response to signals, and succeeded with great difficulty in rescuing the wounded from the rapidly sinking vessel, and in bringing away the dead bodies of those who had been killed. **1904.**

Liverpool S. & H. Society's Silver Camp and Villaverde Medal and Vote of Thanks to Senor Antonio Cordeiro, of Para, Brazil; also **Silver Medal** and **Vote of Thanks** to John Morton Stanton for jumping into the river at Liverpool landing-stage and rescuing a lady who had been carried into the water in a motor car. **1906.**

OCTOBER 23

V.C. General James Blair, C.B., **Bombay Light Cavalry.** (Died 1905.) "Amo probo." Was terribly wounded while engaged in personal encounters with the mutineers on this occasion, also on August 12 of the same year.
Neemuch and Jeerum, Mutiny. 1857.

A Gloucestershire Baby Hero and Martyr: one of the finest Cases in the Book. Archie John H. Walters, aged 6, with a little playmate, lost his way near Bristol late in the day. The children were obliged to spend the night in the open, and Archie took off all his clothing, with the exception of his socks and shirt, and wrapped his friend up, afterwards lying down so as to protect the other child from the cold with his own body. In this position they were found the next morning by some farm labourers. The gallant little fellow died shortly afterwards from the effects of cold and exposure, the result of his self-sacrificing love for his comrade.

1874.

"It is morning: they have found them. Lo! a labourer on his way
Came upon them as still folded in each other's arms they lay.
They are breathing, barely breathing, all unconscious, cold as stone:
Noble Johnnie! pretty Willie! yes, the life has not quite flown.
And they take them to a cottage, and they chafe each frozen limb;
Little Willie has been covered, there is better hope for him.
And the mothers stand there watching, and their tears are falling fast.
Little Willie's eyelids tremble; yes, there's hope for him at last!

. . . .

In the churchyard Johnnie's sleeping, underneath the grassy mould:
No one puts a stone upon it lettered with the tale in gold:—
''Neath this stone a little hero, Johnnie Carr of Bristol, lies,
Who to save his little playmate gave his life a sacrifice.'

Children! think how, when the nations gather round the mighty throne,
He who gave His life for others will claim Johnnie for His own.
Think how full of strange, sweet wonder will the gracious tidings be,
'What thou didst to little Willie, that I count as done to Me.'"

—*Bishop Walsham How.*

A Northamptonshire Baby Hero. Seventeen years later another six-year-old laddie, Edward G. Budworth, of Long Buckly, gallantly gave his life by jumping into a stream swollen by the rain, in an attempt to rescue his little sister, aged three, who had fallen into the water. The force of the current took him off his legs, and both children were washed down stream and drowned. **1891.**

OCTOBER 24

V.C. Major-General Eustace H. Sartorius, C.B., **59th (E. Lancashire).** (Born 1844.) Brother of the late General Reginald W. Sartorius, V.C. With a few men led a successful attack on the stronghold of Tazi, situated on the summit of a precipitous height, when he was badly hurt on both hands by sword cuts. General Sartorius had previously saved three lives from the sea at Broadstairs, and holds the **Royal Humane Society's Medal** for this gallant act. **Shah-jui, Afghan War. 1879.**

Albert Medal of the Second Class to Mr. John H. Wood, for his gallantry in rescuing a boy washed off the pier at South Shields during a gale. **1885.**

Albert Medal of the Second Class, also **Stanhope Medal** to George H. Smith, for great gallantry on the occasion of an accident which occurred in one of the brick kilns at Woburn Sands. Part of the roof gave way, and a man who was working on the top of it fell to the bottom of the kiln, and was partially covered by a large quantity of hot ballast and bricks. Smith, who was passing at the time, heard what had happened, and immediately climbed through the wicket. This he accomplished with great difficulty, as it was partially choked; and after removing some of the bricks from the man, he fastened a rope round his arm-pits, by which he was drawn out of the kiln. The poor fellow, however, was so shockingly injured that he died the same day. **1908.**

October 25

BALAKLAVA

This famous battle, with its two magnificent cavalry charges, is one of those occasions on which the British army rose to the topmost height of chivalric attainment. First came the charge of the Heavy Brigade—the Scots Greys and the Inniskillings—led by Brigadier Scarlett, who dashed upon the Russian forces and drove them back.

"The charge of the gallant three hundred, the Heavy Brigade!
Down the hill, down the hill, thousands of Russians,
Thousands of horsemen, drew to the valley—and stay'd;
For Scarlett and Scarlett's three hundred were riding by
When the points of the Russian lances arose in the sky.

. . . .

But they rode like Victors and Lords
Thro' the forests of lances and swords
In the heart of the Russian hordes,
They rode, or they stood at bay—
Struck with the sword-hand and slew,—
Down with the bridle-hand drew
The foe from the saddle and threw
Underfoot there in the fray—
Ranged like a storm or stood like a rock
In the wave of a stormy day;
Till suddenly shock upon shock
Stagger'd the mass from without.
Drove it in wild disarray,
For our men gallopt up with a cheer and a shout,
And the foemen surged and waver'd and reel'd.
Up the hill, up the hill, up the hill, out of the field,
And over the brow and away."

. . . .

Later on, as the result of an order which had been misunderstood, Lord Cardigan led the "Charge of the Light

Brigade," who rode unflinchingly into the awful death-trap; 670 rode into the "Valley," and 198 returned.

"Forward, the Light Brigade!
Was there a man dismay'd?
Not tho' the soldier knew
Some one had blunder'd:
Their's not to make reply,
Their's not to reason why,
Their's but to do and die,
Into the valley of Death
Rode the six hundred.

. . . . .

Cannon to right of them,
Cannon to left of them,
Cannon behind them,
Volley'd and thunder'd.
Storm'd at with shot and shell,
While horse and hero fell,
They that had fought so well,
Came thro' the jaws of Death,
Back from the mouth of Hell,
All that was left of them,
Left of six hundred!"

—*Alfred Tennyson.*

V.C. Sergeant-Major J. Grieve, **2nd Dragoons.** In the heavy cavalry charge, seeing one of his officers surrounded by the enemy, rode to his aid, decapitated one, disabled two, and put the rest to flight.

V.C. Sergeant H. Ramage, **2nd Dragoons.** Carried a wounded man into shelter, rescued another from seven of the enemy, and captured a Russian. Ramage's Cross was sold for £61 in 1903.

V.C. Major J. Berryman, **17th Lancers.** (Died 1896.)

V.C. Quartermaster-Sergeant J. Farrell, **17th Lancers.** (Died 1865.)

V.C. Riding-Master J. Malone, **13th Hussars.** A noble trio who rode in the "600" and showed the greatest courage and humanity to Captain Webb, who was mortally wounded. Despite the dying officer's commands to look to their own safety, they remained with him, and finally conveyed him out of immediate range of the Russian guns. Berryman was "mentioned" four times during the campaign.

V.C. Lieutenant-Colonel A. R. Dunn, **11th Hussars.** Killed in the Abyssinian War, 1868. "Vigilans et audax." One of the "600," who saved two lives from the enemy.

V.C. Private S. Parkes, **4th (Light) Dragoons.** Had his sword destroyed by Russian fire while dismounted, and engaged in defending another man in the same plight from six Russians. **Crimea. 1854.**

October 26

V.C. Surgeon-General Sir James Mouat, K.C.B., **6th Dragoons.** (Died 1899.) By dressing the wounds of Colonel Morris, 17th Lancers, under galling fire, saved that officer from dying of hæmorrhage.

V.C. Quartermaster C. Wooden, **17th Lancers.** Associated with General Mouat, whom he helped in carrying Colonel Morris into shelter.

V.C. Admiral Sir William N. W. Hewett, K.C.B., K.S.C.I., **Naval Brigade.** (Died 1888.) Defended one gun of his battery against the Russians after the order to "spike the guns and retire" (which he disbelieved) had been given. Also "mentioned" for exceptional pluck at Inkermann.

V.C. Lieutenant-General G. L. Goodlake, **Coldstream Guards.** (Died 1900.) "Omnia bona desuper." For extreme courage in defending, with a handful of men, a picket against a superior number of the enemy in the Windmill Ravine. In November this brilliant officer again distinguished himself.

V.C. Private W. Stanlack, **Coldstream Guards.** Associated with General Goodlake, V.C., in enabling that officer to effect a surprise by crawling up to within six yards of a Russian sentry.

V.C. Lieutenant-Colonel J. A. Conolly, **49th (Royal Berks).** (Died 1888.) For a splendid defence of an outlying picket, fighting hand to hand with the Russians until he fainted from loss of blood and was carried into shelter.

V.C. Corporal J. Owens, **49th (Royal Berks).** (Died 1901.) Associated with Colonel Conolly in forcing back the enemy.

The Great Sortie, Sevastopol, Crimea. 1854.

London Fire Brigade Silver Medal to John M. Scott, who saved four lives at a fire in Oxford Street. **1880.**

OCTOBER 27

V.C. Major C. FitzClarence, **Royal Fusiliers.** (Born 1865). On October 14th, with a few unseasoned men, relieved an armoured train in great peril. On this date led a night sortie and drove out the Boers from their trenches; and on December 26th again distinguished himself, on this last occasion being badly wounded in both legs.

Game Tree Hill and Mafeking, Boer War. 1899.

Albert Medal of the Second Class to Henry Benton for great heroism in saving the life of a fellow-workman named John Green, who had been partially buried by a heavy fall of roof in the Cadeby Main Colliery. **1908.**

Royal Humane Society's Bronze Medal to Alfred Barrie, aged 11, who, when bathing with a friend named William Milne, aged 10, in shallow water at Colombo, Ceylon, supported the latter after they had been washed by a huge wave into seven feet of water, and with great difficulty brought him safely ashore. **1899.**

OCTOBER 28

V.C. Hon. Major James Miller, **Ordnance Department, Bengal.** Saved the life of Lieutenant Glubb, who was severely wounded, by carrying him out of action near Agra, and was subsequently wounded himself.

Mutiny. 1857.

Royal National Lifeboat Institution's Gold Medal to Captain J. A. W. O'Neil Torrens, Royal Scots Greys, who in the absence of the regular crew of the lifeboat collected a volunteer crew of soldiers, and went out through a gale in Dublin Bay to the assistance of a wrecked schooner near Pigeon House Fort. They succeeded in rescuing the only two members of the schooner's crew who were alive. **1881.**

OCTOBER 29

An old Yorkshireman drowned in trying to save a Child. At Siddals Bridge, seeing a little boy fall into the river Derwent, Samuel Simpson, aged 71, pulled off his coat and plunged in after the child. Some men with great difficulty brought the old man out, but he died of exhaustion before medical aid arrived. The child was drowned. **1851.**

London Fire Brigade Martyr. Martin E. Sprague, whilst engaged in searching for people reported to have been buried in the ruins of a house in New Church Court, Strand, was crushed to death by the collapse of the roof. His widow was pensioned by the Brigade. **1895.**

OCTOBER 30

V.C. Lieutenant-Colonel G. V. Fosbery, **4th Bengal European Regiment.** Inventor of the "Paradox" gun. (Died 1907.) Gazetted for fine courage in scaling a precipitous hill, where only a few could mount at a time, and in face of terrible odds recapturing the "Crag Picket."

V.C. Lieutenant and Adjutant H. W. Pitcher, **Bengal Staff Corps.** Displayed extreme gallantry in both the capture and re-capture of the "Crag Picket," being badly hit on the latter occasion. **Umbeyla, N.-W. India. 1863.**

V.C. Captain J. Norwood, **5th Dragoon Guards.** Rode back from a patrol party 300 yards, under heavy Boer fire, to a wounded trooper. Then dismounting, he carried the man on his back out of range, and remounting his horse—which he had been leading with his disengaged hand—went back to his troop. **Ladysmith, Boer War. 1899.**

A little Heroine of Twelve. Kate Griffiths, aged 12, with great pluck rescued Jennet E. Phillips from drowning at Croesor, Merioneth. **1900.**

October 31

A Cornwall Engine-driver's splendid Act. Thomas Cotterill, while in charge of the mail train from Falmouth to London, found that owing to a defective rail his entire train had left the metals near Penryn. The engine rolled over until it was completely upside down, but Cotterill clung on in order that he might shut off steam, and by so doing avert a serious danger to the passengers. His heroism cost him his life, for he was so fearfully scalded that he died the following day. **1898.**

Royal Humane Society's Silver Medals to Chief Officer Mr. G. D. Connell, and 4th Officer Mr. A. W. Webster, of the ss. *Chupra.* On the occasion of a fire in the hold of their vessel at Bombay, three natives who had gone down were overpowered by the fumes. Mr. Connell twice descended, each time bringing up one of the men, and a third time he went down, accompanied by Mr. Webster. He then lost consciousness and had to be brought up by the latter, who ventured again into the hold, and finally succeeded in bringing out the third man, who was, however, dead. **1906.**

NOVEMBER

"*Now Victory to our England,*
And where'er she lifts her hand
In Freedom's fight, to rescue Right,
God bless the dear old Land."

—GERALD MASSEY.

NOVEMBER

November 1

Two London work-a-day Heroes. John Dennell and John Fennell, two middle-aged labourers, lost their lives in a splendid effort to save a comrade, who had become senseless from foul gas, in a sewer at Compton Street, Goswell Road. All three were suffocated. **1852.**

Irish Lifeboat Disaster: Three Men lost. Galbraith H. Grills, chief officer of the coastguards, William M'Neill, and William M'Allister lost their lives when with the Portrush lifeboat going to the rescue of a schooner in distress. The lifeboat capsized three times in a tremendous sea, and was finally driven ashore near Port Ballintrae. **1889.**

"There needs not a great soul to make a hero; there needs be a God-created soul which will be true to its origin—that will be a great soul!"—*Carlyle.*

November 2

Four Volunteer Lifeboatmen drowned at Scarborough. Lord Charles Beauclerc, Mr. W. Tindall, T. Brewster, and John Burton were crushed to death or drowned in a fearful hurricane, while endeavouring to save life on volunteer lifeboat service in Scarborough harbour. **1861.**

Heroism in a Lancashire Colliery. On the occasion of a fire in the Nut Grove Colliery, St. Helens, John Campbell, William Naylor, and William Foster, with heroic devotion, went through dense sulphurous smoke in order to warn the miners of their peril. All three were overcome by the vitiated atmosphere, which even on the following day was so foul that several gentlemen who ventured in search of the gallant fellows became insensible, and had to be taken up to the surface. **1868.**

Seven gallant Seamen drowned off Santander while engaged in Rescue Work. "It is with sorrow that I communicate the death by drowning of seven brave Englishmen, who fell a sacrifice to their self-devotion in trying to save the crew of the Spanish schooner *Union*, which was wrecked yesterday at the entrance to this port. These heroes manned the *Minos* lifeboat, on hearing that a vessel was in distress, and proceeded to the rescue. It was blowing a fearful gale from the Atlantic upon the doomed barque, which was still afloat, but in the midst of the breakers, clinging desperately to her moorings. She was going to pieces and the crew were perishing, as the devoted band of brave Englishmen approached the frail craft. They paused a minute on the edge of the surf, and then, taking advantage of a momentary lull, dashed in to save; but, alas! all perished. The weight and strength of the sea were too great. A huge wave threw the boat against the wreck, and nothing more was seen of her crew."—Letter from the English Vice-Consul at Santander sent to *The Times*, November 3rd. The names of the heroic men were: George Freeman, master of the *Minos*, of Liverpool; William Smith, master of the *Woolsington*, of Newcastle; J. M. Reed, John Parkes, A. Thomas, seamen; and Messrs. Webb and Brookes, divers. **1871.**

"So you who are snug in your homes, when you hear the signal-gun's call,
Just give a thought to the men who may be bidding good-bye to their all;
Who go forth on their errand of mercy, to succour those in need,
To battle with the wind and wave, and the raging ocean's greed."

—*Will Nicholls, Son of a Lifeboat Coxswain.*

NOVEMBER 3

Suffolk Boatman gives his Life in an Attempt to save a Boy. Thomas Cable, jun., of the Coastguard Service, who had always been conspicuous for bravery in saving life, perished while trying to rescue a boy who had been left behind on a brig wrecked at Low Lightbeach, Aldborough, when the rest of the crew were saved. The noble fellow tied a rope round his body, and dashed through the raging sea in a terrific gale to the lad's rescue, whom he succeeded in reaching; but the rope then broke, and Cable was carried under the ship's bottom and instantly crushed to death. **1855.**

Royal Humane Society's Bronze Medals to Commander H. Edwards, R.N., and A.B. James Mutch, of H.M.S. *Agamemnon*, for bravery in plunging overboard at midnight in the Downs and rescuing a man who had fallen from the ship. **1908.**

Carnegie Hero Fund. £5 awarded to Police-Sergeant J. Cullen, of Langford, near Bristol, who received injuries from the wheel of a cart to which a runaway horse was attached. Cullen, at the risk of his life, succeeded in checking the animal's career before he was dragged down and run over. By his prompt and fearless act, a number of children playing in the roadway were saved. **1908.**

NOVEMBER 4

Albert Medal of the Second Class to John Dineen, Chief Mate of the ss. *Albatross*, of London, for gallantly rescuing a shipwrecked crew who were stranded on the Tongue Sand. **1888.**

Miss Florence Nightingale reached on this date Scutari, where her noble work on behalf of our soldiers began. Miss Nightingale is happily still among the survivors of that campaign, in which our men suffered untold agony from lack of sufficient accommodation for the sick, wounded, and dying. **1854.**

"SANTA PHILOMENA"
(Saint Nightingale)

Lo! in that house of misery
A lady with a lamp I see,
Pass through the glimmering gloom,
And flit from room to room.

And slow, as in a dream of bliss,
The speechless sufferer turns to kiss
Her shadow, as it falls
Upon the darkening walls.

. . . .

On England's annals, through the long
Hereafter of her speech and song,
That light its rays shall cast
From portals of the past.

A Lady with a Lamp shall stand
In the great history of the land,
A noble type of good
Heroic womanhood.

—*H. W. Longfellow.*

Death of a Sussex Lifeboatman. Edward Robust was drowned at Winchelsea through the capsizing of the lifeboat, which was on its way to the assistance of a wreck. The boat righted, and the rest of the crew got back into her; but Robust, who tried to swim ashore, was drowned. The crew were eventually brought off the wreck with great difficulty. **1882.**

November 5

BATTLE OF INKERMANN: EIGHTEEN VICTORIA CROSSES AWARDED

V.C. Midshipman E. St. John Daniel, **R.N.** Gazetted for many deeds of indomitable pluck, of which one was that of bringing in powder from a wagon under severe fire, and another that of saving the life of Captain Peel, V.C. (see October 18).

V.C. Seaman J. H. Gorman, **R.N.** (Died 1889.)
V.C. Seaman T. Reeves, **R.N.**
V.C. Seaman M. Scholefield, **R.N.**

Three survivors out of five naval heroes, who mounted a *banquette* under furious fire, and by loading the rifles of disabled soldiers kept up a sharp hail of bullets on the Russians.

V.C. Captain A. Henry, **R.A.** In conjunction with a gunner named Taylor, who was killed, defended a gun against a host of the enemy, who closed upon them and bayonetted them. Although stabbed by twelve hideous thrusts, Henry recovered. Six months later he was promoted to the rank of captain.

V.C. Lieutenant-Colonel F. Miller, **R.A.** For a splendid defence of a gun which was in danger of capture by an overwhelming force of Russians.

V.C. Colour-Sergeant J. Prettyjohn, **R.M.L.I.** (Died 1887.) Went alone ahead of the men and opened fire, killing four Russians, thus checking the approach of the main body.

V.C. Colonel Lord Percy, **Grenadier Guards.** "Esperance en Dieu." Gazetted for splendid gallantry at the "Sandbag" Battery. Also, later in the engagement, rallied a number of men of various regiments who were short of ammunition, and led them through severe fire to where a fresh supply was obtained.

V.C. Lieut.-Colonel Sir Charles Russell, Bart., **Grenadier Guards.** "Promptus."

V.C. Captain A. Palmer, **Grenadier Guards.** With another V.C. hero named Norman (see December 19), and a gallant man named Bailey, dislodged a party of Russians from the "Sandbag" Battery, where Palmer saved Sir Charles Russell's life. Bailey was the first man inside, but was killed.

"For the Colonel rides before,
The Major's on the flank,
The Captains and the Adjutant
Are in the foremost rank;
But when it's 'Action front!'
And there's fighting to be done,
Come one, come all, you stand or fall
By the man who carries the gun."

—*Arthur Conan Doyle.*

V.C. General Sir Mark Walker, K.C.B., **Cambridgeshire Regiment.** (Died 1902.) "Vincit veritas." In a dense fog this young soldier (then a lieutenant) led his company with fixed bayonets straight into two heavy columns of Russian infantry, who were so panic-stricken by the furious onslaught of the little band of Englishmen that they fled.

V.C. General Sir Hugh Rowlands, K.C.B., C.B., **41st (Welsh Regiment).** (Died 1909.) "A soldier of whom the Welsh nation felt proud."—*Daily Telegraph*, August 2, 1909. For a brilliant defence of a picket under severe fire, and for saving—in conjunction with Private McDermond, V.C.—Colonel Hely, who was lying wounded and hemmed in by the enemy.

V.C. Private J. McDermond, **47th (Lancashire).** Assisted General Rowlands in rescuing Colonel Hely by killing the Russian who had rendered him *hors de combat.*

V.C. Sergeant-Major A. Madden, **41st (Welsh Regiment).** With a small party captured a Russian officer and fourteen men.

V.C. Sergeant G. Walters, **49th (Royal Berks).** Decorated for the plucky rescue of Brigadier-General Adams from a perilous position.

V.C. Private T. Beach, **55th (Border Regiment).** Rescued Colonel Carpenter, who was wounded, from the Russians, two of whom he despatched.

V.C. Major-General the Hon. Sir H. H. Clifford, K.C.M.G., **Rifle Brigade.** "Semper paratus." In addition to saving a soldier's life, led a dashing charge, thus driving the enemy back.

V.C. Private John Byrne, **68th (Durham Light Infantry).** After the retreat was sounded turned back and carried a disabled comrade into safety. Also distinguished himself in May 1855.

Bugler Thomas Keep, **Grenadier Guards,** aged 10 (not gazetted). While the long stubborn battle raged, with shells bursting all around him, set to work, built a fire, and made a quantity of tea. Armed with his pannikin, the plucky little red-coated figure flitted here and there carrying warm, refreshing drink to our maimed and stricken soldiers. Perhaps this tiny, humble hero may take precedence of many others in records not of man's making or rewarded by earthly badges.

Crimean War. 1854.

"We gathered round the tent-fire in the evening cold and gray,
And thought of those who ranked with us in Battle's rough array,
Our Comrades of the morn who came no more from that fell fray!
The salt tears wrung out in the gloom of green dells far away—
The eyes of lurking Death that in Life's crimson bubbles play—
The stern, white faces of the Dead that on the dark ground lay
Like Statues of Old Heroes, cut in precious human clay—
Some with a smile as life had stopped to music proudly gay—
The household Gods of many a heart all dark and dumb to-day!
And hard hot eyes grew ripe for tears, and hearts sank down to pray."

—*Gerald Massey.*

Devonshire Lifeboat Work. While a demonstration was taking place in Torbay, with the town and shipping illuminated, on the occasion of laying the foundation stone of a monument to William III., signal lights were shown by the *Gwen Jones* schooner, and these were mistaken at first for part of the festivities. A gale was blowing, accompanied by a very high sea, and the coastguard on duty made out that the vessel was labouring heavily and was signalling for assistance. The lifeboat, therefore, put off to the rescue, and succeeded in taking off the schooner's crew of four men. **1889.**

NOVEMBER 6

London Fire Brigade Silver Medal to Samuel Eade, who, at a fire in Commercial Road, London, finding a child on the second floor, carried it to the window and passed it down the escape. While making a further search flames enveloped the fire-escape, and Eade, carrying a second child whom he had discovered, was obliged to force his way down the burning staircase. **1892.**

Carnegie Hero Fund. £40 awarded to William J. Clark, who contracted a severe attack of typhoid fever as the result of immersion in the foul water of the river Lee at Cork. Mr. Clark, fully clothed, sprang from the ss. *Nugget*, of which he was first mate, and rescued a little boy who was being carried away by the current. The child also had typhoid, but both ultimately recovered. **1908.**

NOVEMBER 7

V.C. Major H. Z. C. Cockburn, **Royal Canadian Dragoons.**

V.C. Lieutenant-Colonel R. E. W. Turner, D.S.O., **Royal Canadian Dragoons.**

V.C. Major E. J. Holland, **Royal Canadian Dragoons.**

Three gallant Canadians whose deeds at Komati River equalled any achieved by sons of the Mother Country in her hour of adversity. Major Cockburn with a few men kept a large number of Boers at bay, and saved the guns, which were in jeopardy, the whole of his valorous little band being killed or wounded. Colonel Turner accomplished a similar feat while suffering from two severe wounds. Major Holland gave splendid help, and when one of the guns was in such peril that there was no time to bring it in on its carriage, lifted it bodily, and carried it, under terrible fire, into safety.

Boer War. 1900.

A Yorkshire Boy drowned in trying to save his Mother. While getting water from the river Rother at Woodhouse, near Sheffield, Mrs. Dunn fell in. Her son Harry, aged 15, who could not swim, rushed to her assistance, but was forcibly restrained by a neighbour. At that moment the poor woman, who was being carried away by the strong current, called out, and the devoted son wrenched himself free, and struggled to reach his mother. The stream, however, was too powerful for him, and both sank. **1883.**

Splendid Rescue by heroic Welsh Quarrymen. When the *Ocean Queen* struck on the rocks opposite Llandulas quarry in a terrible gale, four workmen, named John Jones, John Roberts, and two named William Williams, after making six unsuccessful attempts to launch a small coble, at last reached the wreck, from which they brought the crew safely ashore. **1890.**

"Wake again, the harp of Wales,
As of yore!
Long as storm shall rend the sails,
And Atlantic billows roar,
Long as wrecks ashore are rolled
Shall your dauntless deed be told,
Gallant heroes of the quarry by the shore."

—"Ballads of Brave Deeds," *Canon Rawnsley.*

A gallant little Staffordshire Lad. Thomas H. Barker, aged 8, lost his life in an heroic effort to save his brother, aged 3, who had fallen into a pool at Weir Longton. The younger child was eventually saved by a man, but Tom sank and was drowned. **1898.**

November 8

V.C. Thomas A. Kavanagh, **Assistant Commissioner in Oude.** "Lucknow Kavanagh." (Died 1882.) The name of this civilian hero of the Victoria Cross has become a household word, and his magnificent feat will not soon be forgotten. Leaving Lucknow on this date (or November 9) disguised as a *bud-mash*, or native soldier, he went through a country swarming with ferocious and suspicious mutineers, to communicate news of vital importance to Sir James Outram. Knowing well the fearful risk he ran of being captured and put to death by the most fiendish and prolonged tortures the inhuman Sepoys could devise, he dared them all, and accomplished his heroic purpose. The disguise Mr. Kavanagh wore is treasured in the Dublin Museum as a memento of one of Ireland's bravest sons.

Mutiny. 1857.

A Yorkshireman gives his Life in attempting to save a Boy. Ernest Wookey, seeing a boy overcome by poisonous fumes fall from a ladder into an empty vinegar vat of 30,000 gallons' capacity, at the Victoria Vinegar Brewery, Sheffield, went down to his assistance; but, being himself overpowered by the noxious vapour, fell a distance of 25 feet, and perished before help could be given. **1900.**

Lloyd's Silver Medals to Mr. F. H. Gething, 2nd; and Mr. G. Parry, 3rd officer; also **Bronze Medals** to Boatswain W. Flynn, Able Seamen W. Morgan and F. Costello of the ss. *Don Hugo*, for extraordinary bravery and perseverance in saving life from a wrecked dredger

THE BRITISH GOVERNMENT'S MEDAL TO FOREIGNERS.

LLOYD'S MEDAL.

near Cape Roca. The lifeboat in which the rescue party went out was smashed, and all her crew cast into the water; whereupon life-lines with buoys were thrown from the steamer, and eventually all on the dredger, with one exception, were saved. **1908.**

NOVEMBER 9

Wexford Lifeboat Rescue. During a south-easterly gale, signals of distress were seen in the direction of the Dogger Bank, and with all haste the lifeboat was launched to render aid. When crossing the bar rough and broken seas were encountered, and the greatest difficulty was experienced in reaching the vessel, which proved to be the ketch *Elizabeth*, of Bude. The plucky lifeboatmen stuck to their task, however, and finally succeeded in rescuing the crew of three hands, together with their dog. **1906.**

Royal Humane Society's Bronze Medal to Lieutenant H. Greenwood, R.N., of H.M.S. *Vernon*, for pluckily jumping into the sea at the entrance to Portsmouth harbour, and supporting a fisherman (who had been thrown into the water after the sinking of his boat) until they were both picked up. **1908.**

NOVEMBER 10

V.C. Private F. Wheatley, **Rifle Brigade.** One of eight men who were gazetted for the perilous feat of picking up a live shell and throwing it out of danger.

Sevastopol, Crimea. 1854.

Lifeboat Catastrophe: Gorleston Crew lose Four Men. William Whiley, Edward Drene, Aaron George, and Alfred Woods were drowned after rendering assistance to the ss. *Akaba*, the lifeboat *Refuge* having been dashed against the steamer, deprived of her rudder, and capsized in Yarmouth harbour. The state of the weather at the time may be judged by the fact that as the *Refuge* was lying alongside the *Akaba* a terrific sea *lifted her right on to the deck of the latter.* **1888.**

Carnegie Hero Fund. Award to the widow of James Lyttle, who was killed while removing an obstruction from the line in Ireland to avoid a catastrophe to an oncoming train. He left a widow and six young children. **1908.**

November 11

Albert Medal of the Second Class to Lawrence Hennessy, R.N., who saved four lives from a schooner, totally wrecked in a tremendous gale at Seabrook at 4.45 A.M. He accomplished many gallant feats the same day, and at 9 P.M. took out the lifeboat to a wreck near Folkestone, from which 27 lives were saved. **1891.**

Five Heroes of the Merchant Service drowned. While going in a boat to search for Peter Conway, carpenter of the *Rokeby Hall*, who had fallen overboard, the following men were drowned by the swamping of their craft by a huge wave: J. W. Spencer, mate; W. Paton, M. Ryan, B. Stevens, seamen; and W. P. Eddy, apprentice. Another boat was launched, but it was too late to save any of the victims. **1877.**

Two Kentish Coastguardsmen drowned on Volunteer Lifeboat Service. In a fearful storm, with the waves

NOVEMBER

Hugh Rowlands

Florence Nightingale

E. J. Holland
Major

R. E. W. Turner
Lieut Col.

T. Henry Kavanagh

John Paton VC

Nowell Salmon

F. D. M. Brown

running mountains high, a vessel was seen making signals of distress off Littlestone; and in the absence of the regular lifeboat crew, Daniel Nicoll and Henry Reeves, with other volunteers, put out in the coastguard lifeboat to the rescue, but their frail craft capsized in the raging sea. Nicoll and Reeves lost their lives, while the rest of the gallant volunteers were rescued in an exhausted condition. The dead men were buried with full military honours. **1891.**

November 12

Albert Medal of the First Class to Dr. David Lawson, who nearly lost his life from an attack of diphtheria, contracted while sucking out the mucus accumulated in the trachea of a child. **1880.**

Albert Medal of the Second Class to Pioneer David T. Davies, and also to Sergeants Henry Pickersgill and William Wilson, Coldstream Guards, in recognition of bravery displayed on the occasion of a fire in Wellington Barracks, London. **1890.**

London Fire Brigade Silver Medals to John Snow and Samuel Ross, who rescued two children from the top floor in Wellington Barracks by passing them down the fire-escape. Ross was so terribly burned that he died. **1890.**

November 13

"The Men who never turn back." Magnificent heroism of Norfolk Lifeboatmen in the Caister Disaster. Nine lives lost. Gold Medal of the R.N.L.I. presented by the King to James Haylett, aged 78. During a terrific storm the crew of the lifeboat *Beauchamp*, of Caister, made repeated efforts to put off to the aid of a distressed fishing-boat near Barber Sand. It was three hours before she was finally launched, and no more was seen of her for four hours; then cries were heard, and those who had been waiting saw the *Beauchamp* being washed inshore keel upwards. As she came nearer a tremendous wave tossed the doomed boat high in the air, and the faces of her crew could then be seen. Regardless of danger, brave rescuers dashed through the billows, clutching at the drowning men, and eight lives were saved; but the gunwale of the boat was driven into the soft sand, pinning down several helpless victims. Foremost among the rescuers was James Haylett, aged 78, a former coxswain, who had remained on watch, wet through and without food, after toiling with those who launched the *Beauchamp* on her fatal voyage. The gallant veteran plunged into the sea and succeeded in saving two men, one being his son-in-law. This splendid old hero, who had seen half a century's lifeboat service and saved hundreds of lives, had five near relatives in the boat, of whom three perished. **1901.**

THE OLD COXSWAIN'S MOTTO

In Memoriam Caister Lifeboat Disaster
13th and 14th November 1901

("The Caister men never turn back." As reported at the Inquest, 15th November.)

(*The old Coxswain speaks*)—

"What is this we have done? Why, our duty, and nothing more—
Our sons will do it again, as their fathers have done before.
It is not for the sake of bragging; we are sailors, one and all—
They signalled peril out yonder, and we—we answered the call;

For in face of the storm, in face of the wind, in face of the rising
flood,
We Caister men never turn back. For why? It is not in the
blood.

. . . .

I have fought in a hundred fights when battling with the sea,
They are gone, the young and strong ones, but to live in our
memory;
Here they sleep by the wind-swept shore to the dirge of the
moaning waves,
And the Country's tears are the blossoms let fall on the Caister
graves.

They say that the sea is cruel; they may be right or wrong—
It is not for us to think—we are bound to be hale and strong.
Aye, sir, I've paid my tribute, and I humbly bows my head;
But I keep a good lookout to seaward, for the sake of them that
is dead.
Aye, I'm proud of our Caister manhood, I'm proud of such acts
of love,
When I think of the names recorded in the Log Book up above;
And I'm proud of the words you quote, in the name of myself
and crew,
But not because I spoke them, but because them words is true!
For in face of the storm, in face of the wind, in face of the rising
flood,
We Caister men never turn back. For why? It is not in the
blood!"

November 1901. —*R. Andre.*

London Fire Brigade Silver Medal to William Wright for conspicuous bravery in saving three lives at a fire in Blackheath Road. **1880.**

NOVEMBER 14

V.C. General Sir John Watson, G.C.B., **Punjab Cavalry.** "In recto decus." Was severely wounded during a fierce fight with the leader of a large force of Sepoy cavalry, whom he defeated. **Lucknow, Mutiny. 1857.**

A gallant Derbyshire Man. Samuel Andrews of the Pyebridge Chemical Works, Alfreton, lost his life in trying to rescue two workmen from suffocation in a tar still. Two other men narrowly escaped a similar fate, being rescued only just in time. **1893.**

An heroic Gloucestershire Waterman. Charles Cullimore and several companions were crossing the mud on the Bristol shore of the Severn to reach their boat, when the flood tide swamped and drowned several of them. Cullimore could easily have escaped, but remained to help his friend, Thomas Jordan, who could not get along, and perished with him. **1902.**

November 15

London Fire Brigade Silver Medal to Charles Foster, who, at the risk of his own life, saved three others at a fire in St. Dunstan's Hill, City. **1877.**

Lifeboat Rescue Work at Southend, Cantyre. The lighter *Gnome* having lost her rudder during a stiff gale, was drifting helplessly before the wind, and her only boat was smashed by the terrible sea. The lifeboat *John R. Kerr* put off to her assistance, and found the rolling sea breaking right over her. With great difficulty the crew were rescued, the operation lasting nearly twenty-four hours. **1902.**

"I laugh at the storm whose shadowy form
Raves shrieking in my ear;
And the flying scud as it fires my blood—
The Lifeboat knows no fear!
And I face the blast, a sail at my mast,
I rush through the angry foam;
Like a bird I soar, o'er the ocean's roar—
The seething sea 's my home."
—"The Lifeboat," *Harold E. Jones, M.D.*

NOVEMBER 16

SECOND RELIEF OF LUCKNOW.

V.C. Admiral of the Fleet Sir Nowell Salmon, G.C.B., **R.N.** (Born 1835.)

V.C. Boatswain's mate John Harrison, **R.N.** (Died 1865.)

These naval heroes, by climbing a tree at the Shah Nujjiff under furious fire, poured down such a hail of lead on the enemy below that the place was shortly captured.

EIGHT HEROES OF THE SECUNDRA BAGH.

V.C. Major Sir W. G. D. Stewart, Bart., **93rd (Argyll and Sutherland).** "Virescit vulnare virtus."

V.C. Sergeant J. Paton, **93rd (Argyll and Sutherland).**

V.C. Colour-Sergeant J. Munro, **93rd (Argyll and Sutherland).**

V.C. Private D. Mackay, **93rd (Argyll and Sutherland).**

V.C. Private J. Kenny, **53rd (Shropshire Light Infantry).**

V.C. Private C. Irwin, **53rd (Shropshire Light Infantry).**

V.C. Sergeant S. Hill, **90th (Scottish Rifles).**

V.C. Private J. Smith, **102nd (Madras Fusiliers).**

Of the above eight, six were selected under Rule XIII. of the Victoria Cross Warrant.

Major Stewart, by a brilliant charge, captured two guns.

Paton crawled, under murderous fire, to a wall where he discovered a breach; and it was through this that the relieving troops entered. This brave non-commissioned officer's career is perhaps unique, he having taken part in thirty-one engagements from February 1854 to March 1858. He was in the "thin red line" which faced the Russians at Balaklava.

Kenny carried ammunition under appalling cross-fire.

Irwin, though badly hit in the shoulder, was one of

the first to force a passage into the building under fearful fire.

Munro and Hill each saved an officer's life.

Smith's prowess was similar to that displayed by Irwin.

Mackay, after a desperate struggle with the mutineers, captured two of their standards.

V.C. Commander T. J. Young, **R.N.** Recommended by Captain Peel, V.C., for the Decoration, for intrepid valour at the attack on the Shah Nujjiff.

V.C. A.B. William Hall, **R.N. (Naval Brigade).** Served with conspicuous courage with the guns at the attack on the Shah Nujjiff. One of the three coloured men decorated with the Victoria Cross.

V.C. Lieutenant-General J. C. Guise, C.B., **90th (Scottish Rifles).** (Died 1895.) Displayed superb courage on many occasions, and was selected under Rule XIII. of the Victoria Cross Warrant by about forty officers to receive the trophy "For Valour."

V.C. Lieutenant A. K. Ffrench, **53rd (Shropshire Light Infantry).**

V.C. Lance-Corporal J. Dunley, **93rd (Argyll and Sutherland).**

V.C. Private P. Grant, **93rd (Argyll and Sutherland).**

V.C. Gunner J. Park, **Bengal Artillery.**

Elected under Rule XIII. Lieutenant Ffrench was one of the first to enter the Secundra Bagh, he being in command of a Grenadier company.

Dunley protected Captain Burroughs against a crowd of rebels.

Grant saved Colonel Ewart's life after the latter had captured a colour.

Park likewise displayed exceptional valour.

V.C. Lieutenant F. D. M. Brown, **European Bengal Fusiliers.** "Est concordia fratrum." Seeing a wounded soldier of his regiment lying within fifty yards of the mutineer cavalry, ran to the spot and carried the man into shelter. **Mutiny. 1857.**

"Still stand thy ruins 'neath the Indian sky,
Memorials eloquent of blood and tears!
Oh! for the spirit of those days gone by
To wake a strain amid these later years
Worthy of thee and thine! I seem to see,
When thinking on thy consecrated dead,
From thy scarred chambers start
The heroes whom thy fiery travail bred
And made thee—for us English—what thou art!"
—*J. R. Denning.*

Albert Medal of the Second Class to Inspector Cullinan for jumping on to the four-foot way at Ennis Station, Ireland, and into the six foot, dragging a woman whose clothing had already been caught by an approaching train. **1905.**

London Fire Brigade Silver Medal to A. Saftery—so seriously burned that he lost the power of speech for several days, after ascending a fire-escape enveloped in smoke to rescue a man from the second floor of a burning house in Bermondsey Street. A stream of water had to be directed upon the escape as the heroic fireman descended with his prize. **1906.**

NOVEMBER 17

V.C. Ensign Pye, **3rd (Shropshire Light Infantry).** Carried ammunition under fearful fire at Lucknow, and was noted for steady and brave conduct on many occasions throughout the terrible siege.

V.C. Private P. Graham, **90th (Scottish Rifles).** Under heavy fire at Lucknow carried a wounded comrade into shelter. **Mutiny. 1857.**

Albert Medal of the Second Class to Captain Herbert C. French, R.A.M.C., for diving 36 feet from H.M.S. *Wakool* in the Straits of Malacca (infested by sharks and water snakes) to rescue a fireman who had jumped overboard. Both were subsequently picked up in an exhausted condition. **1902.**

NOVEMBER 18

V.C. Lieutenant-Colonel T. B. Hackett, **23rd (Royal Welsh Fusiliers).** "Virtute et fidelitate."

V.C. Private G. Monger, **23rd (Royal Welsh Fusiliers).** Seeing a young corporal of their regiment lying wounded under heavy fire, the above pair rushed to the rescue, and carried the man into cover. Later in the day Lieut.-Col. Hackett climbed on to the roof of a burning bungalow, and, under fierce, concentrated fire, extinguished the flames by tearing off the thatch, and so prevented the fire spreading generally. **Lucknow, Mutiny. 1857.**

Order of St. John of Jerusalem in England: Bronze Medal to James Bridge, a railway porter, for an extremely fine effort at Birscough Junction to save the life of another porter who had slipped and fallen stunned in front of a train travelling at fifty miles an hour. The man was killed by the engine, and Bridge, who had jumped on to the metals and tried to pull him out of danger, escaped by a hairsbreadth. **1907.**

NOVEMBER 19

A Leicestershire Mother's last Act of Love. Mrs. S. Wilcox, while crossing some flooded land with her seven-year-old boy in her arms, was swept off her feet and drowned. The child was washed against a post in a shallow spot, and was found unconscious, but recovered. 1883.

A Posse of Medical Heroes in Ireland. Dr. William Smyth, medical officer to the Burton-Port Dispensary district, County Donegal, gave his life in heroic efforts to save those of his patients suffering from typhus fever on the island of Arranmore. Each day he rowed alone four miles across the stormy waters to visit the wretched victims of the epidemic, who were huddled three and four in a bed in hovels so dark that in some cases he had to carry a candle to find them. In the utter absence of ventilation and sanitation, the only hope for the wretched people lay in removing them to the mainland for proper nursing. But no one would lend the doctor a boat large enough, or help him, owing to the terror of contagion, until Dr. Brendon McCarthy, Medical Inspector to the Local Government Board, arrived. These two devoted men brought the typhus-stricken people down to the beach, embarked with them on a crazy boat, and rowed them across the Sound. The boat sank five minutes after her arrival, but the patients were landed safely, and nearly all recovered. Of the two gallant men who faced the double danger of pestilence and drowning, one (Dr. Smyth) fell a victim to the disease from which he saved so many, and died on this day, leaving a widow and eight young children. His predecessor, Dr. John A. Spencer, had died on September 3, 1882, under exactly similar circumstances; and two other Donegal doctors, viz. Dr. Charles Doherty and Dr. O'Sullivan, also died of typhus fever contracted in the discharge of their duties, the former in Glenties Fever Hospital on December 12, 1897, and the latter at Ardura, on June 7, 1898. 1901.

NOVEMBER 20

V.C. Colonel Sir. W. J. M. Cuninghame, Bart., **Rifle Brigade.** "Fortitudine." For distinguished gallantry at the Russian rifle-pits. Took part in the battles of Alma, Balaklava, and Inkermann.

V.C. Colonel C. T. Bourchier, **Rifle Brigade.** When Lieutenant Tryon fell, this young soldier—then a lieutenant himself—took command, and led his men to the "wasps' nests."

V.C. Lieutenant-General Sir W. O. Lennox, K.C.B., **R.E.** Was complimented by the French officer, Maréchal Canrobert, for his "cool and gallant conduct" in repelling the enemy's repeated attacks.

Rifle-pits, Sevastopol, Crimea. 1854.

V.C. Colonel A. F. Picard, C.B., **R.A.**
V.C. Lieutenant-Colonel W. Temple, B.A., M.B., **R.A.**
Displayed extreme courage during the attack on Rangiriri, where they saved many wounded men from the Maoris, both heroes having to traverse the entrance to the Keep under an avalanche of fire. **New Zealand. 1863.**

Albert Medals of the First Class to Captain Peter Sharp and John B. McIntosh, who were fearfully injured by the flames caused by a terrible explosion of petroleum aboard a French vessel near Bayonne, towards which they had taken a boat in the hope of saving any survivors. The mate of the vessel sprang overboard from the flaming craft, and was picked up by this noble pair.

1878.

A Kentish Volunteer drowned on Lifeboat Rescue Work. During a hurricane of great severity, a barque

NOVEMBER

[illegible]

W. Temple M.B.
Lieut. Colonel

H. N. D. Prendergast

R. K. Ridgeway
Colonel

Francis Chandler

Francis Fitzpatrick

Thomas Flawn V.C.

sent up signals of distress, in response to which the Dungeness lifeboat was launched in a heavy sea. In spite of their efforts, the fury of the gale drove them wide of the barque, and the boat had to be run ashore west of Dungeness. A volunteer crew of coastguards and fishermen then got out the R. A. O. Buffaloes' Lifeboat, and dragged her over the shingle to the windward of the doomed ship. She had just reached the barque when a terrific sea capsized her. Five men managed to get back into the boat when she righted herself, others being dashed ashore by the furious waves; but one man, John S. Barrett, aged 34, lost his life. A second crew manned the boat, but the storm beat her ashore. Finally the Dover lifeboat, which had been telegraphed for, succeeded in rescuing the crew of the stranded vessel.

1893.

NOVEMBER 21

V.C. General Sir H. N. D. Prendergast, G.C.B., **Royal (Madras) Engineers.** Decorated for several acts of intrepidity, one of which was the saving of Lieutenant Dew from a mutineer at Mundisore, in accomplishing which deed the brave young officer was severely wounded.

Mutiny. 1857.

Lancashire Lad drowned in trying to save a Companion. Several boys were playing on some ice at Stanley, near Liverpool, when it broke, and they were all immersed. William Hunt went to assist one of them, when the ice again gave way, and both he and the boy he tried to save were drowned. The other lads got safely ashore. **1880.**

Carnegie Hero Fund Bronze Medallion and £5 to a fisherman named Thomas Herkes, who saved a woman from drowning in Victoria Harbour, Dunbar, at midnight. This is the brave fisherman's sixth rescue.

1908.

NOVEMBER 22

V.C. Sergeant T. Grady, **4th (Royal Lancaster).** With another man, repaired a breach under heavy fire, his companion in this act not being gazetted. He also showed great courage in remaining on duty while severely wounded, in order to encourage his comrades in preventing the guns from being spiked. **Crimea. 1854.**

V.C. Midshipman A. Mayo, **R. (Indian) N.** At Dacca, under terrible fire, headed a charge against two guns, which he captured. Mr. Mayo was only 17 years of age when gazetted, there being only one younger hero to receive the honour, viz. Drummer Magner, aged 14. (See April 13.)

V.C. Lieutenant H. E. Harrington, **Bengal Artillery.** (Died 1861.)

V.C. Gunner T. Laughnan, **Bengal Artillery.**

V.C. Gunner H. McInnes, **Bengal Artillery.**

V.C. Rough-rider E. Jennings, **Bengal Artillery.**

All elected under Rule XIII. of the Victoria Cross Warrant for conspicuous bravery at Lucknow.

Mutiny. 1857.

V.C. Colonel R. K. Ridgeway, C.B., **Bengal Staff Corps.** Was severely wounded in the shoulder while making a fine attempt to destroy a barricade at Naga Hills.

India. 1879.

V.C. Private C. T. Kennedy, **Highland Light Infantry.** Was severely wounded while carrying a message across an open space swept by terrible fire. This brave man had previously saved a comrade's life by carrying him nearly a mile under fire to shelter. He was killed in 1907 while trying to stop a runaway horse. **Boer War. 1900.**

Edward Medal of the Second Class to Henry Benton, a miner, of Denaby, Yorkshire, for conspicuous heroism at Cadeby Colliery. He was directly responsible for saving the life of a fellow-workman named Green, when hundreds of tons of the pit roofing fell in. **1908.**

Yorkshire Miner suffocated after saving Three Lives. Joseph Mitchell, aged 55, lost his life at Messrs. Day & Twibell's Colliery, Barnsley, when trying to save some of his mates after an explosion which caused thirteen deaths. Mitchell had succeeded in saving three lives, when, on again descending, he was overcome by the noxious fumes, and died before reaching the fresh air. **1841.**

NOVEMBER 23

V.C. Captain L. C. Maygar, **Victorian Mounted Rifles.** (Born 1871.) Seeing a man dismounted and in great peril, took him up on his own horse, which bolted. Lieutenant Maygar (as he then was), having secured the horse, placed the other man on it and made his own way to shelter on foot. **Geelhoutboom, Boer War. 1901.**

Edward Medal of the First Class to Francis Chandler for his great bravery in saving life in a disaster which occurred at the Hoyland Silkstone Colliery. Chandler, who is 60 years of age, was engaged with five others in repairing an underground boiler-house, when a fall of roof took place, which broke an iron girder and damaged the boiler, from which there was at once a tremendous rush of steam. All the men were scalded or hurt; one was killed on the spot, and three others died afterwards. Every lamp was extinguished; and, although badly hurt, Chandler crept three times in the dark through the steam, at the risk of his own life, to rescue others who could not move. He then went to the surface for rescuers, whom he led to the scene of the disaster. One of Chandler's sons was killed, and a second was seriously injured on this occasion. This was the first award of the Edward Medal, "The Miners' V.C." **1907.**

Surrey Nurseryman suffocated in trying to save Life. Charles Mason lost his life at Windlesham, near Bagshot, while attempting to rescue a well-sinker, who had become unconscious owing to foul air. Both men were suffocated, and a brother of Mason, who also went down to them, would have shared the same fate, had he not taken the precaution to tie a rope round his body, by which he was hauled to the surface insensible, recovering afterwards. **1869.**

A Mate killed in trying to save the Crew of his Vessel. T. H. Wolcott, of the ss. *Uppingham* of London, lost his life in a splendid attempt to swim ashore with a line, when his ship struck on the rocks below Hartland Quay, North Devon, during a violent gale. The waves were so terrific when Wolcott plunged in that he was literally dashed to pieces on the rocks. Many of the crew were saved later by means of the rocket apparatus and boats. **1890.**

NOVEMBER 24

Two Northumberland Lifeboatmen drowned. Edmund Robson and James Grant lost their lives in a terrific gale, while on duty in the Tynemouth lifeboat.

1864.

London Fire Brigade Silver Medal to Samuel Goodall, this being the last of three occasions on which the heroic fireman displayed great bravery, saving in all eight lives.

1878.

"Life is a leaf of paper white
Whereon each one of us may write
His word or two, and then comes night.
Greatly begin, though thou have time
But for a line—be that sublime;
Not failure, but low aim is crime."

—*Lowell.*

NOVEMBER 25

A Naval Lieutenant's Heroic Death. Lieutenant W. P. L. Heyland, R.N., possessor of silver and bronze medals for saving life on two occasions, met his death through jumping overboard from H.M.S. *Minotaur* to rescue a drowning man in a heavy sea. Lieutenant Heyland had succeeded in giving the man a line, and was himself trying to seize a Jacob's ladder which had been lowered to him, when a tremendous sea washed over him. Torpedo-Instructor Triggs pluckily descended the ladder and hauled up the man who had fallen overboard, but the gallant young officer perished. **1880.**

Wreck of the *Sardinia*: Board of Trade and Liverpool S. & H. Society's Silver Medals, and many other acknowledgments, to Miss Kate Gilmour, stewardess, for her splendid bravery in saving life on the occasion of the burning of the ss. *Sardinia* at Malta. She was everywhere to be found where service was required, did all that was possible to help passengers and crew, and was the very last person to leave the vessel. **1908.**

NOVEMBER 26

Eleven gallant Worthing Fishermen. In Broadwater Churchyard, near Worthing, is a memorial to eleven gallant fishermen, who perished in a terrible storm, while going to the assistance of the *Lalla Rookh*, two miles from shore. **1850.**

NOVEMBER 27

Albert Medal of the First Class to Ronald Maclean (gazetted in 1890), for a long course of magnificent rescue work from 1872 to 1883, whereby he saved many lives from drowning. One fine case was that of going far into the boiling surf in a fearful gale to bring in the crew of a stranded barque on this date. **1872.**

Albert Medals of the Second Class to James K. Chapman and Thomas McCormack. While workmen were engaged painting the inside of an iron tank in a steamer lying in dry dock at Jarrow, a man named Graham was overcome by the fumes given off by the anti-corrosive paint, as also was Archibald Wilson, who attempted to save him. McCormack then went to Wilson's assistance, but was himself rendered insensible. James K. Chapman next entered the tank, and having pulled McCormack out, went in again after the others. He was, however, overcome by the fumes, but was eventually rescued, as also was Graham. Wilson, who first attempted the rescue, lost his life.

Carnegie Hero Fund Bronze Medals to T. McCormack and J. K. Chapman; also an award to the widow of Archibald Wilson. **1908.**

London Fire Brigade Silver Medal to G. Hellyer, who saved eight lives from a fire in Southwark. **1877.**

NOVEMBER 28

V.C. Drummer T. Flinn, **64th (N. Staffs).** While severely wounded made a splendid dash for the rebels' guns at Cawnpore, and courageously fought two of the rebel gunners. **Mutiny. 1857.**

V.C. Private F. Fitzpatrick, **Connaught Rangers.** Cross sold for £42 in 1906.

V.C. Private T. Flawn, **Connaught Rangers.**

Gazetted for rescuing Lieutenant J. C. Dewar—severely wounded—from about 40 of the enemy, armed with spears, who were in pursuit of them. One of these gallant Irishmen kept up a brisk fire on the savages, while the other carried the young officer into safety.

Sekukuni's Town, Basutoland. 1879.

"The soldier's trade, verily and essentially, is not slaying, but being slain. This, without well knowing its own meaning, the world honours it for . . . the reason it honours the soldier is because he holds his life at the service of the State. Reckless he may be—fond of pleasure or of adventure—all kinds of by-motives and mean impulses may have determined the choice of his profession, and may affect (to all appearances exclusively) his daily conduct in it; but our estimate of him is based on this ultimate fact—of which we are well assured—that put him in a fortress breach, with all the pleasures of the world behind him, and only death and his duty in front of him, he will keep his face to the front; and he knows that his choice may be put to him at any moment—and has beforehand taken his part—virtually takes such part daily—does in reality die daily."—*John Ruskin*, "The Roots of Honour: Unto this Last."

Albert Medal of the Second Class to Hereward Hewison for the splendid rescue of his brother from the teeth of a shark at New South Wales. He gallantly fought the monster off his victim. **1894.**

"Unarmed and naked, lion-brave,
He rushed to join the fierce, unequal fight;
Flashed back the water's crimson wave,
And robbed the ravening sea-hound of his right.

. . . .

Then, while the waves for joy broke loud,
He pushed his fainting brother safe ashore,
Nor knew a whole wide world was proud
Of him who dared, as sea-Kings dared of yore."
—"Ballads of Brave Deeds," *Canon H. D. Rawnsley.*

London Fire Brigade Silver Medals to Thomas Stoneman and William Gordon for a most gallant rescue of a woman and child at a fire in Farm Street, Goswell Road. **1883.**

A Kentish Foreman's heroic Death. Mr. Henry Hill, aged 60, lost his life in a gallant attempt to save some workmen who were overcome by carbonic acid gas in a limekiln at Borstal, near Rochester. **1902.**

NOVEMBER 29

Wells Lifeboat Tragedy: 11 out of a Crew of 13 drowned. Robert W. Elsdon, John Elsdon, Samuel Smith, Charles Smith, William Field, George Jay, William Green, Charles Hinds, John Stacy, Frank Abel, and William Wordingham, an hour after saving the crew of a wrecked vessel, went to the assistance of the brig *Ocean Queen*, which they were unable to reach owing to the falling tide. While sailing for the harbour a heavy sea capsized the lifeboat, which drifted on its side over 150 yards. Afterwards the boat righted, bringing one man (Bell) inside the boat, while the others, clinging outside, or struggling in the water, were unable to get in owing to the weight of their sea-boots and wet clothing. A man named Kew swam ashore in an exhausted state, but the others were drowned. The crew of the *Ocean Queen* walked ashore at low tide. **1880.**

Royal Humane Society's Bronze Medal to Hassan Ali Ghoraib, who swam ashore with a line, and was thereby the means of saving the whole crew of the tug-boat *Darfeel*, which went ashore at Ras-el-Ghain, on the coast of Tripoli. **1907.**

NOVEMBER 30

Albert Medal of the Second Class to John Donovan, R.N., for great pluck in saving life from a stranded barque at Courtmacshery Bay, Ireland. **1866.**

A Nurse's Heroism. Margaret A. Allen, a nurse from Westminster Hospital, volunteered for service during a severe outbreak of typhoid at Luton. After untiring devotion to the sufferers, just as the epidemic was dying out, she contracted the disease herself, and, utterly weakened and worn out by her noble self-sacrifice, died on this day. 1895.

"I was sick, and ye ministered unto Me."

Royal Humane Society's Bronze Medal to A.B. Thomas C. Spencer, who, on a dark night, sprang 30 feet into the shark-infested harbour of Freemantle, W. Australia, and swam to the landing-stage with a man who had fallen overboard. 1905.

DECEMBER

"Not once or twice in our rough island story
The path of duty was the way to glory."

—TENNYSON.

DECEMBER

DECEMBER 1

Postman's Park Hero and Martyr. Tablet 36. George F. Simonds, a general dealer, of Prebend Street, Islington, died from the effects of terrible injuries received while attempting to rescue an old woman, whom he thought had been left in a burning house in St. Peter's Street, but who had already escaped. **1886.**

Royal Humane Society's Bronze Medal to Private George Fidgett, 1st Battalion Royal Fusiliers, who, at great personal risk, rescued Lance-Corporal D. Firth from drowning in the river Nile at Manchea. **1886.**

DECEMBER 2

V.C. Captain J. Cook, **Bengal Staff Corps.** After leading a superb charge, under terrific fire, at Peiwar-Kotal, nearly lost his own life while saving another officer. He was mortally wounded the following year at Cabul.

Afghanistan. 1878.

V.C. Major-General F. J. Aylmer, C.B., **R.E.**
V.C. Major G. H. Boisragon, **Indian Staff Corps.**

Associated in two daring attempts, the last of which proved successful, to blow up the gate of Nilt Fort. Major-General (then Colonel) Aylmer was badly hit in the hand. Eventually, Major Boisragon collected a relief party, and the fort was captured. Major-General Aylmer also saved a life under exceptionally gallant circumstances at the relief of Chitral.

N.-W. India. 1891.

Albert Medal of the Second Class to Stoker James Sutherland, R.N., for exceptional bravery in rescuing a man from the hold of a torpedo-boat destroyer, which was full of steam and water. **1901.**

Kentish Lifeboat Tragedy: Nine Volunteers lay down their Lives. W. Cook, sen., W. Cook, jun., R. Cook, G. W. Ladd, H. R. Brockman, W. R. Gill, Y. B. Dyke, E. R. Crunder, and E. C. Koughton, who formed part of the volunteer crew of the Margate lifeboat *Friend of all Nations*, lost their lives by the capsizing of that boat while on her way to relieve the crew of a distressed vessel. Four men only managed to cling to the bottom of the boat, and were washed ashore with her. The *Friend of all Nations* had been out all the two previous days, and, in addition to saving life, had kept four vessels from destruction. Mr. Koughton was cashier at Lloyd's Bank, and superintendent of the Ambulance Brigade. Queen Victoria sent a message of sympathy and £35 towards the relief of the widows and orphans of the gallant men.

1897.

DECEMBER 3

A gallant Kentish Sailor. Henry King, a seaman, lost his life in helping to save the shipwrecked crew of an Aberdeen vessel, who had taken to a boat. A boat from his own brig—the *Rubicon*—put off to help the other, and all the men were saved, but King was washed overboard and drowned. **1867.**

A Lancashire Heroine. Jemima Isherwood, with her mother and sister, was on a frozen pond at Westleigh, near Bolton, when the ice broke and the latter fell through. The mother rushed to save her, but again the ice gave way, and she too disappeared. Jemima now made a fine attempt to rescue the two drowning women, in which she lost her own life. The others were afterwards rescued.

1869.

Royal Humane Society's Bronze Medal to P.-C. J. Cameron, who dived a depth of 7 feet in the foul water of the river Lea at Bow Bridge, and brought up a woman from the bottom in an unconscious state. **1906.**

December 4

Wilson's Last Stand. When Major Wilson, Captain Borrow, with Trooper Abbott and 35 of his comrades, were surprised and massacred by 4000 Matabele at Shangani River, the opportunity of showing British pluck brought forth a noble response. Their horses being all slain, officers and men fought desperately for three hours. Their last round of ammunition being spent, standing shoulder to shoulder, the survivors lifted their caps, sang "God save the Queen," and fell dead under a torrent of assagais. **1893.**

"There on the piteous bank,
Bleeding haunch, heaving flank—
        Too fierce for sorrow,
Each man his rifle laid,
Each for swift dying prayed,
But till Death came obeyed
        Wilson and Borrow.

. . . . . .

Facing the warrior flood,
Fearless of fate, they stood,
        Shoulder to shoulder.

Sang the old country's song
That keeps the nation strong
In loyal pride.
'Send her victorious,
Happy and glorious,
Long to reign over us'—
And singing, died."
—"Ballads of Brave Deeds," *Canon Rawnsley.*

Albert Medal of the First Class to William H. Pearce, for gallantry in saving life in New South Wales. Pearce was fireman on an engine, the boiler-plate of which collapsed, causing a great escape of steam. Both he and the driver were very severely scalded, but with great bravery Pearce, after lifting the latter into a place of safety, stuck to his post, and at peril of his life opened the cock of the air-pipe, thus applying the automatic brakes and bringing the train to a standstill. **1907.**

Carnegie Hero Fund Memorial Medallion to the relatives of Mr. Charles Gotts, a well-known Norfolk football referee, who allowed himself to be crushed to death in order to save his young brother and another boy. They were sinking a well when the shoring timbers began to give way. Charles was half-way up the ladder when he was caught by the falling débris. He could, however, easily have shaken himself free, but this would have meant the boys below being crushed by the falling earth and timbers. Calling to his brother, "Look after the lad," he remained motionless while the two boys were drawn up. A few minutes later a second fall of earth crushed the brave fellow's life out of him. **1908.**

"Knight of a better era
Without reproach or fear,
Said I not well that Bayards
And Sidneys still are here?"
—*Whittier.*

DECEMBER 5

V.C. Sergeant W. McWheeney, **44th (Essex).** Distinguished himself on several occasions. Saved a life, and was specially "mentioned" as "always vigilant and active," &c. **"The Quarries," Crimea. 1854.**

Royal Humane Society's Bronze Medal to J. Francis, Boy Bombardier, R.G.A., for rescuing first his mother and then his father from the river at Cork. The father fell into the water, though not out of his depth, and the mother, not knowing this, jumped in to try and save him. She got into difficulties in deep water, and was rescued by her son, who afterwards went in again and brought his father out. **1907.**

DECEMBER 6

Fine Heroism of a Canadian Gentleman. While a party of young people were skating on the Ottawa River, near to Kettle Island, close by the confluence of the Gatineau, Miss Bessie Blair and Mr. Creelman, who were in advance, came upon treacherous ice, and were thrown into deep and swiftly flowing water. Mr. Henry Harper, M.A., C.C.S., who was 40 yards behind, hurried to the spot, and, lying down on the ice, tried to save the girl by means of his stick. Failing in this, and undeterred by Mr. Creelman's warning shout, "For God's sake, Harper, don't come in here," the gallant young fellow threw off his fur cap and heavy clothing, and replying, "What else *can* I do?" plunged into the water, and struck out to the girl who was struggling in the terrible tide of the great river. Neither was seen alive again. Mr. Creelman had a miraculous escape from the fate which overtook his friends. **1901.**

Liverpool S. & H. Society's Silver Medal and Vote of Thanks to Lieutenant Frederick Storey, R.N.R., of the ss. *Mauretania*, for gallantly diving into the Sandon Dock, and rescuing a man from drowning. **1907.**

DECEMBER 7

Albert Medal of the First Class to Mr. Edward B. March, British Vice-Consul at St. Sebastian, who swam with a rope to a vessel stranded on the coast of Spain. He also dived under the ship's keel, and brought up a lad, who, together with the rest of the crew, reached the shore in safety by means of the rope. The sea was intensely cold at the time, and Mr. March suffered greatly from his long immersion. **1867.**

Six Suffolk Lifeboatmen lost on Rescue Work. Millar Ward, jun., Tom Morris, Will Ward, Charles Crisp, Jack Butcher, and Dogger Downing were drowned at Aldeburgh through the capsizing of the lifeboat on the shoals in a heavy sea. Twelve of the crew were dragged ashore in an exhausted condition, but the above-named were pinned under the capsized boat and drowned. Several women distinguished themselves in the rescue of the twelve men saved. **1899.**

DECEMBER 8

A gallant Durham Seaman. George Cowell, seeing a sloop in a dangerous position near the entrance of the

Tees, put off alone in a small boat to her assistance, but in the noble attempt his boat capsized, and he was drowned. The Royal National Lifeboat Society voted £10 for the relief of his widow. **1866.**

Royal Humane Society's Bronze Medal to Alexander Chalmers, who plunged into the sea from the pier-head at Drummore, Wigtownshire, fully clothed, and rescued a man named J. Galloway, who had fallen into the water. **1907.**

DECEMBER 9

V.C. Colonel J. A. Wood, **Bombay Native Infantry.** Received seven wounds while making an assault on the fort of Bushire, which he took, utterly defeating the enemy. **Persia. 1856.**

Forfar Labourer's magnificent Heroism. While William B. M'Leish and William Brown were sinking a well at Hillpark, the ground fell in upon them. M'Leish was uppermost, his body free, but his feet entangled and badly injured beneath a beam of wood. Brown was unhurt. Help promptly arrived, but it was found so dangerous to touch the well itself, that a tunnel had to be made in order to reach the imprisoned men, to whom food was conveyed through a pipe from time to time. It was five days before the victims were extricated from their awful position, when M'Leish was found to be dead. The splendid courage and self-sacrifice of this case lies in the fact that M'Leish could easily have been rescued at once, but as the cutting through of the beam pinning down his legs would probably have meant death to Brown, this humble hero refused to have his own life

[illegible]
5th Gurkha Rifles

John Shaul. Bugle Major

Donald D. Farmer. V.C. C. Sergt.

A. G. Hammond

Fred Roberts.

H. N. Schofield

H. L. Reed

G. E. Nurse. V.C

saved at the cost of his comrade's, who was alive when liberated. 1845.

"Heroism is the self-devotion of genius, manifesting itself in action."—*Hare.*

A double Lancashire Lifeboat Tragedy: 26 Lives lost. The entire crew of the lifeboat *Laura Janet* of St. Anne's-on-Sea, and part of the crew of the lifeboat *Eliza Fernley* of Southport—26 men in all—were lost in rescue work rendered to the barque *Mexico*, in distress off the estuary of the Ribble. The Lytham boat had saved 12 of the *Mexico's* crew, and returned in safety, and the Southport boat had also gone out, with the result recorded. The *Laura Janet* then put off in a tempestuous sea, and was not seen again until the afternoon of the following day, when she was found bottom up near the wreck. A subscription was raised, headed by her late Majesty Queen Victoria, for the widows and orphans of these noble fellows, realising over £20,000. 1886.

DECEMBER 10

Albert Medal of the Second Class to Private James Spring, **East Yorkshire,** for conspicuous courage in saving a life in St. Andrew's Docks, Hull. 1887.

London Fire Brigade Silver Medals to William Nicholls and James Pelley, who saved two lives at a fire in Villiers Street, Strand. 1877.

DECEMBER 11

V.C. The Reverend J. W. Adams, B.A., **Chaplain Cabul Field Force.** The only clergyman ever gazetted—"Padre" Adams, also known as the "Fighting parson." Besides rescuing two drowning soldiers on this date, had performed a great service a year earlier by finding a lost column near Peiwar Kotal. **Afghanistan. 1879.**

V.C. Captain H. E. M. Douglas, D.S.O., **R.A.M.C.**
V.C. Sergeant J. D. F. Shaul, **Highland Light Infantry.**
While the fearful massacre of the Highland Brigade was proceeding, this brave and humane pair showed the greatest devotion to the dying, under a fearful torrent of bullets. **Magersfontein, Boer War. 1899.**

"THE CRITIC ON THE HEARTH.

"Ye gentlemen of England
Who live at home at ease,
And fight—on maps—the battles fierce
Which rage across the seas,
Who criticise the generals
Who bear the battle's brunt,
What lamentable circumstance
Has kept *you* from the front?

There, you'd out-Buller Buller,
And take the shine off 'Bobs,'
And be so very useful
For those little kopje jobs.
Come out, and show Great Britain
The way to do the trick—
Ye gentlemen of England
Who wield—a walking-stick.

Ye amateur tacticians
Who theorise at home,
Whilst volunteers are thronging
To the battle o'er the foam,

At whose vicarious prowess
Imagined hosts retire,
'Neath showers of tobacco smoke
Before a club-room fire.

Ye veterans of tea-fights,
Versed in the arts of war,
Of battling with confetti
On sunny Sussex shore,
Come out, and show your science
The enemy to baulk,
Ye gentlemen of England
Who stay at home—and talk."

—(Reproduced by the kind permission of the proprietors of *Punch*.)

Heroic Warwickshire Workmen. Thomas Casey and James Chew lost their lives in an heroic attempt to save a man who had been overcome by the fumes from the foul water in a gasometer in which he was working, at Saltley, near Birmingham. Another man, named R. Smith, rendered assistance, and he and the man who was first affected recovered. **1889.**

DECEMBER 12

Twenty-six Yorkshire Miners sacrifice their Lives. After a disastrous explosion at the Oaks Colliery, Barnsley, a gallant party of 26 men, who descended to render any assistance possible, perished in their heroic efforts, bringing the total number of lives lost on this occasion up to 361. Where all concerned proved their mettle by laying down their lives it is scarcely possible to select any name for special mention; but Mr. P. Jeffcock and Mr. John Smith, two mining engineers, were particularly gallant in refusing to escape from the deadly choke-damp while any chance of helping remained. **1865.**

Carnegie Hero Fund. An award of £5 and Memorial Medallion to the widow of Alfred F. Davies, of Edgbaston, Birmingham, who died a few hours after receiving terrible injuries in trying to stop a runaway horse in Heath Green Road. **1908.**

DECEMBER 13

V.C. Lieutenant-Colonel W. H. Dick-Cunyngham, **Gordon Highlanders.** Under most fearful fire in the Sherpur Pass, made a fine rally of his men, and carried a successful attack. Lieut.-Col. Dick-Cunyngham was killed in the Boer War, 1899. **Afghanistan. 1879.**

V.C. Colour-Sergeant D. Farmer, **Cameron Highlanders.** After carrying Lieutenant Sandilands—who was wounded—out of fire at 20 yards range, returned to his post, and was taken prisoner. **Boer War. 1900.**

Albert Medal of the First Class to Mark Addy, oarsman, who saved at various times no less than 36 persons from drowning from the dangerous waters of the river Irwell. Addy was presented with several other medals for saving life, and was gazetted on this date. **1878.**

A Plymouth Widow's Devotion. Eliza Kirby, on the occasion of a terrible fire at Low Street, whereby 12 persons—mostly children—perished, lost her life by going through the blazing building to warn the other inmates of their danger. Mrs. Kirby's room was on the ground floor, and the passage was already on fire when she departed on her self-sacrificing errand of mercy. **1885.**

Royal Humane Society's Bronze Medal to John Quin, aged 12. A little girl on her way to school fell into the canal at Leigh, the water being 8 feet deep, and a dense fog prevailing at the time. At great risk, John Quin sprang in, fully clothed, and rescued her. **1905.**

December 14

V.C. Major-General W. J. Vousden, C.B., **5th Punjab Cavalry.** (Died 1902.) Showed the greatest courage and skill in bringing a handful of men through a large force of Afghans.

V.C. Colonel Sir Arthur G. Hammond, K.C.B., D.S.O., **Bengal Staff Corps.** (Born 1843.) "Pro Rege et Patria." Saved a wounded Sepoy's life; also checked the advance of the enemy.

V.C. Sergeant G. Sellar, **Seaforth Highlanders.** Badly wounded by an Afghan while leading an attack.

Heroes of the attack on Asmai Heights, Afghanistan. 1879.

A noble Doctor. In 1866 Nathaniel Heckford, M.D., M.R.C.S., was surgeon and doctor at the London Hospital, where he carried off gold medals for both medicine and surgery in that year. Having completed his hospital training, he abandoned what would have undoubtedly proved a brilliant and lucrative West-end practice, and devoted money, time, genius, health, and finally life itself to ministering to the poor and sick children of East London. At his own cost he established a little hospital of ten beds in a warehouse at Ratcliff Cross, which he and his young wife opened on the anniversary of their wedding day, January 28, 1868. The devoted pair constituted the entire staff: he was physician, surgeon, dispenser, druggist; she, nurse, dresser, and everything else. Happily their noble example attracted others to join them, and the work thus begun grew and developed into the present East London Hospital for Children, where a tablet to Dr. Heckford's memory now stands. But the tremendous work, privation (at times his balance at the bank was under £3), anxiety, and self-denial proved too great a strain for the fragile body in which glowed so fine a soul. The doctor developed consumption, and in his thirtieth year, on this day, passed into rest. **1871.**

"Inasmuch as ye have done it unto one of the least of these My brethren, ye have done it unto Me."

Carnegie Hero Fund Bronze Medallion and £1 a week for one year to Nurse Wharton, who saved a child from a burning hotel at Aberavon. She could have escaped easily, but went back to the top floor through the stifling smoke to fetch her little charge. When she again attempted to descend she was forced back by an onrush of flame. Kicking the glass out of the window, she got on to the window ledge, 40 feet from the ground, and a sheet being held out below, she dropped the baby into it. The child escaped unhurt, and the gallant nurse then leaped for her own life, but the sheet was not strong enough to bear the strain. She sustained a broken thigh and also severe internal injuries. Everything she possessed was lost in the fire, and a subscription was afterwards raised on her behalf by W. Williams, Esq., Mayor of Aberavon. **1908.**

DECEMBER 15

THE BATTLE OF COLENSO

Colenso! The day on which English soldiers vindicated, once and for all, the honour of their nation, and, from the nadir of bitter disaster, rose to the very zenith of heroism. Amid that unspeakable horror of guns, standing defenceless in a shambles of gunners and horses crushed together in hideous heaps, at the mercy of an invisible enemy, deeds were done which shall cause the hearts of patriotic British people to thrill with pride as long as the race endures. Seven Victoria Crosses were awarded under Rule XIII. in connection with the tragedy of "Black Friday."

> "The earth is covered thick with other clay
> Which her own clay shall cover, heaped and pent,
> Rider and horse;—in one red burial blent."
>
> —*Byron.*

THE SILENT HERO

V.C. Lieutenant the Hon. F. H. S. Roberts, **King's Royal Rifles.** (Born 1872.) Only son of Field-Marshal Earl Roberts, V.C. Was mortally wounded while helping to bring in one of the two guns which were rescued. This is the first instance of the little brown badge being awarded to father and son. The gun this lamented young officer laid down his life to save from the disgrace of capture was afterwards presented to the hero's father.

V.C. Major H. L. Reed, **Royal Field Artillery.** (Born 1869.) "Memor et fidelis." Severely wounded in the rescue of the guns.

V.C. Major H. N. Schofield. Helped to extricate and bring in the two guns which were saved.

V.C. Colonel W. N. Congreve, M.V.O., **Rifle Brigade.** "Non moritur cujus fama vivit." While severely wounded, went with Colonel Babtie from shelter into a hurricane of lead, and helped to carry Lieutenant Roberts out of danger.

V.C. Sergeant G. E. Nurse, **Royal Field Artillery.** (Born 1873.) Showed the greatest coolness and courage in assisting Colonel Congreve, V.C.

V.C. Colonel W. Babtie, C.M.G., **R.A.M.C.** Disregarding the inferno of one of the most awful deluges of shot and shell ever encountered in British warfare, went among the ghastly heaps of shattered men and horses to minister to the wounded and dying.

V.C. Private G. Ravenhill, **Royal Scots Fusiliers.** (Born 1872.) Took part in rescuing one of the two guns brought in. His Cross was sold at Sotheby's for £43 on this date in 1908. **Boer War. 1899.**

Stanhope Medal to Lieutenant W. B. Huddlestone, Royal Indian Marine, who sprang from the survey ship *Investigator* after a gunner who had fallen overboard, and kept him afloat until they were picked up, although two sharks were close by. **1890.**

Stanhope Medal to Mr. J. Shearme, fourth officer of the P. & O. ss. *Malacca*, which was at anchor off Woosung, China, when a man slipped between the vessel and a lighter alongside. It was a very cold, dark night, and there was a five knot tide running, but despite the difficulty and peril, Mr. Shearme succeeded in effecting a rescue. **1902.**

DECEMBER 16

A Gloucestershire Father's Heroism. Edward Drew, a railwayman, was working at Wickwar Station, when his little boy strayed on to the rails as a down train was approaching. Drew snatched the child from the rails and got on to the six-foot way, when an up train, emerging from the tunnel, struck him, and carried both father and child some little distance. When picked up the man was dead, and the little lad died shortly afterwards in Gloucester Infirmary. **1871.**

A Lancashire Workman's Bravery. George Cross lost his life at Eccleshill Ironworks, Darwen, in attempting to save a comrade who had been overpowered by foul air in the engine-house. Several other men, at great personal risk, tried to save the unfortunate couple, both of whom were suffocated. **1874.**

Stanhope Medal to Alfred Collins, master of the fishing lugger *Water Nymph*, who plunged from his boat with a line to the rescue of a boy who had fallen overboard, and with great difficulty swam with him to the lugger, where they were hauled aboard. This brave deed was enacted on a dark night in a strong gale, seven miles east of the Eddystone. **1884.**

DECEMBER 17

Albert Medal of the First Class to T. A. Whistler, first mate of the ss. *Ennersdale.*

Albert Medal of the Second Class to able-seaman H. Pochin.

A boy having fallen into the sea—which was intensely cold—off Cape Horn, Pochin sprang after him, but, being seized with cramp, was sinking, when Whistler in his turn went overboard to the rescue, seized Pochin, and kept him afloat 40 minutes, menaced all the time by a huge albatros hovering over them. Both men were unconscious when ultimately picked up by a boat. **1885.**

Carnegie Hero Fund. £5 award to Michael Forde, a railway porter, who jumped off the platform before a moving train at Tipperary station, and, at imminent peril to himself, pulled a would-be suicide off the metals just in time. **1908.**

DECEMBER 18

V.C. Captain T. J. Crean, **R.A.M.C., Imperial Light Horse.** (Born 1873.) Was twice most terribly wounded by fire at 150 yards' range while ministering to our stricken men at Tygerskloof. **Boer War. 1901.**

Yorkshire Miner killed while trying to save his Mate. John Roebuck was suffocated by choke-damp while trying to rescue his mate in a colliery at Neville Green, Leeds. Several other miners and the manager tried to save the unfortunate men; but their efforts were unsuccessful, and the bodies were not recovered until the following day. **1883.**

DECEMBER 19

V.C. Private W. Norman, **7th Fusiliers.** While on sentry duty, captured two Russians within 300 yards of their own picket. **White Horse Ravine, Crimea. 1854.**

V.C. Captain H. A. Carter, **Indian Mounted Infantry.** "Sacro gratus cineri." Rode back 400 yards towards a large force of Dervishes, before whom his section was retiring, took up a dismounted Sepoy, and carried him into safety, hotly pursued by the enemy.

Jidballi, Somaliland. 1903.

DECEMBER

W. N. Congreve.

W Babtie

George Ravenhill VC

Thomas J. Crean

H. A. Carter

Alfred Ernest Ind V.C.

Horace R. Martineau

Albert Medals of the Second Class to Captain R. W. E. Knollys, Indian Army, Muhammad Ali of Dir, and Hasil of Chitral, who, after a terrible avalanche in the Lowarai Pass, Peshawar, worked under falling snow; and in imminent peril from further avalanches (it being an almost invariable rule that a second follows when one has occurred), finally rescued three men buried beneath the snow. The gallant trio had nothing but their hands to work with. During the thirteen months preceding this act of heroism four avalanche disasters had occurred in the danger zone of the pass, involving the loss of thirty-six people. **1905.**

Stanhope Medal to Lieutenant L. E. Wintz, R.N., for jumping from H.M.S. *Raleigh*, off the Island of Tenedos, in a stormy sea, and supporting a man who had fallen overboard, until they were both picked up by a boat. **1877.**

December 20

V.C. Major-General G. N. Channer, C.B., **Bengal Staff Corps.** (Died 1902.) Went quite alone to the back of a large stockade, to which he afterwards led his men, and which he captured. By this action many of our soldiers' lives were saved, it being impossible for artillery to approach the spot. **Perak. 1875.**

V.C. Lieutenant-Colonel J. M. Smith, C.I.E., **Bengal Staff Corps.** "Tenax et fidelis." For great coolness and courage in ascending, with a few men, a steep cliff, over which the enemy threw showers of rock. Upon reaching the summit with his gallant little party, they captured the tribesmen's sangar. **Nilt, N.-W. India. 1891.**

V.C. Corporal Shoe-Smith A. E. Ind, **R.H.A. (Pompoms).** "Mentioned" three times for great gallantry. On this date refused to leave his gun, although every other man had been shot, at Tafelkop. **Boer War. 1901.**

Splendid Heroism of a young Yorkshire Mill-Hand. On the occasion of a terrible fire at the Atlas Cotton Mills, Brighouse, it was found that a young girl had been left behind at the top of the building, from which the other hands had with difficulty escaped. James A. Nuttall, aged 19, at once rushed into the mill, fought his way up the flaming staircases, and by an almost superhuman effort brought the girl down in safety. He sustained injuries of the most fearful description, but lived two days. Shortly before his death the young hero was asked if he regretted having sacrificed his life. "No, not for a moment," he replied; "how could I know a helpless girl was in such danger and not go to her rescue?" **1898.**

The Order of St. John of Jerusalem in England. Certificate of Honour to Stewart Rowley, a porter at Bishopsgate Street Station (Metropolitan Railway), for gallant conduct in rescuing a man who had fallen on to the permanent way (then equipped for electric working). With great difficulty Rowley dragged the man over the negative running rails into the six-foot way while two trains, running in opposite directions, passed through the station. Rowley was badly shaken and suffered from slight electric shocks. **1907.**

December 21

Albert Medal of the Second Class to J. Crowden, R.N., who suffered severely from serious injuries received, as well as from the effects of long immersion in the sea, while engaged in most heroic rescue work from a wrecked schooner at Muchals. **1868.**

Albert Medal of the First Class to Albert V. Hardwick. In a dense fog at Finsbury Park (London) Station, a lady fell from the platform in front of an approaching train. With superb courage, Mr. Hardwick leaped on to the line, seized the prostrate woman, and pressed her body and his own at full length between the rail and the wall, over which the platform projected a little. The train passed, and to the amazement of a crowd of onlookers both were found quite uninjured. **1904.**

"A brave soul is a thing which all things serve."
—*Alexander Smith.*

Suffolk Lifeboat Fatality: four Lives lost. Thomas Cable, P. Green, J. Pearce, and J. Wythe perished while engaged on life-saving duty at Aldeburgh, through the capsizing of the lifeboat in a terrible storm. **1859.**

December 22

A Lancashire Boy Hero. While William Bennison, aged 11, and his brother Charles, aged 9, were sliding on a reservoir at Walden, near Bolton, the younger boy fell through the ice, and William, in attempting to rescue him, was also dragged in. Both were drowned. **1891.**

Postman's Park Hero and Martyr. Tablet 4. P.-C. George S. Funnel was fatally injured while rescuing three women from a burning house in Wick Road, Hackney. The brave fellow lived eleven days after accomplishing this heroic deed. **1899.**

Two Somersetshire Heroes. Laurence Hussey, aged 15, lost his life at Chard in a gallant attempt to save another lad from drowning; and a railway stoker named Pearce narrowly escaped the same fate in his efforts to save the two boys. A handsome granite drinking fountain was erected at Chard in memory of young Laurence Hussey's noble act, the inscription of which begins: "In memory of a brave deed bravely done," &c. **1901.**

DECEMBER 23

A brave Manchester Servant. Mary Williamson, an elderly woman, after having been rescued from a blazing building in Shucle Hill, went back to try and save others, and in so doing lost her life. **1847.**

Gallantry of Captain and Three Fishermen of Caithness. Captain John Cormack of the *Iona* of Wick, and William Gum, Robert Bain, and John Sutherland, fishermen, with five others, in the absence of the lifeboat, went out in a salmon coble to the assistance of a schooner wrecked near Reiss Sands, in "a storm of unparalleled magnitude and duration," accompanied by a heavy fall of snow. Three men were taken into the coble, which was afterwards swamped, and the three sailors and four of their rescuers perished. **1876.**

Royal Humane Society's Bronze Medal to Zamblett Chase for going into a pond at High Halden, where the water was 8 to 10 feet deep, on a dark night, and bringing out a man named Hook, who had accidentally fallen in. Hook, however, died from the effects of his immersion. **1907.**

DECEMBER 24

London Fire Brigade Silver Medal to Michael Roach, who, having heard that a child was on the second floor of a burning house in Ladywell Road, managed to enter the room, despite the fact that the ladder used fell short of the window by 3 feet. The child was found and brought to the ground, but had been suffocated by the smoke and heat. **1893.**

Kingstown Volunteer Lifeboat Crew of Fifteen Men drowned. During one of the most furious gales ever experienced, the vessel *Palme* signalled for help from opposite Blackrock railway station. The lifeboat *Civil Service*, manned by a volunteer crew, put off to her assistance, and when next seen was lying bottom upwards, having been capsized by the terrific sea. The names of her noble crew were: Henry Williams, W. Dunphy, F. M'Donnell, J. Barkley, J. Baker, P. Power, G. Saunders, A. Williams, E. Crowe, F. Saunders, H. Underhill, E. Shannon, E. Murphy, T. Dunphy, and J. Ryan. **1895.**

December 25

CHRISTMAS DAY

"And a little Child shall lead them."

Some gallant Kentish Boys and Girls. George Cheesman, aged 16, and his sister Ellen, aged 14, were drowned on the Old Mill Pond at Leeds, near Maidstone, in a noble endeavour to save a friend who had fallen through the thin ice. Several other young people, in their anxiety to render assistance, went to the spot, and all were precipitated into the water. A boy and girl named White, and a younger brother of the Cheesmans, were rescued by a farm bailiff by means of a hop pole, but George and Ellen Cheesman were carried under the ice and perished. **1879.**

A little Renfrew Hero. Samuel M'Girr, seeing his elder brother fall through the ice on a pond at Williamsburg Waterworks, ran to his assistance; but the ice on which he was standing also gave way, and he fell into the water and was drowned. The other lad was eventually saved. **1887.**

A Mother's Heroism in Glamorganshire. Mrs. Hopkins, wife of a draper at Neath, rescued her child from a room which had been set on fire by the explosion of a paraffin lamp, and carried it into safety downstairs. In so doing her night-dress caught fire, and she expired shortly afterwards from her terrible injuries. **1899.**

DECEMBER 26

V.C. Sergeant H. R. Martineau, **Protectorate Regiment.** Was fearfully wounded—subsequently losing his left arm—while trying to carry a wounded comrade out of action.

V.C. Lieutenant H. E. Ramsden, **Protectorate Regiment.** Carried his brother—shot through both legs—a long distance under heavy fire until he obtained help. This is the second case of a Victoria Cross being awarded for saving a brother. The first was that of Sir C. J. S. Gough. **Game Tree, Boer War. 1899.**

An heroic Check-Taker of Durham. During a panic at Gateshead Theatre, a mad rush was made by the audience—of whom the majority were children—for the exits. Thomas Forster, knowing that a crush on the stairs would cause a catastrophe, endeavoured to stop the deadly rush from the gallery. He was, however, overpowered by the struggling, terrified mass of men, women, and children, and was swept off his feet and trampled beneath the onrush. Nine children were killed, but the gallant check-taker was the only adult who lost his life. **1891.**

A Lincolnshire Hero. Thomas Whitehouse, seeing a lad with his foot wedged in the points just in front of an express train at Gainsborough, with a superhuman effort dragged him clear just in time to save his life. **1895.**

> " He has clutched the lad—must he vainly strive?
> He will lever his body with good head-thrust;
> The train roars in!—are they dead or alive?
> They are safe in the six-foot's smother and dust!"
> —" Ballads of Brave Deeds," *Canon H. D. Rawnsley.*

A tiny Hero of Staffordshire. While Arthur Foster, aged 8, with his brother William, was sliding on a pool at Cobridge, near Burslem, the latter fell through the ice. Arthur went to his assistance, but was also immersed, and disappeared. William was finally rescued by a man named Clarke, who was unaware that Arthur was in the water, and the poor little fellow was drowned. **1901.**

Postman's Park Military Hero and Martyr. Tablet 47. Private John Slade, Royal Fusiliers, sacrificed his life at Whitehouse Street, Stepney. In a house set on fire by a broken paraffin lamp he rushed up the stairs to rouse his relatives. He saved the life of one by dragging him through the flames into the street; but perished in an heroic attempt to save another. **1902.**

December 27

A brave Warwickshire Brother. Thomas W. Wing, aged 29, with his brother and two other young men, was skating on the river Avon at Portobello, just below its confluence with the Leam at Warwick, when the ice broke, and all fell into the water. Thomas Wing succeeded in getting his brother Daniel out on to the ice, which again broke, and once more both fell into the water. Daniel was eventually rescued, but Thomas and another young man were drowned. **1890.**

A little Buckinghamshire Hero. Ernest Caulder, aged 8, gave his life in a splendid attempt to save his brother Alfred, aged 11, who had fallen with a sled through thin ice at Burnham. The little fellow crept to the edge of the hole and held his brother up, while the ice was cracking around them. A man shouted to Ernest to run for his life, but the reply came, "I can't leave my brother." The ice was too thin to support the strain; but a little later they rose, Ernest still holding Alfred's coat. A Burnham man named Lawley, coming up at the time, plunged instantly into the ice-clogged water, and brought the bodies out, Ernest still clutching his brother's coat. A soldier from South Africa, who helped to carry home the two, said he had seen no greater act of heroism among the many brave deeds he had witnessed at the front. **1901.**

December 28

Albert Medals of the Second Class to James Vivian Reed and Henry Smith. On the occasion of the terrible earthquake at Messina, the ss. *Afonwen*, of Cardiff, was lying at her moorings there. After having satisfied himself as to the safety of his vessel, Captain W. Owen proceeded ashore with his crew to render any assistance possible. The particular act of gallantry in respect of which these Medals were awarded was performed when a building of five storeys was reached, where, at a great height from the ground, children were noticed crying for help. The interior of the building had for the most part collapsed, and the structure was in a very dangerous state. The children having lowered a string, by means of which a rope was drawn up and made fast, Henry Smith and James V. Reed swarmed up, and succeeded in rescuing all the little ones, besides three persons from the storey above. **1908.**

Stanhope Medal to Gunner W. Hall, **R.E.**, who, after tying a handkerchief over his mouth, made three journeys to an upstairs room in Clerkenwell, and brought down a man, his wife, and three children, who had been overpowered by the fumes of prussic acid. **1898.**

Royal National Lifeboat Institution's Silver Medal to Mr. Henry Nicholas, Coxswain of the Sennen Cove Lifeboat (Cornwall), for magnificent rescue work in connection with the ship *Fairport*, which was riding to her anchors, broadside on to the beach. The lifeboat stood by her, but the sea was so terrific that a tug, which was approaching the vessel, could not get within 200 fathoms of her. Eventually Mr. Nicholas succeeded in getting a rope from the *Fairport* to the tug, and by this means the towing hawsers were hauled aboard and made fast. Shortly afterwards the vessel slipped her anchors, and was towed away. **1908.**

DECEMBER 29

V.C. Colonel H. G. Moore, C.B., **Connaught Rangers.** "Fortis cadere cedere non potest." Was severely wounded while making a desperate attempt to save a soldier from a large force of Gaikas. The man, however, was killed, despite the gallant colonel's efforts. Col. Moore lost his life in Ireland, while attempting to rescue another from drowning in one of the lakes. **Kaffir War. 1877.**

Edward Medals of the First Class to George Dryburgh and James Dryburgh. When a fire broke out at Lockhead Colliery, Fife, it was feared that a fireman in the pit was in danger. Two men descended to rescue him, but were overcome by the poisonous gas of the mine. Then James and George Dryburgh, at great peril of their lives, went down the shaft, and succeeded in saving their brave comrades. **1907.**

Stanhope Medal to Albert Battison, aged 17, who dived under the ice—which he broke with his head—into 14 feet of water, and brought up a girl, whom he eventually landed safely on the bank of the river Soar at Leicester. **1887.**

Royal National Lifeboat Institution's Silver Medal and £3 to Captain D. Martin; £3 to James Meenan; and 30s. each to ten other men, for most heroic services at Campbeltown in a furious gale, with squalls of hurricane force, snow showers, and very heavy sea. **1908.**

Messina Earthquake. The crew of the steamer *Drake*, at great personal risk, rescued 250 persons at the time of this terrible disaster. **1908.**

December 30

Postman's Park Baby Hero and Martyr. Tablet 23. Henry J. Bristow, aged 8 years, seeing that his little sister of 3 had pulled a lighted paraffin lamp over herself, snatched the child's flaming clothes off and saved her life. The gallant little lad's own clothing, however, ignited, and he was so terribly burned that he died a few days later. **1891.**

Liverpool S. & H. Society's Silver Medals and Votes of Thanks to Captain Harold Davie, of the ss. *Inchdune*, and to Mr. James Gunn, chief officer; also £2 each to the crew of the lifeboat, for the gallant rescue of the captain and crew (eleven in number) of the Norwegian barque *Eliezer*, in mid-Atlantic. This service was rendered during a dark, dirty night, with a heavy sea running. **1905.**

DECEMBER 31

V.C. Lieutenant-General Sir C. C. Fraser, K.C.B., **7th Hussars.** (Died 1895.) "Je suis prest." Although suffering from a wound, plunged into the river Raptee and rescued Captain Stisted and others, who were drowning. This fine act was accomplished under fearful mutineer fire. The **Royal Humane Society** awarded a **Gold Medal** to the hero. **Mutiny. 1858.**

Liverpool S. & H. Society's Silver Medal, Vote of Thanks, and £2 to James Singleton for rescuing a boy who had fallen into the river near the Queen's Dock. 1905.

"LEST WE FORGET

"Far-called, our navies melt away;
On dune and headland sinks the fire:
Lo, all our pomp of yesterday
Is one with Nineveh and Tyre!
Judge of the Nations, spare us yet,
Lest we forget—lest we forget!
. . . .
For heathen heart that puts her trust
In reeking tube and iron shard,
All valiant dust that builds on dust,
And guarding, calls not Thee to guard,
For frantic boast and foolish word—
Thy mercy on Thy People, Lord! Amen."

—*Rudyard Kipling.*

APPENDIX

CASES RECEIVED SINCE THOSE RECORDED

Edward Medals of the First Class to Michael Lyons and John Shields. A subsidence of a mass of ore, weighing about 12,000 tons, occurred at the Mount Morgan mine, Queensland. Five men at work in the excavations were killed, and two—Lyons and Banks—escaped, the latter being seriously injured. Lyons would not leave his wounded comrade, but called up the shaft for help, and with the aid of John Shields, who at once descended, despite the danger from falling débris, Banks was securely fastened to the rope, and all three were drawn up. **Nov. 4, 1908.**

Albert Medal of the Second Class to Mr. Henry Kemp, Superintendent of Police in the Worcestershire Constabulary, for conspicuous gallantry displayed at a fire at Halesowen. **January 1881.**

Albert Medal of the First Class to Mr. Leslie Urquhart, British Vice-Consul at Baku, for marked gallantry in September 1905 in saving the lives of four British workmen, who, during an outbreak, were surrounded by the insurgents and were in imminent danger of losing their lives. Mr. Urquhart, accompanied by two Cossacks and several Tartars, started to relieve the men, but the district was in such a state of unrest that it was not expected that he would live to return. His courageous action was, however, happily rewarded with success.

1905.

The brave Judge of Futtehpore. The infection of mutiny and rebellion travelled westward to the station of Futtehpore; and Robert Tucker, the Judge, standing his ground alone after every other European had fled, refusing to purchase life by apostatising to Mahometanism, was murdered on the roof of the cutcherry after he had himself slain some fourteen of his assailants.

June 7, 1857.

An heroic Peacemaker. Professor Palmer of Cambridge, after having ridden through the desert from Gaza to Suez, conciliating the fanatical tribes which were ready to join forces with Arabi Pasha, again undertook the perilous journey to make final arrangements with the Sheikhs. The second time he was accompanied by Captain Gill and Lieutenant Charrington, and all three were murdered in the Wady Sadr, having been betrayed by their treacherous guide. Their remains were brought to England and interred in the Crypt of St. Paul's. Above their grave is the inscription:

"This tablet has been erected by the country in whose service they perished to commemorate their names, their worth, and their fate." **July 1882.**

Extract from "Antiquities of Bridgnorth, Salop," by the Rev. G. Bellet, A.M., extracted from the Blakeway Papers, in Bodleian Library, Oxford. "There is a story connected with St. Leonard's Church, Bridgnorth (Shropshire) which is worth relating, though I can assign no date or name to it. Two boys were at play in the upper part, when some of the beams or joists gave way. One of the boys had just time to catch hold of the beams with his arms, and the other, slipping over his body, caught hold of his legs. There they hung for some time calling for help, but no one heard them. At length the upper boy said he could hold on no longer. The lower boy said, 'Do you think you could save yourself if I were to loose you?' 'Yes,' said the other; 'I think I could.' 'Well, then,' said the lower one, 'God bless you,' and, loosing his hold, was instantly dashed to pieces. The survivor (upper boy) got up upon the beams, and either climbed to a place of safety or remained until some one came to his assistance." This was heroism of the highest type. Had the name of the hero been known, and the exact spot where this affecting incident occurred, they would have been well worthy of being put on record on a Mural Tablet in St. Leonard's Church.

Bravery of a Civil Administrator. A certain landowner, Sheikh Abd-el-Kader Mohammed Imam, had proclaimed himself a prophet, collected a band of followers, and refused to treat with the Mamur, or native administrator, of the district. He sent a message, however, to say that if Mr. Scott-Moncrieff and the Mamur would come and interview him, unarmed and unattended, he would state his grievances. Abd-el-Kader's three brothers had been invited to attend, but declined to do so, and endeavoured to dissuade Mr. Scott-Moncrieff. He and the Mamur decided to trust the man, and leaving their escort a mile away proceeded to the Sheikh's encampment. According to the evidence of men subsequently taken prisoners, the Sheikh, on being asked to state his grievances, replied that he had none, but that what he was doing was for Allah. He and his followers then fell on the Mamur and Mr. Scott-Moncrieff, who "met his death fearlessly, smiling and folding his arms, while his lips moved as if in prayer." Mr. Scott-Moncrieff was only twenty-four years of age.

(*From a letter to "The Times," May* 27, 1908, *by* SIR COLIN SCOTT-MONCRIEFF.

A gallant Coastguardsman. The brigantine *Osprey*, of Waterford, stranded off Dover during a westerly gale. In reply to signals of distress, the coastguard got a line on board; but after two of the crew had been brought ashore this failed, and an attempt was then made to use the rocket apparatus. After several efforts had failed, a coastguardsman, named Maurice Miller, volunteered to swim through the surf with a rope. He entered the water amid the cheers of the crowd assembled on the beach, and, after much buffeting by heavy seas, reached the vessel and climbed up a line thrown over her side. When communication with the vessel had been thus established, the rest of the crew were brought ashore in the breeches buoy. **Oct. 7, 1909.**

LEAGUE · OF · THE · EMPIRE ·

INDEX OF HEROES

N.B.—*Asterisks mark those whose autographs are included. The folios within brackets indicate the pages on which the autographs are printed.*

www.ingramcontent.com/pod-product-compliance
Ingram Content Group UK Ltd.
Pitfield, Milton Keynes, MK11 3LW, UK
UKHW040014200726
13854UKWH00001B/201

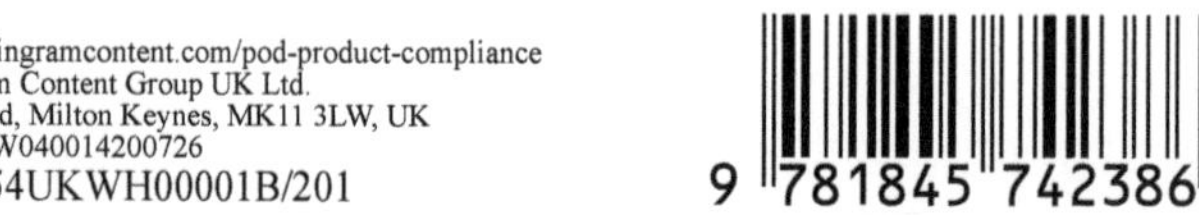

9 781845 742386